RISING
GLOBAL INTEREST
IN FARMLAND

AGRICULTURE AND RURAL DEVELOPMENT

Seventy-five percent of the world's poor live in rural areas, and most are involved in agriculture. In the 21st century, agriculture remains fundamental to economic growth, poverty alleviation, and environmental sustainability. The World Bank's Agriculture and Rural Development publication series presents recent analyses of issues that affect the role of agriculture, including livestock, fisheries, and forestry, as a source of economic development, rural livelihoods, and environmental services. The series is intended for practical application, and we hope that it will serve to inform public discussion, policy formulation, and development planning.

Titles in this series:

Agribusiness and Innovation Systems in Africa

Agricultural Land Redistribution: Toward Greater Consensus

Agriculture Investment Sourcebook

Bioenergy Development: Issues and Impacts for Poverty and Natural Resource Management

Building Competitiveness in Africa's Agriculture: A Guide to Value Chain Concepts and Applications

Changing the Face of the Waters: The Promise and Challenge of Sustainable Aquaculture

Enhancing Agricultural Innovation: How to Go Beyond the Strengthening of Research Systems

Forests Sourcebook: Practical Guidance for Sustaining Forests in Development Cooperation

Gender and Governance in Rural Services: Insights from India, Ghana, and Ethiopia

Gender in Agriculture Sourcebook

Organization and Performance of Cotton Sectors in Africa: Learning from Reform Experience

Reforming Agricultural Trade for Developing Countries, Volume 1: Key Issues for a Pro-Development Outcome of the Doha Round

Reforming Agricultural Trade for Developing Countries, Volume 2: Quantifying the Impact of Multilateral Trade Reform

Rising Global Interest in Farmland: Can It Yield Sustainable and Equitable Benefits?

Shaping the Future of Water for Agriculture: A Sourcebook for Investment in Agricultural Water Management

The Sunken Billions: The Economic Justification for Fisheries Reform

Sustainable Land Management: Challenges, Opportunities, and Trade-Offs

Sustainable Land Management Sourcebook

Sustaining Forests: A Development Strategy

RISING
GLOBAL INTEREST
IN FARMLAND

Can It Yield Sustainable and Equitable Benefits?

Klaus Deininger and Derek Byerlee
with Jonathan Lindsay, Andrew Norton,
Harris Selod, and Mercedes Stickler

THE WORLD BANK
Washington, D.C.

ISBN: 978-0-8213-8591-3
eISBN: 978-0-8213-8592-0
DOI: 10.1596/978-0-8213-8591-3

Library of Congress Cataloging-in-Publication Data

Deininger, Klaus W., 1962-
  Rising global interest in farmland : can it yield sustainable and equitable benefits? / Klaus Deininger and Derek Byerlee.
    p. cm. — (Agriculture and rural development)
  Includes bibliographical references and index.
  ISBN 978-0-8213-8591-3 — ISBN 978-0-8213-8592-0 (electronic)
  1. Land use. 2. Land tenure—Government policy. 3. Right of property. I. Byerlee, Derek. II. World Bank. III. Title.
  HD111.D36 2011
  333.76—dc22

                                                                    2010044273

Cover photo: Klaus Deininger
Cover design: Critical Stages

CONTENTS

BOXES, FIGURES, AND TABLES

Boxes

Figures

Tables

PREFACE

Interest in farmland is rising. And, given commodity price volatility, growing human and environmental pressures, and worries about food security, this interest will increase, especially in the developing world.

Many countries have suitable land available that is either not cultivated or produces well below its potential. This was a development challenge even before the food price rise of 2008. Seventy-five percent of the world's poor are rural, and most are engaged in farming. The need for more and better investment in agriculture to reduce poverty, increase economic growth, and promote environmental sustainability was already clear when there were "only" 830 million hungry people before the food price rise. The case is even clearer today when, for the first time in human history, over a billion people go to bed hungry each night.

One of the highest development priorities in the world must be to improve smallholder agricultural productivity, especially in Africa. Smallholder productivity is essential for reducing poverty and hunger, and more and better investment in agricultural technology, infrastructure, and market access for poor farmers is urgently needed. When done right, larger-scale farming systems can also have a place as one of many tools to promote sustainable agricultural and rural development, and can directly support smallholder productivity, for example, through outgrower programs. However, recent press and other reports about actual or proposed large farmland acquisition by big investors have raised serious concerns about the danger of neglecting local rights and other problems. They have also raised questions about the extent to which such transactions can provide long-term benefits to local populations and contribute to poverty reduction and sustainable development.

Although these reports are worrying, the lack of reliable information has made it difficult to understand what has been actually happening. Against this backdrop, the World Bank, under the leadership of Managing Director Ngozi Okonjo-Iweala, along with other development partners, has highlighted the need for good empirical evidence to inform decision makers, especially in developing countries. One result is this report, *Rising Global Interest in Farmland: Can It Yield Sustainable and Equitable Benefits?* To prepare the report, a multidisciplinary team was tasked with carrying out a multicountry study on large-scale agricultural land acquisition and investment. While this task proved to be less straightforward than originally anticipated, the effort has produced some striking results.

First, the demand for land has been enormous. Compared to an average annual expansion of global agricultural land of less than 4 million hectares before 2008, approximately 56 million hectares worth of large-scale farmland deals were announced even before the end of 2009. More than 70 percent of such demand has been in Africa; countries such as Ethiopia, Mozambique, and Sudan have transferred millions of hectares to investors in recent years.

At the same time, in many cases the announced deals have never been implemented. Risks are often large. Plans are scaled back due to a variety of reasons including unrealistic objectives, price changes, and inadequate infrastructure, technology, and institutions. For example, we found that actual farming has so far only started on 21 percent of the announced deals. Moreover, case studies demonstrate that even some of the profitable projects do not generate satisfactory local benefits, while, of course, none of the unprofitable or nonoperational ones do.

Institutional gaps at the country level can be immense. Too often, they have included a lack of documented rights claimed by local people and weak consultation processes that have led to uncompensated loss of land rights, especially by vulnerable groups; a limited capacity to assess a proposed project's technical and economic viability; and a limited capacity to assess or enforce environmental and social safeguards.

Such problems are not due to a lack of potential. For example, although deforestation associated with the expansion of the agricultural frontier has been a serious problem (and one of the world's largest contributors to greenhouse gas emissions), our analysis shows that the projected increase in the demand for agricultural commodities over the next decade could be met, without cutting down forests, by increasing productivity and farmland expansion in nonforested areas. In particular, none of the Sub-Saharan African countries of most interest to investors is now achieving more than 30 percent of the potential yield on currently cultivated areas. So, increasing productivity on existing farmland would have a much bigger impact than simply expanding the land area at current yields.

There is also considerable scope for a South-South exchange of good practice. Again, when done right, larger-scale farming can provide opportunities for poor countries with large agricultural sectors and ample endowments of land. To make the most of these opportunities, however, countries will need to better secure local land rights and improve land governance. Adopting an open and proactive approach to dealing with investors is also needed to ensure that investment contributes to broader development objectives. Experience in Asia and in Latin America and the Caribbean can provide lessons for Sub-Saharan African countries that have confronted these issues more recently.

A major conclusion of the report is that access to a basic set of good information is essential for all stakeholders. Good public information can help governments formulate policies, identify gaps in implementation, and perform essential regulatory functions. Good public information can help civil society educate local communities about their rights and the potential uses and value of their land, assist in specific negotiations, and monitor agreements so they are indeed adhered to. And good public information can help investors effectively design and implement projects that respect local rights, are profitable, and generate local benefits.

Helping countries reduce poverty and hunger by increasing agricultural productivity is at the core of the World Bank's agenda. In collaboration with partners, the World Bank is ready to contribute to this important agenda by providing information and analysis, helping countries build their institutional and regulatory capacity, and supporting more and better investment in agriculture, especially smallholder agriculture, so that the rising global interest in farmland contributes to results that are sustainable and equitable.

Juergen Voegele
Director
Agriculture and Rural Development Department
The World Bank

Derek Byerlee is a Member of the Science Council of the Consultative Group on International Agricultural Research (CGIAR) and a consultant and adviser to a number of international organizations. Formerly he was Rural Strategy Adviser of the World Bank and Co-Director of the 2008 *World Development Report: Agriculture for Development*. Before joining the World Bank, he was Director of Economics at the International Maize and Wheat Improvement Center, Mexico, and Associate Professor, Michigan State University. For most of his career, he worked in several postings in Africa, Asia, and Latin America, conducting field research on agricultural technological change and food policy. He has published widely in several fields of agricultural development.

Klaus Deininger is Lead Economist in the Development Research Group of the World Bank. His research focuses on income and asset inequality and its relationship to poverty reduction and growth; access to land, land markets, and land reform, and their impact on household welfare and agricultural productivity; land tenure and its impact on investment, including environmental sustainability; and capacity building for policy analysis and evaluation, in Africa, China, India, Latin America, and East Asia. He holds a Ph.D. in Applied Economics from the University of Minnesota and has published more than 50 articles and a number of books, including a 2003 Policy Research Report "Land Policies for Growth and Poverty Reduction." For the past four years, he has also served as the World Bank's adviser on land tenure and land policy.

Jonathan Lindsay is Senior Counsel in the Environmental and International Law practice group of the World Bank's Legal Department, where he specializes in legal aspects of land and natural resource management, and in tenure issues arising in the context of the World Bank's safeguard policies. Prior to joining the Bank, he worked in the Development Law Service at the Food and Agriculture Organization (FAO) for 13 years, providing legislative technical assistance on land, forestry, and common property management issues. His work at the World Bank and FAO has involved extensive involvement in land and natural resource management projects in most regions of the world.

Andrew Norton is Director of Research at the Overseas Development Institute in London. A social anthropologist by training, he carried out his doctoral fieldwork in a farming community in Mali and has since worked extensively on issues of poverty, vulnerability, social protection, citizen participation, political economy analysis, aid effectiveness, natural resource management, and social policy. From 2005 to 2010, he was a Lead Social Development Specialist at the World Bank, where he was responsible for oversight of strategy, social and political analysis, gender, and special initiatives within the Social Development Department, managing a major multidonor work program on Poverty and Social Impact Analysis and leading a number of studies, including on social dimensions of climate change and social guarantees. Before joining the World Bank, he was the Head of Profession for Social Development at the UK Department for International Development.

Harris Selod is a senior economist with the Development Research Group of the World Bank, on secondment from the French Ministry of Foreign and European Affairs. His current research focuses on land governance, land markets, and the spatial organization of rural, urban, and peri-urban areas in developing countries, with a specific interest in West Africa. He has published on a number of topics in regional and public economics, including theories of squatting and residential informality, the political economy of investments in transport infrastructure, the effects of residential segregation on schooling and unemployment, and the impact of land reforms and place-based policies. Prior to joining the World Bank in 2007 as an invited scholar, he was a researcher at the French National Institute for Agricultural Research (INRA) and an associate professor at the Paris School of Economics. He holds a Ph.D. in economics from the University of Paris Panthéon-Sorbonne, graduated in statistics from the Ecole Nationale de la Statistique et de l'Administration Economique (ENSAE) and in business administration from the Ecole Supérieure de Commerce de Paris (now ESPC Europe). He serves as an adviser for the French Ministry of Sustainable Development and has consulted for several governmental agencies in France, including the Conseil d'Analyse Economique (Council of Economic Advisers to the Prime Minister).

M. Mercedes Stickler is an Associate in Ecosystem Services for Development at the World Resources Institute (WRI). Her work focuses on mapping and valuing ecosystem services provided by Kenya's arid and semi-arid lands and includes coordinating the dissemination of these spatial data to secondary and tertiary schools in Kenya. Previously, she was a Junior Professional Associate in the Agriculture and Rural Development Department at the World Bank. Ms. Stickler has spent several years working and studying in South Africa, where she investigated agricultural development issues across Sub-Saharan Africa for the Howard G. Buffett Foundation and also earned her M.Sc. in Environmental Sciences from Rhodes University with the support of a U.S. Fulbright Grant.

ACKNOWLEDGMENTS

This report arose out of an initiative by Managing Director Ngozi Okonjo-Iweala in close interaction with a working group on this topic with broad representation from the World Bank Group. It was prepared by a team led by Klaus Deininger (DECAR) under the overall guidance of Juergen Voegele, ARD Sector Director; Mark Cackler, ARD Sector Manager; with support from Martin Ravallion, DEC Sector Director; and Will Martin, DEC Sector Manager. The core team included Derek Byerlee (consultant), Guenther Fischer (IIASA), Jonathan Lindsay (LEGEN), Andrew Norton (Overseas Development Institute, formerly World Bank, SDV), Harris Selod (ARD), Mahendra Shah (formerly IIASA, new Qatar national food security agency), and M. Mercedes Stickler (World Resource Institute, formerly World Bank, ARD), as well as Diji Chandrasekharan Behr (ARD), Nuria de Oca (SDV), Gerhard Dieterle (ARD), Clemens Gros (SDV), Daniel Monchuk (DEC), and Michelle Rebosio (SDV). Brian Blankespoor, Gloria Kessler, Deepthi Kolady, Katie Lancos, Siobhan Murray, Libei Tian, and Jeremy Weber also contributed to the report. Guenther Fischer and Mahendra Shah applied the global agro-ecological zoning (AEZ) methodology and models for the yield gap analysis, quantification of crop production potentials, tabulations and maps, and analysis of the results.

We gratefully acknowledge the cooperation and valuable inputs for country case studies contributed by the following individuals: **Argentina:** Martín Piñero (Economics and Organization Consultants Group, Grupo CEO); **Benin:** José Tonato (independent consultant); **Brazil:** Túlio Barbosa and

Alberto Coelho Gomes Costa (independent consultants); **Cambodia:** Chan Sophal (Leopard Capital); **the Democratic Republic of Congo:** Angélique Mbelu, Augustin Mpoyi, Patrick Mutombo, Serges Ngwato, and Olivier Nzuzi (Council for Environmental Defense by Legality, CODELT); **Ethiopia:** Imeru Tamrat (Multi-Talent Consultancy); **Indonesia:** Bambang Setiono (Institute for Environmental and Natural Resource Economics, ELSDA); **the Lao People's Democratic Republic:** M. Srinivas Shivakumar (consultant); **Liberia:** Sam Gotomo (Making Enterprises) and Augustine Johnson, Peter Lowe, and J. Christopher Toe (independent consultants); **Mexico:** Gustavo Gordillo de Anda and Brando Flores Pérez (Workshop in Political Theory and Policy Analysis); **Mozambique:** Anna Locke (HTSPE), Simon Norfolk (Terra Firma), and Gil Lauriciano and Rachel Waterhouse (independent consultants); **Nigeria:** Adeolu Ayanwale (Obafemi Awolowo University); **Pakistan:** Gulbaz Ali Khan, Adnan Rasool, and Abid Suleri (Sustainable Development Policy Institute, SDPI); **Paraguay:** Thomas Otter (independent consultant); **Peru:** Victor Endo (Administration del Territorio Consultantes) and Mercedez Callenes, Alvaro Espinoza, and Eduardo Zegarra (Grupo de analisis para el desarollo, GRADE); **Sudan:** Musa Adam Abdul Jalil and Omer Egemi (University of Khartoum), Atta El-Hassan El-Battahani (International Institute for Democracy and Electoral Assistance, IDEA), and Abdelmoneim Taha (Agricultural Research Corporation); **Tanzania:** Thomas Blomley (Acacia Natural Resource Consultants), Razack Lokina and George Senyoni (University of Dar es Salaam), and Daudi Danda, Gabriel Joshua, Lembulung M. Ole Kosyando, Devis Mlowe, and William Ole Nasha (Pastoralists' Survival Options, NAADUTARO); **Ukraine:** Ildar Gazizullin (International Centre for Policy Studies, ICPS) and Alex Lissitsa (Ukrainian Agribusiness Club); **Zambia:** Davison Gumbo (Center for International Forestry Research, CIFOR), Henry Machina (Zambia Land Alliance), Augustine Mulolwa (University of Zambia), and Choolwe Mudenda, K. Ng'omba, and Frightone Sichone (independent consultants).

This report was produced with the collaboration of many partners, including the African Union, the Food and Agriculture Organization of the United Nations (FAO), the International Fund for Agricultural Development (IFAD), the United Nations Conference on Trade and Development (UNCTAD), the International Institute for Environment and Development (IIED), the International Land Coalition (ILC), and a number of development partners, including numerous bilateral organizations, the Working Group on Land of the European Union, and the Global Donor Platform for Rural Development. Many colleagues from inside and outside the World Bank, too numerous to list here individually, contributed to this report through insightful discussions. A selective listing of key contributors to this report is provided on page 195.

We also wish to acknowledge the contribution of the Office of the Publisher, World Bank, in particular, Mary Fisk, who managed the publishing process.

ABBREVIATIONS

AEZ	agro-ecological zoning
CGE	computable general equilibrium
DUAT	direito de uso e aproveitamento da terra (land use right)
EIA	environmental impact assessment
EITI	Extractive Industries Transparency Initiative
FAO	Food and Agriculture Organization (of the United Nations)
FSC	Forest Stewardship Council
GALDC	Government Agricultural Land Disposition Committee
GPS	global positioning system
IFC	International Finance Corporation
IIASA	International Institute for Applied Systems Analysis
LEV	land expectation value
NGO	nongovernmental organization
NPV	net present value
OECD	Organisation for Economic Co-operation and Development
PACRO	Patents and Companies Registration Office
PLIAF	policy, legal, and institutional framework
PROFEPA	Procuraduría Federal para la Protección al Ambiente
REDD	Reducing Emissions from Deforestation and Forest Degradation in Developing Countries
RSB	Roundtable on Sustainable Biofuels

R&D	research and development
RSPO	Roundtable on Sustainable Palm Oil
SNNPR	Southern Nations, Nationalities, and People's Region
UNEP	United Nations Environment Programme
ZDA	Zambia Development Agency

The 2007–08 boom in food prices and the subsequent period of relatively high and volatile prices reminded many import-dependent countries of their vulnerability to food insecurity and prompted them to seek opportunities to secure food supplies overseas. Together with the reduced attractiveness of other assets due to the financial crisis, the boom led to a "rediscovery" of the agricultural sector by different types of investors and a wave of interest in land acquisitions in developing countries. With little empirical data about the magnitude of this phenomenon, opinions about its implications are divided. Some see it as an opportunity to reverse long-standing underinvestment in agriculture that could allow land-abundant countries to gain access to better technology and more jobs for poor farmers and other rural citizens. If managed well, new investments in agriculture could help create the preconditions for sustained, broad-based development. Others say that an eagerness to attract investors in an environment where state capacity is weak, property rights ill-defined, and regulatory institutions starved of resources could lead to projects that fail to provide benefits, for example, because they are socially, technically, or financially nonviable. Such failure could result in conflict, environmental damage, and a resource curse that, although benefiting a few, could leave a legacy of inequality and resource degradation.

Without reliable information on large-scale investment, it is difficult to determine which of these positions is right or to advise countries on how to minimize the risks associated with such investments while capitalizing on any opportunities. This information is often not available to those affected, key decision makers, or the public. This report aims to overcome this information gap and provide key data needed to facilitate an informed debate about large-scale land acquisition. Its main focus is analytical rather than normative, and its purpose fourfold:

- Use empirical evidence to inform governments in client countries, especially those with large amounts of land, as well as investors, development partners, and civil society, about what is happening on the ground.
- Put these events into context and assess their likely long-term impact by identifying global drivers of land supply and demand and highlight how country policies affect land use, household welfare, and distributional outcomes at the local level.
- Complement the focus on demand for land with a geographically referenced assessment of the supply side, that is, the availability of potentially suitable agricultural land.
- Outline options for different actors to minimize risks and capitalize on opportunities to contribute to poverty reduction and economic growth, especially in rural areas.

The World Bank recognizes that large-scale agricultural investment poses significant challenges that can be addressed successfully only if stakeholders collaborate effectively. Together with the Food and Agricultural Organization of the United Nations, International Fund for Agricultural Development, United Nations Conference on Trade and Development, and other partners, it has formulated seven principles that all involved should adhere to for investments to do no harm, be sustainable, and contribute to development. These principles are summarized in box 1.

The principles have already served a useful purpose in reminding countries and investors of their responsibilities and in drawing attention to situations where they were not adhered to. At the same time, countries need to take the lead and strategically determine what type of investment will help them to most effectively pursue their overall development goals. Better understanding of what is happening, the underlying factors, and ways in which key stakeholders can most effectively play their role will be critical to determine how these principles can be made operational in specific country contexts.

To provide an empirical basis that can help countries and other stakeholders to better understand and address the issue, we use a variety of methodological approaches and proceed in a number of steps.

- First, we use experiences of land expansion in Asia, Latin America and the Caribbean, Eastern Europe, and Sub-Saharan Africa to distill lessons that will be useful in light of predicted future commodity- and land-demand.
- Second, we assess the extent to which recent demand for land differs from earlier processes of area expansion and identify the challenges, in terms of land governance, institutional capacity, and communities' awareness of their rights, raised by this. To do so, we use a variety of sources ranging from

1. **Respecting land and resource rights.** Existing rights to land and associated natural resources are recognized and respected.
2. **Ensuring food security.** Investments do not jeopardize food security but strengthen it.
3. **Ensuring transparency, good governance, and a proper enabling environment.** Processes for acquiring land and other resources and then making associated investments are transparent and monitored, ensuring the accountability of all stakeholders within a proper legal, regulatory, and business environment.
4. **Consultation and participation.** All those materially affected are consulted, and the agreements from consultations are recorded and enforced.
5. **Responsible agro-investing.** Investors ensure that projects respect the rule of law, reflect industry best practice, are economically viable, and result in durable shared value.
6. **Social sustainability.** Investments generate desirable social and distributional impacts and do not increase vulnerability.
7. **Environmental sustainability.** Environmental impacts of a project are quantified and measures are taken to encourage sustainable resource use while minimizing and mitigating the risk and magnitude of negative impacts.

intended land acquisitions as reported by the media to official country data and project case studies.

- Third, to properly frame the issue and allow it to be included in countries' development policies, we determine the agricultural potential for land—whether currently cultivated or not—to provide a basis for quantifying the gap between actual and potential yields by current producers, the amount of land that could be available for area expansion, and where investor interest may actually materialize.
- Fourth, we compare countries' policy, legal, and institutional frameworks to help identify good practice in a variety of country contexts to assist countries confronted with this issue in providing a response that will minimize risks and allow them to utilize available opportunities.
- Finally, based on the notion that the scale and nature of the phenomenon require different stakeholders to each contribute their share, we discuss the areas where governments, the private sector, civil society, and international organizations are challenged to contribute.

CROPLAND EXPANSION: DRIVERS, UNDERLYING FACTORS, AND EXPECTED IMPACTS

Large-scale expansion of crop land is not new. From 1990–2007, the land cultivated expanded by 1.9 million hectares (ha) per year, for a total of some

1.5 billion ha cultivated globally. Declines in industrialized and transition countries (–2.1 million and –1.3 million ha, respectively) were more than outweighed by increases of 5.5 million ha per year in developing countries. Cropland expansion, which would have been much larger without productivity increases, was concentrated in Sub-Saharan Africa, Latin America and the Caribbean, and Southeast Asia. Key commodities driving this expansion were vegetable oils, sugarcane, rice, maize, and plantation forests. In addition to overall increases in commodity demand attributable to population and income growth and biofuel mandates, greater trade led to shifts of production to developing countries with high productive potential. For example, since 1990, soybean yields in Latin America increased at twice the U.S. rate from a much lower base, and the yield of fast-growing trees for wood and pulp in South America is three to four times the level that can be achieved in Europe or the United States. By contrast, agricultural area with sufficient amounts of water has not grown much or even shrunk in most countries of the Middle East and North Africa and in China and India.

Expansion of cultivated area seems unlikely to slow. Population growth, rising incomes, and urbanization will continue to drive demand growth for some food products, especially oilseed and livestock, and related demands for feed and industrial products. A conservative estimate is that, in developing countries, 6 million ha of additional land will be brought into production each year to 2030. Two-thirds of this expansion will be in Sub-Saharan Africa and Latin America, where potential farmland is most plentiful. At the same time, in many countries that are of interest to investors productivity on currently cultivated land is only a fraction of what could be achieved. Concerted efforts to allow existing cultivators to close yield gaps and make more effective use of the resources at their disposal could thus slow land expansion sharply while creating huge benefits for existing farmers.

Because investment to expand cultivated area is not a new phenomenon, it is important to draw lessons from past experience. Even a cursory review of recent land expansion across regions highlights the associated environmental and social risks, shows that country policies have an important impact on outcomes, and points to a need for new approaches involving all stakeholders to help achieve sustainable outcomes.

In *Latin America and the Caribbean*, different processes of land expansion can be distinguished with mixed results. The best known is forest clearing for extensive livestock ranching and establishing land rights in the Amazon basin. Net impacts were often negative as most of the land deforested was not put to productive use. A second process was the expansion of soybeans and other crops in the *cerrado* (savanna) region of Brazil, based on public investment in research and development (R&D) that allowed cultivation of acid soils previously unsuitable for agriculture, use of appropriate varieties, and adoption of conservation tillage. While this was a major technological success, direct impacts on rural poverty were reduced because capital subsidies encouraged more highly mechanized forms of cultivation. Public and private sector players in Brazil and neighboring countries now recognize that agricultural investment and expansion pose serious environmental challenges and that action will be needed to reduce detrimental impacts. These actions include rehabilitation of degraded lands, stricter enforcement and monitoring of "legal reserves" (minimum levels of forested areas on agricultural properties), better delineation of protected areas, and environmental zoning. In Peru's Pacific Coast,[1] auctions of 235,500 ha of public land brought in almost US$50 million in investment over the past 15 years, generating large numbers of jobs and underpinning the country's emergence as a major force in high-value agro-exports (see box 2).

In *Southeast Asia*, area expansion has been pronounced for oil palm, generally under large estates, often with smallholders attached to them in Indonesia and Malaysia. Rice cultivation, entirely based on smallholders, has also expanded significantly in countries such as Thailand and Vietnam. The oil palm industry has grown rapidly in response to global demand, high returns to investment, and low labor costs. In Indonesia, planted area more than doubled from about 2.9 million ha in 1997 to 6.3 million ha in 2007, with significant smallholder participation and creation of an estimated 1.7 million to 3 million jobs. In response to policies that aimed to foster development of the industry by giving away land (and the trees on it) for free, large areas with high biodiversity value have been deforested without ever having been planted with oil palm.

Box 2   Using Auctions to Transfer Public Land in Peru's Coastal Region

Peru uses a public auction mechanism to divest public lands for investment. The government first regularizes any land rights to determine if anyone has claims to it that may need to be respected. This also enables to government to determine what types of rights are eligible for transfer.

When the government initiates the auction, the intention to divest the land and the terms of the bidding are published publically for at least 90 days. Bidders must prequalify for the auction by posting a bond of at least 60 percent of the minimum bid price plus the intended amount of investment. The successful bidder must deposit the land payment and a letter of credit covering the proposed investment amount with the government.

Where an investor expresses interest in public land, the investor is required to present a business plan to a board of public and private sector specialists. If the project is considered viable, the proposal is published for at least 90 days to allow other investors to present offers. If any investor comes forward, the public bidding process above is initiated. If no other investor shows interest, the initial investor can proceed.

This has given rise to concerns about oil palm expansion contributing to the loss of biodiversity, greenhouse gas emissions, and social conflict due to a failure to recognize local land rights. With expected further increases in palm oil demand, directing plantation expansion away from standing forest toward degraded grassland areas will be important. Estimates suggest that the area available under these degraded areas is at least double what is needed to satisfy increased demand over the next decade. A number of economically viable options to use these areas are available, most importantly the use of payments for environmental services and REDD (United Nations Collaborative Program on Reducing Emissions from Deforestation and Forest Degradation in Developing Countries) to improve incentives for establishing oil palm on degraded rather than forest land. Applying these mechanisms successfully, however, requires that the rights of existing occupants on degraded lands be identified and compensated.

Thailand and Vietnam have clarified property rights and used public investment to provide smallholders with access to technology. The small and medium farmer-driven expansion of rice exports—and subsequently exports of other commodities with higher value added—in these countries indicates that these policies had a major impact on poverty reduction and gradual increases of farm size as nonagricultural growth accelerated as well. It also illustrates that increases in production are by no means contingent on large-scale land acquisition. In fact, in the rubber sector, production has shifted primarily from large plantations to smallholders. Some countries, such as Cambodia, with relatively abundant land resources but production based mainly on smallholders, have more recently also tried to attract outside investment with mixed success.

In most of Africa, area expansion has been based on smallholder agriculture in the context of population growth.[2] While countries on the continent range from very land scarce (such as Malawi and Rwanda) to relatively land abundant (such as the Democratic Republic of Congo, Tanzania, and Zambia), large-scale investment has been limited. A key reason for this was that policy distortions against agriculture, especially exports and low public investment in rural areas, have reduced investment incentives, thus limiting the development of Africa's agricultural potential. Elimination of many of these policy interventions over the past two decades has allowed agricultural growth to accelerate and paved the way for renewed investor interest in the continent. Even so, many attempts to jump-start agricultural growth through large-scale farming, as in Sudan, Tanzania, and Zambia, were largely unsuccessful. In some of these, neglect of existing rights prompted conflict over land and further undermined investment incentives. Associated negative impacts were made worse by poor technology and management.

Also, structural issues arising from this long-standing neglect of technology, infrastructure, and institutions continue to limit competitiveness. In many cases, they contributed to disappointing performance of commercial cultivation of bulk commodities, where Sub-Saharan Africa can have a comparative advantage. Instead, success with export agriculture was limited to higher-value crops, such as cotton, cocoa, coffee, and more recently horticulture. At the same time, such gaps also affect smallholder performance. In fact, none of the Sub-Saharan African countries (for example, Mozambique, Sudan, Madagascar, or Zambia) that recently attracted investor interest achieved more than 25 percent of potential yields, and area cultivated per rural inhabitant remains well below 1 ha. If technology, infrastructure, and institutions can be improved, higher global demand for agricultural commodities can bring large benefits to existing producers and countries. The challenge for public and private sector is to identify ways to address these challenges effectively in a way that provides local benefits.

Eastern Europe and Central Asia represents a unique situation, where investments in very large farms contrast with an overall contraction of agricultural land use. In the Russian Federation, Ukraine, and Kazakhstan, the area sown to grains has declined by 30 million ha since the end of the Soviet era. These croplands were mostly returned to pastures or fallow, due to lack of suitable technology and market access. Large farms were better able to deal with financing, infrastructure, and technology constraints of the transition, leading to considerable concentration. For example, the 70 largest producers in Russia and Ukraine control more than 10 million ha. They have been a key driver of increases in grain production in Russia, Ukraine, and Kazakhstan, the region's three most land-abundant countries. There remains considerable scope for improving technology to increase yields.

In general, given the large differences in labor intensity across crops, the social and equity implications of cropland expansion will depend on the type of crop grown and the way production is organized. Except for plantation crops, agricultural production across the globe has historically been managed by owner-operated farms, with increases in farm sizes largely driven by rising nonagricultural wages. Recent developments in technology—such as zero tillage, pest resistant varieties, and information technology—made it easier to manage large farms. But true "superfarms" emerged only where vertical integration of operations well beyond the production stage allowed large firms to better overcome the obstacles created by imperfections in other factor markets, especially marketing and access to finance. Owner-operated farms, linked to processors and exporters via contracts or other forms of productive partnerships (including producer organizations), will therefore continue to be a key pillar of rural development.

ARE RECENT PROCESSES OF LAND ACQUISITION DIFFERENT FROM PAST ONES?

Countries attracting investor interest include those that are land abundant and those with weak land governance. The 2008 commodity boom dramatically increased interest in agricultural land as a potential investment, especially in Sub-Saharan Africa. According to press reports, foreign investors expressed interest in around 56 million ha of land globally in less than a year. Of these, around two-thirds (29 million ha) were in Sub-Saharan Africa. Countries with fairly abundant nonforested, noncultivated land with agricultural potential attracted more interest. However, countries with poorer records of formally recognized rural land tenure also attracted interest, raising a real concern about the ability of local institutions to protect vulnerable groups from losing land on which they have legitimate, if not formally recognized, claims. Especially in these countries, public disclosure, broad access to information on existing deals, and vigilant civil society monitoring are needed, along with other efforts to improve land governance, including the overall policy, legal, and regulatory framework for large-scale land acquisition. Moreover, actual farming has so for started on only 20 percent of the announced deals, indicating that these is a large gap between plans and implementation, and ways to transfer land from nonviable enterprises to more capable entrepreneurs may be needed in the future.

Inventory data on land acquisitions highlight the role of policies and domestic players, as well as the limited benefits attained to date. Data from official registries in 14 countries[3] suggest that policies influence the size and nature of large-scale land transfers, whether by lease or by sale. In Tanzania, where land rights are firmly vested with villages, less than 50,000 ha were transferred to investors between January 2004 and June 2009. By contrast, over the same period in Mozambique, 2.7 million were transferred. But a 2009 land audit found that some 50 percent of this transferred land was unused or not fully used. Total transfers between 2004 and 2008 amounted to 4.0 million ha in Sudan, 2.7 million in Mozambique, 1.6 million in Liberia (although many were renegotiations of existing agreements), and 1.2 million in Ethiopia (table 1). Virtually everywhere, local investors, rather than foreign ones, were dominant players. Moreover, in most cases, the expected job creation and net investment were very low.

Data from country inventories highlight serious weaknesses in institutional capacity and management of land information. In many countries where demand has recently increased, limited screening of proposals, project approvals without due diligence, rivalries among institutions with overlapping responsibilities, and an air of secrecy all create an environment conducive to weak governance. Official records on land acquisitions are often incomplete, and neglect of social and environmental norms is widespread. All this implies a danger of a "race to the bottom" to attract investors. Deficient processes for local consultation and unclear boundary descriptions create several problems: they reduce tenure security and investment incentives, increase the likelihood of conflict, and make it difficult for the public sector to collect land taxes and monitor whether investors comply with agreements they had entered into with local people.

Table 1   Large Land Acquisitions in Select Countries

Country	Projects	Area (1,000 ha)	Median size (ha)	Domestic share[a]
Cambodia	61	958	8,985	70
Ethiopia	406	1,190	700	49
Liberia	17	1,602	59,374	7
Mozambique	405	2,670	2,225	53
Nigeria	115	793	1,500	97
Sudan	132	3,965	7,980	78

Source: Country project inventories collected for this study.
Note: Data are for the 2004–09 period except for Cambodia and Nigeria where they cover 1990–2006. Liberian figures refer to renegotiation of concessions that had been awarded much earlier.
a. Domestic share is the proportion of the total transferred area allocated to domestic investors (vs. foreign investors) rather than the share of the number of investments.

Case studies confirm widespread concern about the risks associated with large-scale investments, including the following:

■ Weak land governance and a failure to recognize, protect, or—if a voluntary transfer can be agreed upon—properly compensate local communities' land rights
■ Lack of country capacity to process and manage large-scale investments, including inclusive and participatory consultations that result in clear and enforceable agreements
■ Investor proposals that were insufficiently elaborated, nonviable technically, or inconsistent with local visions and national plans for development, in some cases leading investors to encroach on local lands to make ends meet
■ Resource conflict with negative distributional and gender effects.

In many of the case studies, progress with implementation was well behind schedule. As a result, local people had often suffered asset losses but received few or none of the promised benefits. Yet field visits by local collaborators also found that investments can provide benefits through four channels: (i) supporting social infrastructure, often through community development funds using land compensation; (ii) generating employment; (iii) providing access to markets and technology for local producers; and (iv) higher local or national tax revenue. If investments generated profits, social impacts depended not only on the magnitude of benefits, but also on the mix of different types of benefits. For example, entrepreneurial and skilled people could gain from jobs created by an investment, while vulnerable groups or women lost access to livelihood resources without being compensated. This illustrates the importance of clearly addressing distributional issues upfront.

TOWARD A COUNTRY TYPOLOGY—LINKING ENDOWMENTS AND EQUITY EFFECTS

The potential global supply of land suitable for rainfed cultivation is concentrated in a limited number of countries, mainly in Sub-Saharan Africa, Latin America and the Caribbean, and Eastern Europe and Central Asia. Complementing the focus on land demand with spatially referenced information on potential supply can provide valuable information for stakeholders in a number of respects. First, participatory mapping of potentially suitable land can help local communities and governments identify areas where investor interest may materialize. Second, in anticipation of potential demand, countries can initiate priority measures to secure local property rights and educate local people. This can help steer investors away from fragile or low-potential areas where investment could cause environmental damage and disruption to local livelihoods. Third, information on productive capacity and land values from such an exercise can help local communities appreciate alternative options for using their land and guide them towards a fair value for land transfers.

Globally, more than half of land that could potentially be used for expansion of cultivated area is in ten countries, of which five are in Africa. The currently noncultivated area suitable for cropping that is nonforested, nonprotected, and populated with less than 25 persons/km^2 (or 20 ha/household) amounts to 446 million ha (table 2). This is equivalent to almost a third of globally

Table 2 Potential Availability of Uncultivated Land in Different Regions

	Total area (1,000 ha)	Share of land with travel time to market (%)	
		< 6 hours	> 6 hours
Sub-Saharan Africa	201,546	47	53
Latin America and the Caribbean	123,342	76	24
Eastern Europe and Central Asia	52,387	83	17
East and South Asia	14,341	23	77
Middle East and North Africa	3,043	87	13
Rest of world	50,971	48	52
Total	**445,624**	59	41

Source: Fischer and Shah 2010.
Note: Data identify uncultivated land with high agro-ecological potential in areas with population density of less than 25 persons/km^2.

cropped land (1.5 billion ha). More than half of this area is in ten countries, six of which (Sudan, the Democratic Republic of Congo, Mozambique, Madagascar, Chad, Zambia) are in Africa. But relatively more land in Africa is located far from infrastructure.

Classifying countries by the availability of land for rainfed cultivation and the share of potential output achieved on areas currently cultivated (the yield gap) can provide input into planning and help identify options, including providing incentives to existing small-scale producers to use development of land to contribute to countries' overall development. Figure 1 illustrates this relationship for a select sample of countries by plotting relative land availability compared to currently cultivated area (in logs) against the potential for increasing yields.

In many countries, both those with and without land available for expansion, there is large scope to increase productivity on currently cultivated land, something that could have major impacts on poverty. Broadly, countries with relatively little or no available additional suitable land for cultivation (for example, Burundi, the Arab Republic of Egypt, India, Malawi, and Rwanda) are on the left half of the graph, and those with relatively more land (for example, Argentina, Brazil, Russia, Sudan, Uruguay, and Zambia) are on the right. Countries also vary widely in the extent to which they realize potential yields. Large gaps in productivity, with current farmers achieving less than 30 percent of potential yields—as found in most of Sub-Saharan Africa—point to deficiencies in technology, capital markets, infrastructure, or public institutions, including property rights. In countries with large amounts of suitable land currently not cultivated, area expansion will have little developmental impact if it fails to address the factors that underlie such widespread failure to make full use of the productive potential of currently cultivated land. Careful analysis of these factors as part of a broader country-level agricultural and rural development strategy that identifies a proper space for private investment can help realize this potential by attracting investment that will also help existing smallholders realize the productive potential of their land.

At the global level, the typology can be used to classify countries into four types corresponding to the quadrants in figure 1.

Type 1: Little land for expansion, low yield gap: This group includes some countries in Asia, Western Europe, and the Middle East with high population density and limited land suitable for rainfed cultivation. Agricultural growth has been, and will continue to be, led by highly productive smallholder sectors that may shrink as nonagricultural employment grows. Investors increasingly provide capital, technology, and access to markets through contract farming to meet demand for high value products. As countries reach the stage of declining agricultural population due to rural-urban migration, land consolidation facilitated by efficient land markets will gradually increase farm size.

Type 2: Suitable land available, low yield gap: This group includes countries, mainly in Latin America, where land is fairly abundant and technology is

Figure I   Potential Land Availability vs. Potential for Increasing Yields

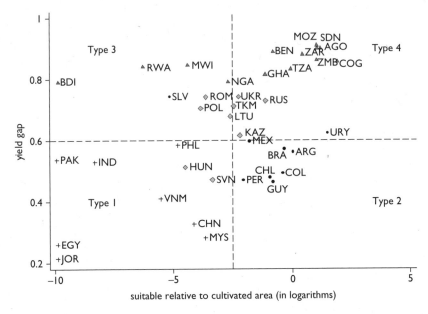

Source: Authors based on Fischer and Shah 2010.

advanced, often a result of past investment in technology, human capital, and infrastructure. Here, savvy investors have recently exploited opportunities for area expansion. A proper regulatory role by the public sector is needed to ensure that areas with high social or environmental value are protected and to provide the basis for well-functioning factor markets, especially land markets.

Type 3: Little land available, high yield gap: This group includes many densely populated developing countries. While little additional land is available, yields far below potential lock many smallholders in poverty. Especially given limited scope for nonagricultural development to absorb labor in the short run, increasing agricultural productivity will be critical for poverty reduction. This will require public investment in technology, infrastructure, and market development to raise smallholder productivity. Private investment through contract farming can promote diversification into high value and export markets.

But the limited availability of nonagricultural employment implies that potential productivity benefits from large-scale mechanized farming are likely to be outweighed by undesirable social and equity effects. Care is thus needed to protect property rights and ensure that other markets work well to prevent large-scale land acquisitions from pushing people off the land. The situation is different if incomes and employment in the nonagricultural sector grow rapidly, land markets are working well, and population growth is low. This situation prevails in parts of Eastern Europe, where movement of the rural population out of agriculture creates scope for land consolidation and a transition to larger operational units.

Type 4: Suitable land available, high yield gap: This group includes countries with large tracts of suitable land, but also a large proportion of smallholders with very low productivity. If labor supply constrains smallholder expansion and in-migration is limited, larger farm sizes enabled through mechanization could be a viable strategy. This situation could create opportunities for outside investors. The public sector needs to establish the institutional framework and provide complementary infrastructure as well as information on business models and contractual arrangements to maximize spillovers and local multipliers.

Commodity-level analysis illustrates the size of opportunities and the importance of technology. In many African countries with large amounts of suitable but currently uncultivated land, transfers of technology could provide large benefits to local populations. To reduce risks and increase benefits, greater effort will be needed to identify local comparative advantage, assess the technical viability of proposed investments, improve weak institutional frameworks for land governance, and level the playing field for smallholder competitiveness.

A closer look at the underlying data (yield gap, availability of uncultivated area, and area cultivated per rural inhabitant as a proxy for farm size) for some countries in Sub-Saharan Africa and Latin America and the Caribbean points to large variations even within regions. Sub-Saharan African countries differ widely in the availability of suitable area—from Rwanda and Malawi, where virtually all the suitable land is cultivated, to Mozambique, Sudan, and Zambia, where vast tracts of suitable nonforested and unprotected land are not cultivated (figure 2). None of these countries cultivate more than about one ha of land per rural person or attain more than 25 percent of potential output. This suggests that other constraints prevent farmers from making the most effective use of available land. Understanding these constraints and identifying ways to address them will be critical to identifying the types of investments that could best help reduce poverty. Identifying constraints should precede efforts to attract outside investors. As in most countries the area already cultivated exceeds the amount of suitable land that could still be brought under production, addressing these constraints could also lead to output increases much greater than would be possible by expanding cultivated area without improving productivity.

Whether and how land is transferred to investors will have potentially far-reaching impacts on the dynamics of farm size distribution. Projections of future population growth and the scope for employment generation in

Figure 2 Yield Gap, Availability of Uncultivated Land, and Area Cultivated per Rural Inhabitant, Selected Countries in Sub-Saharan Africa

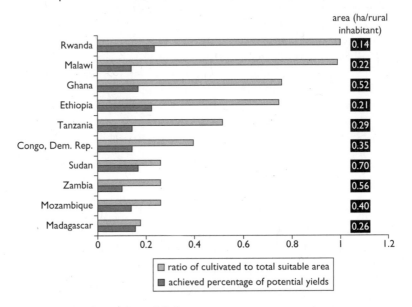

Source: Authors based on Fischer and Shah 2010.

the nonagricultural economy would be useful to trace out options for the evolution of farm sizes. Land-abundant Sub-Saharan African countries have a choice between establishing an agricultural sector founded on broad-based ownership of medium-size farms (much larger than those currently operated and expanding over time) or a dual structure where a few mega farms coexist with many small producers. Given the long-term impacts associated with such choices, clear elaboration of the issues in an informed public debate about the development paths open to a country is needed.

In contrast to Sub-Saharan Africa, Latin America is characterized by greater variation in availability of area for expansion, yield gaps, and area cultivated per rural individual (figure 3). Area cultivated per rural inhabitant ranges from 0.2 ha in Haiti to 8.8 ha in Argentina. Some countries in the region, such as Argentina, Brazil, and Uruguay, combine large areas for expansion with other factors attractive to potential investors. These include high levels of technology and human capital, competitive land markets, and a supportive investment climate. The Latin American experience can provide valuable lessons for countries where demand for land has emerged more recently. South-South exchanges to understand what influences investor choices between locations would be useful for countries to develop incentives that will prevent them from attracting investments that are poorly conceived or unable to compete in countries with more mature land markets.

Figure 3 Yield Gap, Availability of Uncultivated Area, and Area Cultivated per Rural Inhabitant for Selected Countries in Latin America and the Caribbean

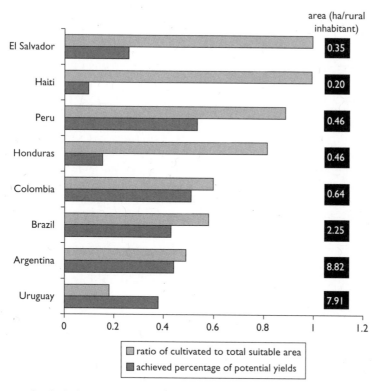

Source: Authors' calculations based on Fischer and Shah 2010.

THE POLICY, LEGAL, AND INSTITUTIONAL FRAMEWORKS

Variation in legal and institutional frameworks is wide. This is especially true regarding the extent to which property rights are recognized, and the openness, capacity, and coordination of different public institutions responsible for guiding investment and ensuring compliance with regulations. Five areas are relevant.

Rights Recognition

Rights to land and natural resources need to be recognized, clearly defined, identifiable on the ground, and enforceable at low cost. These include rights to lands managed in common areas, state lands, and protected areas. This is to ensure that local people benefit from investments, and that investors enjoy tenure security that encourages them to make long-term investments. There are now many examples of cases where relatively land-abundant countries have improved their legal and regulatory framework to recognize customary rights and allow their registration. Low-cost and participatory tools to do so, either at individual or group level without eliminating secondary rights, have been applied successfully in cases such as Ethiopia, Mexico, and Vietnam with positive impact. They demonstrate that, if transparent and accountable structures can be relied upon, registration at group level can be a cost-effective way to protect rights over large areas quickly, greatly empowering rights holders.

Voluntary Transfers

Transfers of land rights should be based on users' voluntary and informed agreement, provide them with a fair level of proceeds, and should not involve expropriation for private purposes. To create these preconditions, local people need to be aware of their rights, the value of their land, and ways to contract, and have assistance in analyzing investment proposals, negotiating with investors, monitoring performance, and ensuring compliance. Compensation may occur in several ways, either through the provision of equivalent land, the setting up of a community fund to provide public services, an equity stake in the investment, or monetary transfers (including the payment of a land rent). To provide a basis for negotiation of a fair level of compensation, it is necessary to be able to assess the value of the land used by the investor.

Transparency

To effectively perform their respective functions, all stakeholders, in particular, governments, need access to accurate and up-to-date information on opportunities, actual transfers, and the technical and economic impact of large investments. In many cases, lack of such information makes it difficult to identify and utilize opportunities, ensure a level playing field, and enforce regulation and contracts properly. Investors unaware of the location of high potential land that current owners might be willing to transfer may design projects that are ultimately not viable or, if institutions are weak, that could cause great damage. Communities that have not been educated about their rights or potential land values will be less likely to anticipate and contest investments that are not sustainable or may lead to conflict. Weak or nonexistent information on project performance or technical parameters imposes costs on all parties and makes it difficult to quickly restructure or liquidate investments that are underperforming or that violate environmental and social safeguards.

Information on prices, contracts, rights, and, ideally, on land use plans should thus be publicly available to help local people to monitor performance of investments and public institutions to properly do their job. Information on land use, existing rights, and land suitability will allow governments to devise strategies and revise them during implementation. The availability of these types of information will also be useful to investors who want to know what approaches and technologies have or have not worked in the past. Public availability of information on rights and written agreements will help communities and civil society to ensure that contracts are enforced and promises kept. A clear format in which information is reported, accessed, and used can help to move toward this goal and thus shape regulation, assess performance, and encourage policy debate.

Technical and Economic Viability

For investments to provide local benefits, mechanisms need to be in place ensuring technical and economic viability, consistency with local land use plans and taxation regimes, and transfers of assets from nonviable projects. This should also include the scope for investment and associated land governance issues in countries' broader development strategies that identify areas or crops where investment can provide the highest benefits based on agro-ecological endowments and existing land use intensity. This information can then be used to establish parameters and minimum criteria for investor applications. This exercise could be combined with mapping and documenting existing rights on a systematic basis, as well as educating local populations on how to manage their land most effectively. This will allow proper measures to be taken to scrutinize each project's technical viability, including reviews by private sector experts or practitioners engaged in large-scale farming elsewhere. These procedures should include a competitive and incentive-based approval process that involves an up-front declaration of projected capital investment and job generation. There is a need to improve the public sector's capacity for processing investments by reducing red tape and ensuring that incentives, if deemed necessary, are fair, free of distortions, and administered transparently.

Environmental and Social Sustainability

Even investments that are highly profitable for an investor will generate sustainable social benefits only if they are not associated with environmental externalities or undesirable social and distributional changes within or beyond the immediate project area. Ideally, investors should take these considerations into account on their own in the context of project preparation. However, experience indicates that this is often not the case and that therefore a regulatory framework to ensure such negative effects do not outweigh potential benefits will be essential. In particular, areas not suitable for expansion need to be protected from encroachment and any indigenous or other rights on them respected. Environmental norms need to be clearly defined and compliance with them monitored, with ways for recourse in case of noncompliance. Large investments will also need to consider social impacts in advance and make relevant information on potential impacts available to stakeholders in order to allow informed decisions.

CONCLUSION: MOVING FROM CHALLENGE TO OPPORTUNITY

The earlier evidence suggests that large-scale expansion of cultivated area poses significant risks, especially if not well managed. As the countries in question often have sizable agricultural sectors with many rural poor, better access to technology and markets, as well as improved institutions to improve productivity on existing land and help judiciously expand cultivated area, could have big poverty impacts. Case studies illustrate that in many instances outside investors have been unable to realize this potential, instead contributing to loss of livelihoods. Problems have included displacement of local people from their land without proper compensation, land being given away well below its potential value, approval of projects that were only feasible because of additional subsidies, generation of negative environmental or social externalities, or encroachment on areas not transferred to the investor to make a poorly performing project economically viable.

Many countries with large amounts of currently uncultivated land suitable for cultivation also have large gaps between potential and actual yields. Thus, even without any expansion of cultivated area, large increases in output and welfare for the poorest groups could be possible through efforts to enable existing farmers to use currently cultivated land more productively. The associated need for investments in technology, infrastructure, market access, and institutions all suggest that private investors can contribute in many ways, not all of which require land acquisition. Especially in countries with large amounts of currently noncultivated land with potential for rainfed cultivation and a large yield gap, ways to better utilize existing endowments and help producers move closer to realizing their potential will need to be part of a long-term strategy. Often this can be through partnerships between the public and private sector.

To counter the negative outcomes that can result from participants being ill-informed, all involved will need to contribute to better information access and land and water governance. This requires making information on deals, land availability, and future plans accessible to all interested parties and using such information as an input into analysis and policy advice. Exploring options for doing so and drawing on lessons from other sectors or initiatives could help move in this direction and avoid doing harm by shedding light on these important issues. More immediately, using information on recent and proposed land transfers available at the project level could also help promote more effective monitoring of performance and continued feedback to decision makers in the public and private sectors. This information could help them make more informed decisions so that the opportunities opened up by increased global interest in land and agriculture can benefit local people and reduce poverty.

Governments can help to promote this agenda by identifying strategic priorities to assess ways to bring productivity closer to the potential and to identify whether, given available resources and necessary trade-offs, large-scale investment could help generate employment, improve food security, and foster technology transfer and local development. Based on an assessment of agro-ecological potential, this can include identification of public infrastructure or technology investments that could complement private sector efforts through a participatory process of land use planning. Such a process would also provide valuable information to landholders when deciding whether they want to transfer land to investors. It will require informing and educating communities, ideally through a participatory dialogue that includes all stakeholders and draws on lessons from global experience.

Even if large-scale land acquisition is not a desirable option, it will, in many cases, be necessary to improve land governance to ensure that the pressures from higher land values do not lead to dispossession of existing rights. To ensure that existing rights are protected and a level playing field exists to make voluntary transfers feasible, three priority areas need to be covered. First, have state land identified geographically and ensure that mechanisms for its management, acquisition, and divestiture, as well as the imposition of land use restrictions, are transparent and justified. Second, make information on land rights that is complete and current available to all interested parties in a cost-effective manner. Finally, ensure that accessible mechanisms for dispute resolution and conflict management are in place.

If large-scale investment and land transfers are part of a country's strategy, actions will be needed to improve the capacity of government institutions to administer and manage large-scale land transfers. This must also entail learning from experience through a variety of mechanisms, including an audit of existing contracts. Such analyses could provide guidance on appropriate regulations and standards, environmental safeguards, and ways to ensure that approved investments are economically viable and that they generate local benefits. Capacity building is required to accomplish the following:

- Establish effective consultation that enables representative participation, provides relevant information, records reservations and decisions, and develops an agreed approach to monitoring and remedies.
- Streamline and review institutional responsibilities to strengthen coordination between agencies and their capacity to develop and monitor transparent land transfer mechanisms, as well as design environmental and social assessments.
- Develop more open modalities of land acquisition including, for example, an auction model.
- Strengthen records management including, for example, developing and maintaining an inventory of state land and transfers in a central database—a task that can be conducted at lower cost with the benefit of new technologies.
- Ensure proper technical review and screening of proposed projects as part of due diligence. There is also scope for review and possibly refinement of

incentives for investors to promote positive outcomes—examples include encouraging investment in areas where land rights have been clarified or infrastructure is in place, or offering tax holidays only after certain milestones are achieved.

Responsible investors interested in the long-term viability of their investments realize that adherence to a set of basic principles is in their best interest; many have committed to doing so under a range of initiatives, including ones with a governance structure incorporating civil society and governments. Expansion of membership and scope of these initiatives is desirable. At the same time, there is an urgent need to make such principles operational, disseminate good practice, and provide feedback to public sector officials. This needs to be combined with effective disclosure mechanisms, including third-party verification and ways to ensure compliance. Translating practices adopted by industry leaders into regulations could help to quickly improve performance on the ground.

Civil society and local government can build critical links to local communities in three ways: educating communities about effectively exercising their rights; assisting in the design, negotiation, implementation, and monitoring of investment projects where requested; and acting as watchdogs to critically review projects and publicize findings by holding governments and investors accountable and providing inputs into country strategies.

International organizations can do more to support countries to maximize opportunities and minimize risks from large-scale land acquisition in four ways. First, they can assist countries to integrate information and analysis on large-scale land acquisition into national strategies. Second, they can offer financial and technical support for capacity building. Third, there is scope for supporting stakeholder convergence around responsible agro-investment principles for all stakeholders that can be implemented and monitored. Fourth, they can help establish and maintain mechanisms to disseminate information and good practice on management of land acquisitions by incorporating experience and lessons from existing multi-stakeholder initiatives.

Building on the work done thus far, the World Bank is committed to work together with its partners to help countries integrate investment into their rural development strategies and spending plans, strengthen land governance and relevant institutions, establish complementary infrastructure, and support multistakeholder initiatives to facilitate monitoring and sharing of experience.

NOTES

1. Peru uses very transparent and competitive processes for divestiture of state lands for agricultural use along the Pacific Coast. In the Amazon, processes for land transfer are less open and have many loopholes.

2. Large farms had been established during colonial times and were often either subjected to redistributed land reform or nationalized (Binswanger, Deininger, and Feder 1995). Even for industries with significant upstream processing (for example, cocoa) most production is done by smallholders rather than in big estates.

3. These countries are Cambodia, the Democratic Republic of Congo, Ethiopia, Indonesia, the Lao People's Democratic Republic, Liberia, Mozambique, Nigeria, Pakistan, Paraguay, Peru, Sudan, Ukraine, and Zambia.

REFERENCES

Binswanger, H. P., K. Deininger, and G. Feder. 1995. "Power, Distortions, Revolt, and Reform in Agricultural Land Relations." In *Handbook of Development Economics*, ed. T. Behrman and T. N. Srinivasan. North Holland: Elsevier.

Fischer, G., and M. Shah. 2010 "Farmland Investments and Food Security: Statistical Annex." Report prepared under World Bank and International Institute for Applied System Analysis contract, Luxembourg.

Introduction

Although fairly short-lived, the 2007–08 commodity price boom and the subsequent period of high and volatile prices reminded many import-dependent countries of their vulnerability in food security and prompted them to secure their food supplies overseas. Together with the financial crisis, the boom led to a "rediscovery" of the agricultural sector by different types of investors. One of the more permanent effects of the food and financial crisis was that it prompted some food import-dependent countries to reconsider their policies to reduce vulnerability from what is considered to be an "undue dependence" on imports. Investment in agriculture, while still small compared with other economic sectors, has been growing rapidly (UNCTAD 2009), and land has become the focus of a new wave of long-term investors (de Lapérouse 2010). Highly publicized were the land acquisitions by foreign investors in Africa and Asia, often for speculative purposes, at very low prices, and in ways that appeared to be not conducive to local welfare or inconsistent with basic human rights.

Given the number of actors involved, the political overtones, and the potentially far-reaching impact of such land acquisitions on local livelihoods and long-term development paths, the phenomenon has attracted considerable attention from public officials, policy makers, think tanks, nongovernmental organizations, and the public. Contributions have highlighted the size of the phenomenon (Kugelman and Levenstein 2010), its link to food security (French Inter-Ministerial Food Security Group 2010), the importance of building on countries' existing commitments in human rights and food security (De Schutter 2010), and the need to identify principles to guide large-scale land acquisition. Multilateral and bilateral agencies aimed to anchor such investment more firmly in the existing guidelines for foreign investment, including those by the Organisation for Economic Co-operation and Development and to help countries adapt their policy frameworks accordingly.

Increased investor interest in agriculture provides opportunities to developing countries with large primary sectors and high levels of rural poverty, gaps in productivity, and large amounts of land (box I.1). It affects the work of development institutions and provides an opportunity for them to demonstrate leadership and act as a catalyst in a number of ways (Songwe and Deininger 2009). This study was initiated to overcome the information gaps that undermined stakeholders' efforts to deal with this phenomenon. It is thus analytical rather than normative, and its main purpose is threefold:

- Use empirical evidence to inform governments in client countries, especially those with large amounts of land, as well as investors, development partners, and civil society, about what is happening on the ground.
- Put these events into context and assess their likely long-term impact by identifying global drivers of land supply and demand and highlighting how country policies affect land use, household welfare, and distributional outcomes at the local level.
- Complement the focus on demand for land with a geographically referenced assessment of the supply side, that is, the availability of potentially suitable land for rainfed cultivation.

Box I.I   Who Demands Land?

On the demand side, three broad groups of actors can be distinguished. A first group includes governments from countries initiating investments, which, especially in the wake of the 2007–08 food crisis, are concerned about their inability to provide food from domestic resources. A second group of relevant players are financial entities, which in the current environment find attractive attributes in land-based investments. These include the likely appreciation of land, the scope to use it as an inflation hedge, and the projection of secure returns from land far in the future, something of great importance for pension funds with a long horizon. Although land markets are quite illiquid, some of the more active investors might also benefit from steps to improve the functioning of land markets and, in some cases, use sophisticated quantitative techniques to identify undervalued land. Third, with greater concentration in agro-processing and technical advances that favor larger operations, traditional agricultural or agro-industrial operators or traders may have an incentive to either expand the scale of operations or integrate forward or backward and acquire land, though not always through purchases.

- Outline options for different actors to minimize risks and capitalize on opportunities to contribute to poverty reduction and economic growth, especially in rural areas.

Based on initial findings from this empirical research, the World Bank has contributed to the formulation, jointly with partners, of a set of principles for responsible agricultural investment that respects rights, livelihoods, and resources (box 1 in the overview) (FAO and others 2010). The government of Japan, together with other institutions (such as the United States and the African Union), has been fostering debate on these principles with the goal of developing a consensus around them, receiving broad informal support from other governments that view the principles as a starting point.

These principles have already served a useful purpose in reminding countries and investors of their responsibilities and drawing attention to policies that seemed to violate them. At the same time, the real challenge is to make them operational in a country setting. Empirical evidence is urgently needed to assess whether and under what conditions such investment can serve broader social goals, to provide guidance on how to implement them in practice, and to assess compliance. Observers noted that a broad consultation about these principles has yet to happen. Concern has also been expressed that the way the principles are currently framed creates the impression that their purpose is to promote investor interest rather than to help countries formulate strategies and implement regulations that would protect local rights and allow them to confront the "land rush" in a way that promotes sustainable poverty reduction. Although this was not the goal in designing the principles, there is a need to ensure that their application assists countries in making strategic decisions about large-scale agro-investments.

To do justice to the complexity of the phenomenon and the fact that in many cases information is not readily available, we use a range of methods:

- Compiling country inventories of large land transfers during 2004–09 in 14 countries based on data officially available to in-country consultants,[1] complemented by analysis of media reports on large investments in 2008–09
- Assessing the policy, legal, and institutional framework for large-scale land acquisition based on compilations of background information by a country coordinator and panels with representation from a wide range of stakeholders to arrive at a consensus ranking[2]
- Identifying by country and region the available land that might attract investor interest in the future, based on a global assessment of agro-ecological suitability for rainfed farming given current land use, infrastructure access, and population density
- Reviewing historical land expansion processes and predicted rates of expansion of cultivated area depending on different demand drivers.

Three insights are worth noting. First, access to information emerged as much more of a problem than anticipated. Even for data that should not be subject to any restrictions of confidentiality or within government departments, limited data sharing and gaps and inconsistencies in record keeping implied an astonishing lack of awareness of what is happening on the ground even by the public sector institutions mandated to control this phenomenon. This lack or dispersion of information makes it difficult to exercise due diligence and to responsibly manage a valuable asset. More importantly, it makes it easy to neglect local people's rights and creates a lack of openness that can lead to bad governance and corruption and jeopardize investors' tenure security. Improving the quality of data recording could thus have high payoffs. Measures in this direction, straightforward from a technical point of view, are a priority for outside support in the short term.

Second, while some countries have transferred large areas to investors, the extent to which such land is actually used productively remains limited. Country collaborators had great difficulty identifying operating investments. In many cases, it appeared that investors either lacked the necessary technical qualifications or were interested more in speculative gains than in productive exploitation. Land taxation and the ability to revoke unused concessions, options available according to many countries' legislation but rarely exercised, should help to avoid such behavior. But gaps in information management imply that taxes are rarely collected. And the shortage of monitoring capacity, together with the fact that those involved are often powerful politically, implies that few concessions have been revoked. Impartial ex ante review of investors' technical proposals, which could be outsourced if needed, is a more cost-effective way to avoid having large tracts of land held in less than fully productive ways in expectation of speculative gains.

Third, it was surprising that in many cases the nature and location of lands transferred and the ways such transfers are implemented are rather ad hoc—based more on investor demands than on strategic considerations. Rarely are efforts linked to broader development strategies, careful consideration of the alternatives, or how such transfers might positively or negatively affect broader social and economic goals. Only in a very few cases have countries started to establish an inventory of currently uncultivated land with potential for cultivation, its suitability, its current use, and the rights to it. Without such information, it will be difficult to protect existing rights, attract capable investors, fully exploit potential complementarities between private investment and public goods, and ensure that the investment will contribute to poverty reduction and overall development. As agriculture is typically a very competitive business with thin margins, a more strategic approach to land transfers that first considers the relative allocation of land to different commodities will likely also be important for profiting from these investments.

The report is structured as follows.

Chapter 1—Land expansion: Drivers, underlying factors, and key effects. The chapter quantifies past land expansion and, based on key drivers, highlights predictions for current and potential future demand for land expansion. It uses differences in regional experience to highlight how policy affects the nature, magnitude, and impact of investments and to demonstrate risks and opportunities. This is linked to determinants of the agricultural production structure and the implications for fair land valuations.

Chapter 2—Is the recent "land rush" different? To provide an answer to this question, we rely on press reports on demand for land, inventories of registered transactions, and case studies based on field visits to assess social impacts of actual investments on the ground. Media reports highlight the magnitude of investor interest, the pervasive implementation gaps, and the focus on countries with weak land governance. Project inventories point toward the overriding importance of policies, illustrated by differences in the amounts of land transferred and the number of jobs or land-related investment generated. Case studies show that investments can bring significant benefits, but that they can also impose high costs borne disproportionately by vulnerable groups. This implies that, in many cases, potential benefits from such transfers are not realized or outweighed by negative impacts. As such, measures may be needed to improve capacity on all sides and monitoring of actual outcomes to bring about improvements.

Chapter 3—The scope for and desirability of land expansion. The focus of the debate thus far has been almost exclusively on investors' demand for land rather than the potential for expanding rainfed cultivated area or increasing productivity on currently cultivated area from a country perspective. Adopting the latter will help in at least two ways. First, it highlights the fact that any investments need to help countries achieve their development objectives rather than the other way around, that for many countries improving the productivity of smallholder farmers will have a much larger impact on poverty reduction than promotion of large-scale land acquisition, and that if a country decides that attracting investors is in its best interest, ways that such investments benefit local populations must be high up on the agenda. Geographically referenced data on land potential also allows to check whether investors focus on the most productive areas and fully use available potential and to identify hotspots that might attract investor interest in the future.

Second, it suggests how one might quantify, at the country level, the supply of land with unused agro-ecological and economic potential where cultivation would not eliminate environmental services or displace existing land users without their agreement. In addition to agro-ecological potential, this will require data on land rights and global public goods (for example, high biodiversity). In the absence of these, we map as a proxy the currently uncultivated, unprotected, and unforested land in areas of low population density (<5, 10, and 25 persons/km^2)

agronomically suitable for rainfed cultivation of wheat, sugarcane, oil palm, maize, or soybeans at different levels of infrastructure access. We complement this with an assessment of the yield gap, that is, the percentage share of potentially attainable yields actually obtained on areas currently cultivated, to illustrate that area expansion will not always be the most desirable or beneficial option. Even if it is, benefits may be maximized by linking it to ways of increasing smallholder productivity (for example, through technology spillovers or market access). If technology is not widely used locally, this also implies a need for closer scrutiny of investors' technical proposals and more specific descriptions of how spillovers to local producers are expected to occur.

Chapter 4—The policy, legal, and institutional framework. If there is potential for sustainable agro-investment outcomes but outcomes are far from optimal, it is necessary to explore the framework under which these investments are conducted. Broad consensus exists that the framework governing large-scale land acquisition in sample countries should have five attributes:

- Legal recognition and actual demarcation of rights to land and associated natural resources and the way communities are consulted and decisions made.
- Representative mechanisms should ensure that transfers of rights to land and other resources are voluntary and that all interested parties are consulted, not captured by a narrow elite.
- Clear rules and impartial, open, and cost-effective mechanisms should guide interactions with investors.
- The investments' economic viability and consistency with broader goals of food security should be assessed and publicized.
- Adherence to standards for environmental and social sustainability should be ensured during project preparation and implementation.

Extensive review of arrangements in place in 14 countries helps identify good practice examples that have helped achieve good outcomes and thus can guide countries with weak frameworks. At the same time, it points to a large number of gaps that are likely to lead to some of the negative impacts observed in practice. Addressing these quickly, in a way that focuses on high priority areas and complements existing initiatives, will be critical if investments are to live up to their potential rather than cause significant damage and harm.

Chapter 5—Moving from challenge to opportunity. How can governments, the private sector, and civil society address the risks and respond to opportunities opened by large-scale investment? For governments, what is needed to provide the basis for strategic decisions is an assessment of the following:

- Current and potential future comparative advantage in terms of not only availability of suitable land but also infrastructure, evolution of the labor force and human capital, and anticipated changes in the environment

- The institutional framework for investors (and its implementation) and how consistent it is (and its implementation) with the goals of attracting serious investors, respecting land rights and sharing benefits with local people, and monitoring performance
- Potentially available land, existing claims to such land, and the scope and need for employment generation.

We developed a typology of countries by potential availability of land for rainfed cultivation and yield gap to help countries assess the extent to which large-scale investment will be an option and, if yes, how to shape such investment to contribute to national development. In many cases the most desirable mechanism for investment in the agricultural sector will be providing support to existing smallholders. If investment in land acquisition is desirable, attention will need to be given to the gaps identified in case studies and in the review of policy and legal frameworks. Although industry-led initiatives are not always simple to establish, drawing on them for technical guidance and building on accepted financial sector performance standards offer considerable potential. International institutions and civil society actors can complement this with effective mechanisms involving all stakeholders to monitor and improve land governance and increase disclosure and access to information. This would include dissemination, capacity building, and support to implementation and effective monitoring of a common set of standards. Debate on how to shape it, followed by concrete steps, will be a high priority.

NOTES

1. These countries are Cambodia, the Democratic Republic of Congo, Ethiopia, Indonesia, the Lao People's Democratic Republic, Liberia, Mozambique, Nigeria, Pakistan, Paraguay, Peru, Sudan, Ukraine, and Zambia.
2. These countries are Brazil, the Democratic Republic of Congo, Ethiopia, Indonesia, Liberia, Mexico, Mozambique, Nigeria, Pakistan, Peru, Sudan, Tanzania, Ukraine, and Zambia.

REFERENCES

de Lapérouse, P. 2010. "Survey of Global Developments in Private Sector Investment in Farmland and Agricultural Infrastructure." Paper presented at the Annual Bank Conference on Land Policy and Administration, Washington, DC, April 27.

De Schutter, O. 2010. "Large-Scale Land Acquisitions and Leases: A Set of Core Principles and Measures to Address the Human Rights Challenge." Louvain, Belgium: United Nations Special Rapporteur for the Right to Food.

FAO (Food and Agriculture Organization of the United Nations), IFAD (International Fund for Agricultural Development), UNCTAD (United Nations Conference on Trade and Development), and World Bank Group. 2010. "Principles for Responsible

Agricultural Investment that Respects Rights, Livelihoods and Resources." A discussion note to contribute to an ongoing global dialogue, Rome.

Kugelman, M., and S. L. Levenstein. 2010. "Land Grab? The Race for the World's Farmland." Washington, DC: Woodrow Wilson International Center for Scholars.

Songwe, V., and K. Deininger. 2009. "Foreign Investment in Agricultural Production: Opportunities and Challenges." Agricultural and Rural Development Notes, Land Policy and Administration, World Bank, Washington, DC.

UNCTAD (United Nations Conference on Trade and Development). 2009. "World Investment Report 2009: Transnational Corporations, Agricultural Production and Development." New York and Geneva: United Nations.

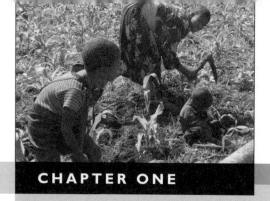

CHAPTER ONE

Land Expansion: Drivers, Underlying Factors, and Key Effects

Land acquisition has evolved over time with variations across regions and commodities in the balance between area expansion and intensification, the role of large-scale and small-scale farming, and the resulting social and environmental impacts. To set the context for recent processes of large-scale land acquisition, this chapter discusses three issues.

- It identifies the magnitude and key drivers of demand growth and area expansion in major commodities over the last decade and reviews estimates of how these may evolve in the near and medium terms. Land expansion, much of it through commercial farming in owner-operated units, is not new and is expected to continue. Given their relative land abundance, such land expansion is likely to be concentrated in Sub-Saharan Africa and Latin America and the Caribbean.
- To illustrate how natural endowments (such as climate or terrain), infrastructure, technology, and institutions affected nature and social as well as economic impacts of land expansion across the main regions, it differentiates structural change in the agricultural sector by region and reviews large-scale cultivation trends across regions.
- To provide the basis for assessing social impacts, it reviews key determinants of the structure of agricultural production—particularly the factors determining the competitiveness of owner-operated family farms and large corporate units—and the implications for determining fair land values and integrating large-scale agricultural investment into country strategies.

PAST AND LIKELY FUTURE PATTERNS OF COMMODITY DEMAND AND LAND EXPANSION

To assess whether the drive toward land acquisition seen after the 2008 commodity price spike is a temporary aberration or part of a longer-term pattern, we review patterns of past land expansion and predictions of future demand for commodities as well as land. Expansion of cultivated area is not a new phenomenon and is likely to continue, although the regional emphasis may shift slightly over time.

Past Processes of Land Expansion

Between 1961 and 2007, the area of cultivated land expanded at some 3.8 million hectares per year (ha/year) globally, compared with a total cultivated area of 1,554 million ha in 2007. This increase was unevenly distributed between developed and developing countries, with small declines in industrial and transition economies and an increase of 5.0 million ha/year in developing countries (table 1.1). Regionally, expansion was most pronounced in Sub-Saharan Africa, Latin America and the Caribbean, and East Asia.

Were it not for advances in productivity, especially the development of land-saving technology, much larger areas would have been brought under cultivation. In fact, 70 percent of the increase in crop production between 1961 and 2005 was due to yield increases, 23 percent to the expansion of arable area, and 8 percent to the intensification of cropping (Bruinsma 2009). Area growth dominated in Sub-Saharan Africa and, though less relevant than yield growth,

Table 1.1 Changes in Arable Area Used for Farming (million ha)					
	Total area			**Change/a**	
Region	**1961–63**	**1989–91**	**2007**	**1961–2007**	**1990–2007**
East Asia	176	223	256	1.7	1.9
Latin America and the Caribbean	104	148	164	1.3	1.0
Middle East and North Africa	86	97	97	0.2	0.0
South Asia	191	204	205	0.3	0.0
Southeast Asia	71	92	103	0.7	0.7
Sub-Saharan Africa	148	179	221	1.5	2.4
Developing countries	704	850	940	5.0	5.3
Industrialized countries	385	395	360	–0.5	–2.1
Transition countries	286	275	254	–0.7	–1.3
World	1,376	1,521	1,554	3.8	1.9

Source: FAOSTAT 2009.

Figure 1.1   Area Expansion and Yield Growth

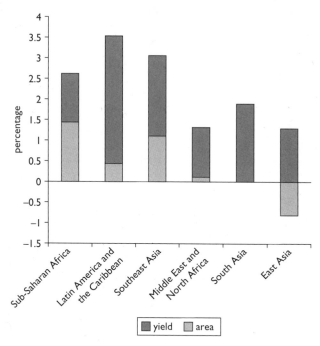

Source: Authors based on FAO figures.
Note: Data are for 1990–2007.

was also a key factor in Latin America and the Caribbean and Southeast Asia (figure 1.1).

Three factors underpin this expansion of cultivated area:

- Demand for food, feed, pulp, and other industrial raw materials, driven by growth of population and income
- Demand for biofuel feedstocks as a reflection of policies and mandates in key consuming countries
- Shifts of production of bulk commodities to land-abundant regions where land may be cheaper and the scope for productivity growth higher than in traditional producing regions already operating at the productivity frontier.

From 1990 to 2007, growth of harvested area for different crops, which could come about either via substitution for other crops or via expansion into previously uncultivated areas, was narrowly concentrated in a few key commodities (table 1.2). With an increase in harvested area of more than 55 million ha, soybean, rapeseed, sunflower (much of it in large-scale operations) and oil palm (about half under large and half under small-scale operations) accounted for

Table 1.2 Key Commodities Driving Land Use Change, 1990–2007

Commodity	Area 2007	Change 1990–2007	Annual change	% large-scale	Key contributors (% of net increase)[a]
Maize	158	27.3	1.6	52	China (29) United States (29) Brazil (9)
Oil palm	14	7.8	0.5	55	Indonesia (50) Malaysia (26) Nigeria (11)
Rice	156	9.0	0.5	4	Myanmar (38) Thailand (21) Indonesia (18)
Rapeseed	30	12.1	0.7	85	Canada (32) India (15) France (8)
Soybean	90	32.9	1.9	78	Argentina (33) Brazil (28) India (19)
Sunflower	27	4.1	0.2	90	Russian Federation (41) Ukraine (38) Myanmar (10)
Sugarcane	23	5.9	0.3	55	Brazil (47) India (29) China (9)
Plantation forestry	139	37.1	2.5	n.a.	China (35) United States (18) Russian Federation (12)

Source: Authors' tabulations from FAOSTAT 2009. Plantation forestry is from FAO 2007 for the 1990–2005 period. Large-scale is based on authors' classification of the most common production scales in the 20 countries with the fastest expansion.
a. This column refers to net changes in cultivated area of a crop that may be due to substitution for other crops rather than area expansion.

more than half of total growth. Demand for these oil crops grew significantly as a result of higher consumption of cooking oil in developing country markets of Asia, greater use of soybeans as feed, and production of biodiesel in the European Union. More than two-thirds of the increase in soybean area was in Argentina and Brazil, while oil palm expansion was concentrated in Southeast Asia. Rising developing-country incomes increased demand for maize as animal feed in Asia (mainly grown by smallholders) and as an input for bioethanol to satisfy biofuel mandates in the United States. Rice is used mainly for human consumption, with changes in area driven by population growth in Asia, and income growth and urbanization in the Middle East and North Africa. Virtually all of the rice expansion was concentrated in small farms. Pastures, natural or improved, account for 3,400 million ha of land use globally and have expanded at about 2.5 million ha/year between 1990 and 2007, with implications for deforestation, biodiversity, and the global carbon balance.[1]

Rising energy prices and public subsidies and mandates, with second-generation (cellulosic) biofuels still at least a decade away, led to rapid increases in the demand for biofuel feedstock starting in 2003. In 2008, the total area under biofuel crops was estimated at 36 million ha, more than twice the 2004 level, with 8.3 million ha in the European Union (mainly rapeseed), 7.5 million ha in the United States (mainly maize), and 6.4 million ha in Latin America and the Caribbean, mainly sugarcane (UNEP 2009). Experts have long been concerned that, by affecting prices, biofuel mandates will have sizable impacts on land use far beyond the countries where they operate (Renewable Fuels Agency 2008). General equilibrium models that allow for trade, substitution among crops, and land use conversion suggest that biofuel mandates may have large indirect effects on land use change, particularly converting pasture and forest land.[2]

Greater global integration and reduction of trade barriers, together with large preexisting differences in productivity across regions prompted shifts of production toward developing countries. Between 1990 and 2007 soybean yields in Latin America and the Caribbean grew at twice the U.S. rate from a much lower base, prompting much new production to shift to countries in Latin America and the Caribbean. Similarly, for wood and pulp, tree productivity is less than 15 m³/ha/a in the United States and less than 10 in northern Europe, compared with 45 m³/ha/a in Brazil, suggesting potential for large future investment in pulp production in the tropics and subtropics.

In addition to food and industrial crops, area used for plantation forestry expanded at some 2.5 million ha/year in 1990–2005. Forest plantations now account for between half and two-thirds (if pulp/fiber is included) of global wood production (Carle and Holmgren 2008) and occupy some 140 million ha globally, 54 percent of it (75 million ha) in developing and transition economies. Developing countries entered the sector late but increased areas dramatically, by 1.5 million ha/a in 1990–2005, to take advantage of high productivity and short production cycles. Some of this expansion has been controversial, as summarized by the characterization of these as "green deserts" with monoculture and limited biodiversity (Cossalter and Pye-Smith 2003). Plantation forestry also expanded in China and in industrial and transition economies where agricultural area declined, partly as marginal lands were removed from agricultural production.

FUTURE DEMAND FOR AGRICULTURAL COMMODITIES AND LAND

Experts agree that population growth, rising incomes, and urbanization will continue to drive demand growth for some food, especially vegetable oils and livestock, with higher derived demand for feed and for industrial products. To cope with a 40 percent increase in world population, production would need to rise by 70 percent, and raising food consumption to 3,130 kcal/person/day by 2050 would require agricultural production to nearly double in developing countries (Bruinsma 2009). With slower advances in technology and greater resource constraints, especially for water, even conservative estimates suggest that past rates of land conversion will be maintained or exceeded until 2030 (box 1.1). So, the "land rush" is unlikely to slow.

Assumptions about yield growth are critical to assess how demand for commodities relates to land demand. Among the major crops, especially rice and wheat, yield growth has slowed sharply since the 1980s, a result of exhausted

Box 1.1   Are Crop Yields Stagnating?

Much of the concern about producing enough food for the future relates to slower yield growth in the major cereals over the past three decades (World Bank 2009a). The 10-year moving average annual growth rates for wheat and rice yields in developing countries declined from 3 percent to 5 percent in the mid-1980s to 1 percent to 2 percent in this decade (box figure 1.1). The trends for maize and soybean are much less pronounced.

Box Figure 1.1   Yield Growth Rates for Selected Crops in Developing and Industrial Countries, 1996–2001

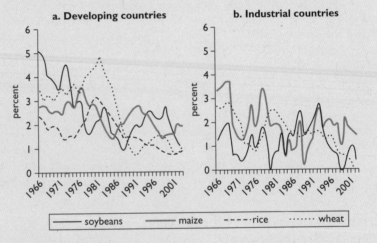

Source: Authors, based on data from FAOSTAT.
Note: Figures show 10-year moving averages of annual growth rates, estimated by log linear trend regression.

green revolution technology, lower grain prices until 2000, slower growth in research and development (R&D) spending in most countries, and land degradation. With few breakthrough technologies on the horizon, the scope for yield gains over 2005–30 seems lower than in the past.

Irrigation has contributed to past growth in crop yields, but water scarcity is slowing the expansion of irrigation in many regions where water is now a major constraint to production. Large areas of China, South Asia, and the Middle East and North Africa maintain irrigated food production through unsustainable extraction of water from rivers or aquifers. The availability of water in these regions will be further reduced by competition from growing urban populations and industrial sectors. In contrast, Sub-Saharan Africa and Latin America and the Caribbean have large untapped water resources for agriculture. With greater efficiency in water use, global irrigated area could expand by 23 million ha and harvested area by 41 million ha by 2030 (Bruinsma 2009).

Climate change will have profound impacts on agricultural production in several ways. While higher temperatures may allow crop cultivation to expand into areas that have traditionally been too cold for crop cultivation, it is likely to reduce yields in hotter climates. Experts also agree that with climate change extreme weather events are likely to create higher variability of output. Even if, as in many parts of Africa, rainfall remains plentiful, it may be concentrated in shorter time periods, creating a need for infrastructure to minimize runoff and the associated soil erosion and to allow storage of water to extend growing seasons. While likely impacts need to be considered on a country-by-country basis, aggregate impacts could be significant. One study estimates that climate change will reduce irrigated wheat yields in developing countries by as much as 34 percent by 2050 (Nelson and others 2009). The Food and Agriculture Organization of the United Nations (FAO) thus estimates annual yield gains of 0.9 percent for cereals, a decline from 1.5 percent over 1980–2005.

Demand for biofuel feedstocks is a major factor for world agriculture with land conversion for biofuels by 2030 estimated to range between 18 and 44 million ha (Fischer and others 2008). If mandates imposed in many countries are maintained, such demand will be inelastic to oil prices in the medium term until, in a decade or so, second-generation biofuels derived from cellulosic material such as leaves, stalks, and straw become viable.[3] Potential impacts on land use could be large (Searchinger and others 2008). Over 2008–18, biofuel feedstocks may account for 52 percent of the increased demand for maize and wheat, and 32 percent of that for oilseeds (OECD and FAO 2010). Biofuel mandates also drive expansion of sugarcane for ethanol. Brazil processes half its cane into ethanol, and the cane area is expected to double by 2017 (BNDES 2008).

Plantation forestry has been one of the land use categories that has expanded fast over the past decades and is expected to continue doing so in the future. But no study of demand for land includes such plantations. Including projected growth of this land use category of 42–84 million ha (the higher figure based on a continuation of past trends) adds significantly to the total demand for land (Carle and Holmgren 2008).

Without accounting for biofuels and forest plantations, or trade and price effects, FAO projections suggest that for 2010–30, after adjusting for increases in cropping intensity, 47 million ha of land will be brought into production globally—a decrease of 27 million in developed countries and transition economies and an increase of 74 million in developing countries. This translates to an annual increase of 1.8 million ha for food and feed only.

Computable general equilibrium (CGE) models allow for adjustments to prices and trade that induce land supply in regions where land is fairly abundant (Keeney and Hertel 2009). Such adjustments increase the estimates, with projected annual land use changes ranging from 4.5 million ha (Fischer and others 2008) to 10 million ha (Al-Riffai and others 2010) or even 12 million ha (Eickhout and others 2009), highlighting the conservative nature of FAO estimates. Plantation forestry could add some 1.5 million ha/year, although part of the required land does not compete with crop uses.

In sum, a conservative estimate is that 6 million ha/year of additional land will be brought into production through 2030, implying a total land expansion of 120 million ha. Projections that allow for trade and price changes can be much larger, with total area increases of up to 240 million ha over the period. The fact that land use is in decline in developed and transition economies implies that more area expansion will shift to developing countries. As land that may be used for expansion is not equally distributed, some two-thirds of land expansion in developing countries is likely to be in Latin America and the Caribbean and in Sub-Saharan Africa.

LESSONS FROM PAST PROCESSES OF LAND EXPANSION: REGIONAL PERSPECTIVES

In each of the world's major regions, area expansion happened in a variety of historical contexts, driven by different actors and with social and environmental impacts profoundly affected by public policies. A review of key factors and differences across regions and commodities helps identify issues deserving attention. It can be useful to help countries where such demand is only now materializing to be aware of some of the pitfalls and ideally take measures to avoid them.

Latin America: Missed Opportunities for Poverty Reduction and Environmental Challenges

Following the liberalization of markets and trade in the 1980s, relatively land-abundant countries in Latin America—including Argentina, Brazil, Paraguay, and Uruguay—capitalized on growing global demand to increase their position in world markets. Higher prices, improved technology, and lower transport costs pushed out the land frontier. Soybean production increased from 33 million tons (t) to 116 million t from 1990 to 2008, making Latin America the world's largest soybean exporter. Beef, sugarcane, and plantation forestry also occupy an important position.

Over the past two decades, Brazil's *cerrado* experienced the world's fastest expansion of the agricultural frontier (World Bank 2009a).[4] Largely uncultivated until the 1970s, it now accounts for more than half of Brazil's soybean area, making it the world's second-largest soybean exporter after the United States. A key factor was technology, particularly the development of varieties suited to the cerrado's low latitudes and acid soils and wide adoption of conservation tillage, which sharply reduced costs. Significant expansion has also taken place in the Argentine *Pampas* as zero tillage and herbicide-tolerant and pest-resistant varieties increased the profitability of soybeans, which then substituted for other crops and pasture. Though concerns have been expressed about the contribution of soybean cultivation to the clearing of the dry topical forests of the cerrado, there is little evidence that such cultivation directly pushed into areas of the Amazon biome on a significant scale.

But rapid agricultural growth has also not always translated into positive social impacts. Land policy failures and large-scale programs of subsidized credit for large farmers at negative interest rates led to mechanized rather than labor-intensive production (Rezende 2005). Employment generation and poverty impacts thus remained far below potential (World Bank 2009a). The exit of small farms contributes to a continued concentration of farm operations with average farm sizes of more than 1,000 ha. A main reason small farmers lost their land is that land records were poor and the protection of land rights limited, leading many to argue that development of the cerrado region, although successful commercially, missed opportunities for social development. To address this problem, Brazil initiated efforts to regularize land tenure and better protect natural areas.

Brazil is the world's largest meat exporter with exports, mostly for beef or chicken, increasing from US$600 million to US$11 billion between 1990 and 2007. The expansion has been fastest in the Amazon, where the cattle population more than doubled from 1990 to 2006 and the pasture area expanded by 24 million ha (Pacheco 2009). But this expansion has come at the expense of tropical forests, with negative social and environmental impacts. Pasture expansion is the most important cause of deforestation, accounting for about two-thirds of the Amazon's forest loss (Pacheco 2009). Based on satellite imagery, Figure 1.2 summarizes key changes in forest and cerrado areas in the state of Mato Grosso between 2001 and 2004 (Morton and others 2006):

- About 2.7 million ha (27,000 km²) of forest was converted to pasture or abandoned, pointing to low efficiency in the use of forest resources.
- About 1.0 million ha (10,000 km²) of forest was converted to cropland, with mechanized large farms and small farms each accounting for about half of observed forest loss.

Figure 1.2 Cropland Expansion, Deforestation in Mato Grosso, Brazil 2001–04

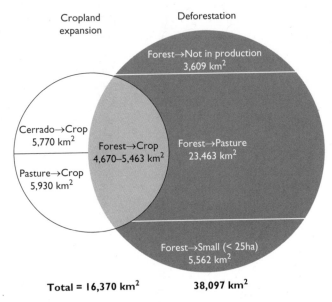

Source: Morton and others 2006.

- About 1.1 million ha (11,000 km²) was brought under crop production from cerrado or degraded pasture that had previously been converted.

A key factor for expanding cattle ranching was policies requiring "productive use" of land to claim ownership. Together with weak institutions and gaps in governance of forest resources and the protection of indigenous peoples' rights, these policies contributed significantly to deforestation (Fearnside 2001). Due to its low fertility, most land was quickly converted into low-grade pastures for cattle ranching or even abandoned, implying that long-term impacts on output or welfare remained limited.

Building on more than 30 years of research and a proactive policy to promote sugarcane, Brazil also developed an advanced sugarcane industry to produce sugar and ethanol, producing 20 percent of the world's sugar and 34 percent of its ethanol in 2005 and accounting for 38 percent of world trade in sugar and 74 percent of world trade in ethanol. In addition to low production cost for sugarcane, the high concentration of sucrose in Brazilian varieties (14 percent) contributes to its competitiveness and has made it one of the lowest-cost global producers.

The expansion of sugarcane suggests that increased productivity can mitigate the environmental effects of agricultural expansion. About two-thirds of the area into which sugarcane expanded has been from converting pastureland, 32 percent from substituting other crops, and only 2 percent from converting natural vegetation. Rapid gains in productivity in both sugarcane and pastures reduced the indirect effects on land expansion, although the resulting higher price of land has probably put pressure on pasture expansion further north to the cerrado and the Amazon biome.

Investments to establish fast-growing plantation forestry on vast expanses of land led to major shifts in land use in some countries. In Brazil, private R&D investment that tripled the productivity of eucalyptus over the past 30 years was a key to developing a competitive industry (Bacha 2008; Doughty 2000). Benefiting from substantial technology transfers from Brazil and international companies, Uruguay started to develop an export-oriented pulp industry in 1990. Targeted subsidies to convert poor quality pasturelands expanded the area under plantation forest from 97,000 ha to 751,000 ha between 1990 and 2005 (Morales Olmos 2007).

Public and private sector players in the region now recognize that agricultural investment and expansion pose serious environmental challenges. They have taken action to reduce detrimental impacts, including better delineating protected areas, using satellite-based technology to monitor deforestation in real time, and prosecuting violators (de Souza and others 2010). The Brazilian government is increasingly using financial incentives, such as the barring of individuals who do not comply with legal requirements (in maintaining minimum levels of forested areas on their property, for example) from access to state-supported credit. It has also initiated a zoning exercise to limit negative environmental impacts of sugarcane and other crops by limiting areas into which these crops can expand. Other initiatives, such as the Roundtable on Responsible Soy and an industry-led boycott on beef from recently deforested pasture, also point toward increased awareness by the private sector of the reputational risks in contributing to unsustainable outcomes. While their impact remains to be seen, they could hold lessons for other regions.

Southeast Asia: Tropical Deforestation with Diverse Social Impacts

Oil palm is regarded as one of the most profitable land uses in the humid tropics (Butler and Laurance 2009). It is highly labor intensive, providing scope for employment generation and positive social impact although this potential was not always achieved and environmental impacts were often negative. The crop expanded rapidly in Indonesia and Malaysia in response to growing global demand for edible oils and strong government support.[5] Malaysia pioneered the commercial oil palm industry (Martin 2003; Rasiah

2006). With rising land and labor costs, the industry moved to neighboring Indonesia, which at 16.9 million tons (Mt) in 2008 is now the world's largest producer, slightly ahead of Malaysia (15.8 Mt), with Malaysia and Indonesia now accounting for 85 percent of global palm oil production. Planted area in Indonesia more than doubled between 1997 and 2007, from about 2.9 million ha to 6.3 million ha. Given the processing requirements and the rapid deterioration of harvested fruit, large-scale production close to the processing unit, often complemented by outgrower schemes, is the norm (see chapter 3). There has also been a strong trend toward vertical integration with refining oil and manufacturing palm oil and palm kernel oil products.

While large units dominate, Indonesia's smallholders account for about a third of production. Average income from oil palm cultivation is much higher than from subsistence farming or competing cash crops (Rist and others 2010). Given the high labor requirements, oil palm expansion in Indonesia helped to significantly reduce poverty with estimates of employment in the oil palm sector ranging from 1.7 million to 3.0 million. Poor planting material, limited access to finance and a noncompetitive market for fresh fruit gives mills considerable market power. This limits smallholder's ability to be successful on their own and implies that most are in formal partnerships with oil palm companies through nucleus estate schemes.

A major social issue in oil palm development is the frequent failure to recognize local land rights. Improving the clarity of rights would allow local people more say in negotiating the terms for making their land available for oil palm—and reduce the costs for companies. Social conflict surrounding oil palm expansion also derives from opaque or poorly understood contractual agreements, lack of consultation, and limited benefit-sharing with local communities (World Bank 2009b). Contracts are often unclear on the terms for transferring land, remunerating outgrowers, and employing local people (Colchester and others 2006). Smallholder associations, greater clarity, and avenues for conflict resolution, could help address these problems.

The oil palm sector has also been criticized for being a major contributor to deforestation and greenhouse gas emissions. Oil palm plantations harbor less biodiversity than natural forests, fail to provide the same environmental services (carbon storage, forest products, soil fertility), and may force smallholders to give up subsistence production and rely on food from the market. Some 70 percent of Indonesia's oil palm plantations (4.2 million ha) are on land previously part of the forest estate; and 56 percent of expansion between 1990 and 2005 was at the expense of natural forests (Koh and Wilcove 2008). To help expand production, the government provided land, in many cases still forested, almost for free, within a legal framework that did not recognize local land rights (Barr and others 2010). Timber sales were expected to finance planting and oil palm establishment. But many companies allegedly use fictitious palm oil schemes to obtain logging licenses without ever establishing oil palm estates. By some estimates up to

12 million ha have been allocated to oil palm and deforested but not planted (Fargione and others 2008).

Approximately 25 percent of oil palm is estimated to have been established on peat. Developing oil palm on peat land causes irreversible damage to vulnerable ecosystems and high levels of carbon emissions; it also requires high levels of management skill to be sustainable. Land use change and deforestation are the largest single contributors to Indonesia's greenhouse gas emissions of 1.7 million Gt in 2007. Studies of the value of carbon stocks in Indonesian forests suggest that payments through programs under the REDD (Reducing Emissions from Deforestation and Forest Degradation) umbrella will be well below the US$22/t at which they could compete with returns from oil palm (figure 1.3). Environmental costs can, however, be reduced, by developing oil palm on *Imperata* grasslands (*alang-alang*) usually portrayed as unproductive wasteland.

At more than 20 million ha, the amount of such land available is well above the 10–20 million ha expected to be needed to meet oil palm demand for the next decade and beyond. Costs of establishing oil palm on these lands are much lower than on secondary forests, and yields are indistinguishable from those on forest land (Fairhurst and McLaughlin 2009). However, as local people and communities may already use degraded lands, bringing these into production will require recognizing such rights and negotiating and sharing benefits with local people. Nongovernmental organizations (NGOs) are implementing demonstration activities that can provide important lessons. For example, the World Resources Institute is conducting community mapping to identify degraded land of interest for oil palm development that could be swapped for planned expansion in forest areas.

Figure 1.3 Range of Returns to Oil Palm and Potential REDD Payments for Forest Conservation in Indonesia

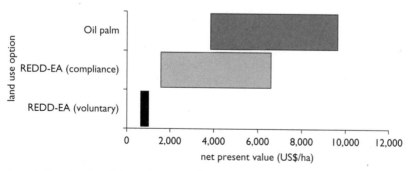

Source: Authors based on Butler and Laurance 2009.
Note: "Compliance" is based on mandated carbon emission reduction in Europe. "Voluntary" is based on voluntary participation in carbon markets, such as the Chicago Board of Trade.

Given the controversies surrounding oil palm, especially the threat to tropical forests, the industry initiated the Roundtable on Sustainable Palm Oil in 2004 to develop and implement palm oil certification. In principle, certification criteria require recognition of local land rights, especially those of local communities, and (since November 2005) ban plantings that "replace primary forest or any area containing one or more High Conservation Values." But applying these criteria to actual operations has been difficult and controversial. Moreover, only 1.6 Mt (4 percent of global production) was certified by April 2009, and demand for certified oil has been slow to develop.

Rubber, although originally grown on large plantations in humid forest areas of Southeast Asia that also suffered from deforestation and neglect of local rights, provides an interesting contrast. Improved clones, techniques suited to smallholder production and processing, and rising labor and land costs led to the rapid expansion of smallholder production. Farms of 2–3 ha make up 80 percent of world rubber production (Hayami 2009). Smallholders in Indonesia produce rubber in diverse natural or improved agro-forestry systems that maintain carbon stocks and species richness. While returns from such systems are lower than those from monocultures, reduced risk and lower initial capital costs more than compensate, and efforts are under way to certify rubber from these systems to obtain a price premium.

Rice, with some additional 10 million ha of cultivated area since 1990, accounted for by far the largest expansion of cultivated area in Southeast Asia and is grown almost entirely by small farmers, in many cases with strong impacts on poverty reduction. For example in Thailand, institutional support through research, extension, credit, and producer organizations was critical in engaging smallholders. In response to land conflicts in the 1970s, a land titling program was initiated to provide tenure security and allow land markets to develop. Until 2004, this program issued 12 million out of a total of 26 million titles countrywide. Thailand also became a major exporter of other commodities (sugar, cassava, maize) in similar smallholder expansions driven by the following:

- Availability of previously uncultivated land, combined with land policies that allowed farmers to expand cultivated area rapidly in response to market opportunities
- Improved agricultural technologies, such as short-duration cassava varieties and improved soil management practices
- Government investment in rail and road infrastructure to reduce the cost of market access
- An undistorted policy environment and supportive investment climate for a rapid supply response by the private sector to market signals (World Bank 2008).

Sub-Saharan Africa: Policy Distortions and Disappointing Performance of Large-Scale Farming

Until the late 1980s, almost all Sub-Saharan African countries had policies that strongly discriminated against agriculture. Overvalued exchange rates lowered real agricultural prices while producer prices of agricultural commodities were suppressed through controlled procurement prices and high export taxes. In the 1980s, net taxation of the sector averaged 29 percent but stood at 46 percent for exportables (World Bank 2009a). At the same time, public expenditure in agriculture fell below 4 percent of national budgets, affecting in particular spending on infrastructure and research. These policies discouraged investment by local farmers and outsiders alike.

After 1990, most Sub-Saharan African countries moved to market-determined exchange rates and open trade regimes. Net taxation of agriculture decreased (though it still exists for export crops), and lower inflation and real interest rates now create a more favorable environment for agricultural investment, especially to the extent that institutional reforms to secure property rights, reduce red tape, and combat corruption were implemented. Several countries have reformed their land laws to protect customary rights, increase incentives for land-related investment, and make land transfers easier. While growth in the sector responded positively, gaps in infrastructure and markets as well as the time required to strengthen property rights and other institutions continue to constrain investment and market development. Most production growth is thus still based largely on land expansion (Fuglie 2008).

Policy bias greatly reduced Sub-Saharan Africa's attractiveness for investment so that, despite relative land abundance, expansion was mainly driven by population growth to provide food to subsistence producers and growing urban populations. Coarse grains, oilseeds, and pulses account for some 90 percent of land expansion since 1990, reflecting slow adoption of improved technology so that increasing food production still depends on area expansion rather than increasing yields. With few exceptions, almost all the expansion has been through smallholders. Little commercial agriculture has taken hold, though experts generally agree that there is large untapped potential.

Where large-scale land acquisition has taken place, experience has not been encouraging: Semi-mechanized sorghum and sesame production in Sudan, which captured investor attention some decades ago, illustrates the risks of large-scale farming and holds lessons for current investors. The scheme expanded rapidly in the 1970s when financing from the Gulf aimed to transform Sudan into a regional breadbasket through favorable access to land and subsidized credit for machinery. It attracted civil servants and businessmen who mostly hired managers for farms 1,000 ha or larger. Existing land rights were neglected on a large scale: while official statistics indicate that some 5.5 million ha were "officially" converted to arable land under the scheme, up to 11 million ha were informally encroached upon (Government of Sudan 2009; UNEP 2007).

Partly because of the resulting tenure insecurity, most of Sudan's semi-mechanized farms rely on low-level technology. Limited use of fertilizer, rotations, or livestock to maintain fertility points to soil mining in a system neither ecologically sustainable nor economically competitive. In an agro-ecological environment comparable to Australia, where yields are 4 t/ha, sorghum yields are only 0.5 t/ha and have been stagnant or declining (figure 1.4). Land rights of traditional users, both small-scale farmers and pastoralists, have been neglected, and encroachment by mechanized farms has contributed to serious conflict (Johnson 2003). Natural vegetation has been destroyed, land degraded, and farms have been abandoned. Land access is a key contributor to broader conflict (Pantuliano 2007).[6]

As there are many parallels to recent expansion of large-scale mechanized farming in Sudan and neighboring countries such as Ethiopia, the lessons from semi-mechanized farming in Sudan could be of wider relevance. With improved technology and farming systems, production could be competitive internationally. But unlocking the agro-ecological potential would require investment in adaptive research and extension, combined with institutional reforms, to provide incentives for sustainably managing land, resolving-conflict, and protecting traditional land users' rights (Government of Sudan 2009).

Large-scale production of low-value bulk commodities in other parts of Sub-Saharan Africa has often been unsuccessful. Efforts to introduce mechanized

Figure 1.4 Yields on Semi-Mechanized Farms, Sudan, 1970–2007 (t/ha)

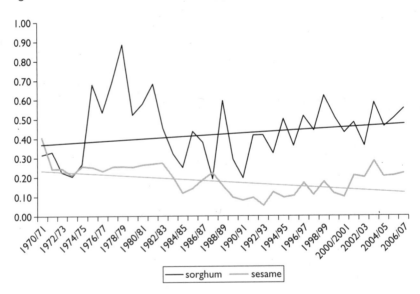

Source: Authors based on Government of Sudan 2009 and official statistics.
Note: Yields are for rainfed production. Dashed lines indicate trends.

rainfed wheat in Tanzania on some 40,000 ha of land that were previously prime grazing grounds for pastoralists illustrate the challenges. Pastoralists tried to use litigation to force a benefit-sharing agreement with wheat farmers, with limited success. After a US$45 million investment, production became only marginally profitable financially, without accounting for the social cost associated with the loss of livelihoods and increased land conflicts. Wheat cultivation was ultimately deemed unprofitable, and production has been declining (Lane and Pretty 1991; Rogers 2004). Similarly, Nigeria's large-scale mechanized irrigated wheat schemes of the 1970s and 1980s have largely been abandoned (Andrae and Beckman 1985).

Maize is Sub-Saharan Africa's most important food crop, and although largely produced by smallholders, large-scale production was attempted throughout the colonial period. Yields on large-scale Sub-Saharan African farms are comparable to or higher than those in Brazil and Thailand. But despite negligible or zero payments for land, production costs in Sub-Saharan Africa are as much as twice those in Brazil and Thailand (figure 1.5). Although maize is competitive with imports in Cameroon, Ghana, and Zambia, it is not competitive as an export because of high transport costs (including unofficial fees). In Zambia, large farms produce at a cost twice the world market price and only the protection provided by high transport costs allows them to turn a modest profit. For rice in Ghana, semi-mechanized, large-scale production could be competitive with imports only if milling rates improve (Winter-Nelson and Aggrey-Finn 2008).

Recently, a surge in demand for sugar and biofuels sparked great interest in sugarcane, either to supply protected and subsidized European markets, as in

Figure 1.5   Maize Production Costs by Country

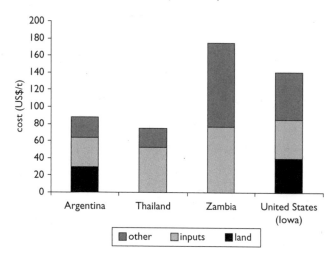

Source: Figures are from Agri Benchmark and World Bank 2009a.

Malawi, South Africa, Swaziland, Zambia, and Zimbabwe, or to benefit from domestic subsidies, as in Sudan. Given the distorted environment the industry's competitiveness is doubtful, especially in view of low processing efficiency and high transport costs (Mitchell 2010). Jatropha, a shrub whose fruits can be used to produce oil for biofuels, has also attracted large-scale investments in Sub-Saharan Africa, partly due to European Union trade preferences. Initial experience failed to meet expectations and lower crude oil prices forced many newly established enterprises to exit the industry. Lack of research on appropriate varieties, management practices, and technologies for oil extraction leaves economic viability and production parameters uncertain (Global Exchange for Social Investment 2008). Jatropha can be a viable fuel substitute in countries or regions with low wage rates and high fuel costs (say, because they are landlocked) (Mitchell 2010). Still, it remains a risky investment.

Production of high-value export crops has resulted in some marked successes. Factors conducive to this were an ideal agro-ecological setting, low if any compensation for land, and cheap labor (Poulton and others 2008). These natural advantages offset a lack of technology, weak institutions, high transport costs, and ill-functioning markets for outputs, inputs, and capital. Indeed, poor infrastructure and the difficulty of assembling sufficient volumes continue to limit the potential for bulk commodity exports from many Sub-Saharan African countries. However, these successes were limited almost exclusively to export crops where values above US$500/t allowed to compensate for high transport and marketing costs.

Experts agree that Sub-Saharan Africa's fairly plentiful endowment of water and land imply that a better policy environment and business climate would create considerable scope to profitably produce bulk commodities. Infrastructure constraints imply that, initially, supply would be limited to domestic and regional markets, worth some US$50 billion a year, which could then provide a springboard for global exports. Investors will need to work with local communities to engage smallholders. And if farming is large-scale, attention needs to be given to the rights of local land users. While still at an early stage, experiences with productive partnerships and between large operations and local smallholders that have been initiated by a number of investors recently could provide valuable lessons and help identify good practice.

Eastern Europe and Central Asia: The Rise of Superfarms

Eastern European countries have undergone major transitions from the former Soviet system of collective and state farms to new agrarian structures. These transitions have unfolded in many ways, depending on countries' factor endowment, the share of agriculture in the overall labor force, infrastructure, and the way the reforms were implemented (Swinnen 2009). In areas of low population density, where collectives were divided into small plots allocated to members, the plots were quickly rented back by companies with access to finance and machinery. These companies were often created from former collective farms whose managers could more easily consolidate land parcels and shares. Services, institutions, and logistics were geared to large-scale production, so smallholder grain production was never a viable option. Where farms were land- and capital-intensive, corporate farming was the dominant organizational structure. On the other hand, many countries where land was split up into smallholder farms also performed well. The diversity is illustrated by the share of area under corporate farms 10 years after the transition, ranging from 90 percent in the Slovak Republic, 60 percent in Kazakhstan, 45 percent in the Russian Federation, to less than 10 percent in Albania, Latvia, and Slovenia (Swinnen 2009).

In Kazakhstan, Russia, and Ukraine, the transition was associated with a 30 million ha decline in area sown, with most of that area returning to pastures or fallow. Large farms were better able to deal with the prevailing financing, infrastructure, and technology constraints. Aided by the phasing out of an inefficient meat industry and the associated demand for grain as feed, the region turned from a grain deficit of 34 Mt in the late 1980s to exports of more than 50 Mt of grain and 7 Mt of oilseeds and derivatives (Liefert and others 2009). In light of the scope for transfer of available technology, Kazakhstan, Russia, and Ukraine, the region's three land-abundant countries, have an opportunity to establish themselves as major players in global grain markets, especially if ways to effectively deal with volatility are found.

Given the slow development of markets, mergers to integrate vertically to help acquire inputs and market outputs led to the emergence of some very large companies. For example, in Russia, the 30 largest holdings farm 6.7 million ha, and in Ukraine, the largest 40 control 4 million to 4.5 million ha (Agri Benchmark 2008; Lissitsa 2010). Many of the agricultural companies are home grown, though often with significant investment from abroad. Several have issued initial public offerings (IPOs). Some Western European companies have also invested directly in large-scale farming in the region. For example, Black Earth, a Swedish company, farms more than 300,000 ha in Russia.

With greater demand and better logistics, there remains substantial potential for intensification and, in some cases, for area expansion. Cereal yields increased 38 percent from 1998–2000 to 2006–08 but are still far below potential. For example, Ukraine's cereal yields are 2.7 t/ha, some 40 percent of the Western European average. The potential to transfer technology and relatively cheap land has been one of the major motivations for foreign direct investment in the region.

In Russia, land is either leased or owned, and in Ukraine (where private land sales are not allowed), all land is leased, usually for 5 years to 25 years. But throughout the region, land rents are still very low relative to land of comparable quality in other parts of Europe. Competitive markets for land shares have yet to emerge, and in many situations imperfections in financial and output markets preclude owner-cultivation as a viable option. So the bargaining power of land owners is often weak, suggesting that rental rates are low and that owners receive few of the benefits from large-scale cultivation.

FACTORS AFFECTING THE ORGANIZATION OF AGRICULTURAL PRODUCTION

To understand factors that may promote or constrain the expansion of area under cultivation and the potential impact of such expansion, it will be useful to discuss how such production is organized and how it has evolved over time.

Why Agricultural Production Is Dominated by Family-Owned and Operated Farms

In most countries, both rich and poor, the average farm size is quite small. The industry is dominated by owner-operated family units that combine ownership of the main means of production with management (table 1.3). The main reason is that, unlike marketing, agricultural production has few technical (dis) economies of scale, implying that a range of production forms can coexist. In contrast, processing and distribution are characterized by significant economies of scale that have given rise to consolidation and often high levels of industry concentration.

Agricultural production, in contrast, is generally in owner-operated farms that are small by comparison. The main reason is the spatial dispersion of production, which requires flexibility and an ability to quickly adjust to microvariations in climate or soil conditions. As residual claimants to profit, family workers will be more likely to adjust and work hard than wage workers, who have an incentive to shirk and require costly supervision. Unless they

Table 1.3 Mean Farm Sizes and Operational Holding Sizes Worldwide			
Region	Mean size (ha)	% < 2 ha	Gini coefficient
Central America	10.7	63	0.75
East Asia	1	79	0.5
Europe	32.3	30	0.6
South America	111.7	36	0.9
South Asia	1.4	78	0.54
Southeast Asia	1.8	57	0.6
Sub-Saharan Africa	2.4	69	0.49
United States	178.4	4	0.78
West Asia and North Africa	4.9	65	0.7

Source: Based on Eastwood and others 2010.

are disadvantaged by policy distortions in favor of large farms (Binswanger, Deininger, and Feder 1995), they will produce more efficiently than wage labor–based operations, which need to spend resources supervising workers (Allen and Lueck 1998; Binswanger and Deininger 1997; Lipton 2009).

A look at the 300 or so publicly listed companies in table 1.4 illustrates this point: Even though farming accounts for 22 percent of the global agricultural value chain, it makes up less than 1 percent of market capitalization. The main reason is the industry's dispersion: with average farm sizes of less than 1,000 ha in the United States and Europe, gaining the scale for a public listing is difficult. As of October 2009, there were only seven publicly listed farming companies worldwide, three in Brazil and Argentina and four in Ukraine and Russia.

Three factors are critical determinants of the evolution of the structure of agricultural production over time: access to credit and insurance; lumpy inputs, such as machinery and skills; and the nonagricultural wage rate. Although small agricultural operations have advantages in accessing labor and local knowledge, in many cases they have difficulty acquiring capital. The high transaction costs of providing formal credit in rural markets mean that the unit costs of borrowing and lending decline with loan size and bias lending against small farmers. Raising interest rates on small loans does not overcome this problem, as it will lead to adverse selection (Stiglitz and Weiss 1981). Moreover, as formally titled land is ideal collateral, the cost of borrowing in the formal credit market will be a declining function of the amount of formally owned land, conferring an additional advantage on borrowers who formally own larger amounts of land. Unless ways are found to provide small farmers with access to finance (through, for example, credit cooperatives), their inability to obtain financing may outweigh any supervision cost advantages they have, thus linking size and efficiency (Chavas 2001).

Table 1.4 Publicly Listed Companies in Agribusiness Value Chains

Item	Global age. value chain (%)	Number of companies	Market cap (%)
Suppliers	22.7	103	39.6
Farming	22.2	7	0.2
Processing	14.8	60	9.7
Logistics	14.7	26	9.7
Packing and distribution	25.6	88	36.8
Integrated	n.a.	16	4
Total	**100**	**300**	**100**

Source: Own computation based on Brookfield 2010.
Note: Global market capitalization is in US$ millions as of October 2009. n.a. = not applicable.

Machinery such as threshers, tractors, and combine harvesters may reach their lowest cost of operation per unit area at a scale larger than the average size of operational holdings. If farms were to rely only on their own machinery, this could produce economies of scale and increase the optimum operational farm size. But machine rental can help small farms use large machinery, circumventing this constraint for all but the most time-bound operations.[7] A second indivisible factor is operators' ability to acquire and process information. This factor, which assumes greater importance with more advanced technology, gives managers with formal schooling and technical education a competitive edge and increases the size of the holdings they manage. It is particularly important for new crops, in which managers skilled in modern methods may enjoy a large advantage (Collier and Dercon 2009; Feder and Slade 1985). Over time, part of this advantage may dissipate, especially if technology is scale-neutral and, aided by public provision of extension services or farmer associations, spreads to small farmers.

Rising wages in the nonagricultural sector will lead farm operators to seek ways to attain incomes comparable to what they can obtain in other sectors of the economy (Eastwood and others 2010). Normally this implies substitution of capital for labor and an increase of farm sizes over time in line with wage rates. As figure 1.6 illustrates, both variables moved together closely in the United States for most of the 20th century, suggesting that the desire to obtain a comparable nonagricultural income was the main factor driving changes in the average size of operational holdings (Gardner 2002). Of course, even large farms are mostly owner-operated rather than company-owned.

Figure 1.6 Evolution of United States' Farm Size and Nonfarm Manufacturing Wage

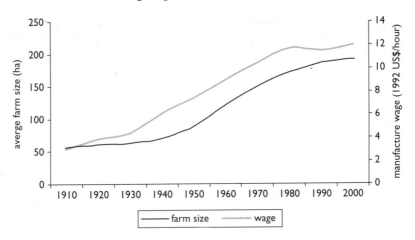

Source: Based on Gardner 2002.

Why Do Large Farms Emerge?

An important exception to the superior performance of owner-operated units of production over those relying on wage labor is in plantation crops, where economies of scale in processing and the need for close coordination with processing make plantations more efficient. The need for quick processing of produce to avoid deterioration, often within 24 hours to 48 hours, requires tight adherence to delivery and harvesting schedules (Binswanger and Rosenzweig 1986). The perishable nature of these crops and the sensitivity of the timing between harvesting and processing transmit economies of scale in processing to the production stage. The potential loss of quality in unprocessed sugarcane due to fermentation, together with high sensitivity of total cost to the cost of transport, requires that production be not only tightly coordinated but also spatially concentrated close to a processing plant. This need usually prompts sugar factories to run their own plantations to ensure at least a base load for processing. In densely populated areas in India and Thailand, for example, mills contract with outgrowers to deliver their cane to the mill and determine which farmers receive technical advice and inputs from the firm.

The advantage of large production of plantation crops is consistent with the fact that firms in the sugar and oil palm sectors, many of them based in developing countries, manage production on enormous areas. For example, Cosan, one of the largest sugar-ethanol producers in Brazil, manages more than 600,000 ha, about half of it on land it owns (the rest is produced by outgrowers). Operational size in the oil palm sector, which includes 8 of the 25 largest agricultural production companies in the world, is also very high. Several large oil palm companies manage plantations of 200,000 ha or more. Although large firms' ability to raise large amounts of capital provides them with significant advantages in establishing plantations in areas of low population density, in-migration, together with family labor's higher incentives, has, in situations with high population growth, led to the gradual replacement of plantations with smallholder production (Hayami 2010), contrary to what is generally observed in annual crops.

A general trend toward larger operational units in developed countries is underpinned by recent innovations in breeding, zero tillage, and information technology that make supervision easier. By facilitating standardization, they allow supervision of operations over large spaces, reducing owner-operator advantages. Pest-resistant and herbicide-tolerant varieties reduce the number of steps in the production process and the labor intensity of cultivation. The scope for substituting information technology and remotely sensed information on field conditions for personal observation to make decisions increases managers' span of control. Also, importing countries' increasingly stringent requirements on product quality and food safety throughout the supply chain increase the advantages of large-scale production and an integrated supply chain. Establishing such a supply chain can be more difficult under smallholder production models, as illustrated by the challenges encountered by the Roundtable on Sustainable Palm Oil in certifying smallholders.

The superior ability of large companies to overcome market imperfections further up in the supply chain can also provide them with a competitive advantage in production, especially if other markets do not function well. This can happen through several channels:

- First, large firms may be able to access global financial markets where funds can often be obtained at much lower cost than in domestic ones. This was important in Argentina during the period of financial repression and continues to be relevant in settings requiring high investments, either to establish new plantations or to make degraded land productive. In addition, as markets for agricultural inputs and outputs often are highly concentrated, large operators are reported to be able to reduce cost on either side of the market by 10–20 percent, giving them an edge in highly competitive global markets (Manciana, Trucco, and Pineiro 2009).
- Second, diversification across space can allow large companies to self-insure, thereby generating opportunities to overcome the difficulties for establishing crop insurance created by covariance of risks. This ability could allow large companies to expand strategically by acquiring assets at relatively low prices in periods of climatic or other distress.
- Third, large firms can substitute for gaps in public services (in transport and logistics or in applied R&D, for example). In Brazil and Ukraine, a number of large companies have constructed their own port terminals for export, shielding them from the limitations imposed by public facilities. Poor integration of agricultural markets across Africa is reported to provide business opportunities for large vertically integrated producers that can operate across many countries. High fixed costs of R&D and significantly reduced public funding for it have stimulated research by private firms, for example, in plantation forestry or oil palm.

Even in production of annual crops, a combination of technical change favoring mechanization and more stringent phytosanitary standards by importing countries, together with large farms and a superior ability to overcome market imperfections, can favor large operations in some contexts. In Ukraine, 85 agriholdings together operate more than 6 million ha of land (Lissitsa 2010). In Argentina, the 30 largest companies control a total of 2.4 million ha (box 1.2). Some large firms, such as the Russian firm Ivolga in grains and El Tejar, which cultivates soybeans and maize in Brazil and Argentina, operate more than 600,000 ha, albeit in operational units rarely larger than 10,000 ha.

On the other side of the spectrum, rice production shows that agricultural produce can be grown competitively on a wide range of sizes depending on local factor endowments and labor costs. With a total export volume of 4.6 million t, Vietnam is a major global exporter and low-cost producer of rice, with an average farm size of 0.5 ha and labor intensive technology (table 1.5). A large effort to secure property rights after decollectivization

Box 1.2 Competitive Land Markets in Latin America

Led by Argentina, farm management companies have emerged that own neither land nor machinery but rent land and contract with machine operators. This business model evolved during Argentina's financial crisis, when having access to outside capital provided a significant advantage. With clear property rights allowing easy contracting, several companies farm more than 100,000 ha, most of it rented, with operational units in the 10,000–15,000 ha range. The largest companies, many of them traded publicly, are vertically integrated into input supply and output markets and operate across several countries. Access to a large pool of highly qualified agronomists who undergo continued training and are organized hierarchically allows adoption of near-industrial methods of quality control and production at low cost.

Competitive land lease markets, with contracts renewed annually, imply that at least part of the savings is passed on to landowners, who generally receive lease payments above what they would have been able to earn by self-cultivation (Manciana, Trucco, and Pineiro 2009). A number of options are used to share risk, including fixed-rent contracts with up-front payment in dollars (all risks to the company), fixed payment in grain equivalents (only the production risks are borne by the company), and sharing production (production and price risk are shared). This model and other innovative ways to harness private investment for agricultural production are expanding into neighboring Uruguay, Paraguay, and lowland Bolivia and Colombia (Regunaga 2010).

Source: Authors.

Table 1.5 Yields and Cost Structure for Major Rice Exporters

	Vietnam	Northeast Thailand	South Thailand	Uruguay
Farm size (ha)	0.5	4	3.4	340
Irrigation	Yes	No	No	Yes
Yield (t/ha)	4.32	2.2	2.62	8.3
Farm price (US$/t)	166	161	199	230
Cost (US$/ha)	372	252	420	1,238
Cost (US$/t)	86	127	160	150
% costs as inputs	47.9	26	27.3	26
% costs as labor	34.6	62	27.2	12
% cost of machinery	12.9	2	34.2	35
% costs as land and water	2.1	3	6.9	26

Source: Authors based on Insituto Nacional de Investigación Agropecuaria Uruguay (INIA); personal communication; Ekasingh and others 2007; IRRI.

expanded labor-intensive rice production as a basis for rapid poverty reduction and subsequent diversification of the rural economy into high-value exports and nonagricultural employment (Do and Iyer 2008; Piongali and Xuan 1992). Uruguay, with different factor endowments, developed a rice industry based on large-scale rice production, with exports of some 1 million t in 2009. Rice farms there average 340 ha of fully mechanized and irrigated production and attain average yields of more than 8 t/ha.

CAN LARGE-SCALE INVESTMENT CREATE BENEFITS FOR LOCAL POPULATIONS?

Small Farmers and Large Investors Can Form Mutually Advantageous Partnerships

Large-scale investment does not necessarily have to result in the conversion of small-scale agriculture to large-scale agriculture. To the contrary, a variety of institutional arrangements can be used to combine the assets of investors (capital, technology, markets) with those of local communities and smallholders (land, labor, and local knowledge). Such arrangements include land rental, contract farming, and intermediate options, such as nucleus-outgrower schemes. Large-scale farming is only one option for farming the land and, as box 1.3 illustrates, small farmers may find it more profitable to retain their activity rather than accept a wage job. In these circumstances it may be advantageous for both smallholders and large-scale investors to enter into partnerships rather than an agreement involving the transfer of land.

As long as property rights to land and, where necessary water, are well-defined and a proper regulatory framework to prevent externalities is in place, productivity- and welfare-enhancing transactions can occur without the need for active intervention by the state. The desirability and the outcomes of partnerships or contracting depend on the institutional context. Parties will be more likely to voluntarily enter (mutually advantageous) contractual relationships if the transaction costs of doing so, particularly those of enforcing agreements, are low. The chosen arrangement will depend on commodity and market characteristics. Contract farming, with investors providing capital and technology, would be expected for crops such as oilseeds or sugarcane because processing makes it easy to enforce contracts, as side-selling is limited. It can also provide opportunities for landless people and women by increasing labor demand, as for example in Senegal (Maertens and Swinnen 2009). When the share of investment is larger—for example, for horticulture, perennials, and oil palm or in cases with high up-front investment in irrigation—land ownership will be more important. This may lead to situations where wage payments and land

Box 1.3 Can Smallholders and Large Farms Coexist?

To explore whether, when smallholders already own and cultivate land, there may be a case to replace them by large cultivation, we use representative farm budgets from areas where smallholders and large farms for the same crop exist side by side (see appendix 2, table A2.5).[a] Three factors are of interest.

First, although yields on smallholder farms are lower than or equal to those on large farms, often by a large margin, lower yields do not necessarily translate into lower efficiency. On the contrary, smallholder farms' costs are lower than or roughly equal (ratio less than 1.1) to those of large farms in two-thirds of the comparisons, suggesting that there is no strong case to replace smallholder with large-scale cultivation on efficiency grounds.

Second, and more important, the data clearly indicate that, even though efficiency is comparable, smallholder cultivation has advantages on equity grounds. Smallholders' income is 2 times to 10 times what they could obtain from wage employment only. This does not imply that there may not be opportunities for productive partnerships between investors and smallholders (in gaining access to technology, for example, as illustrated by the poor performance of some smallholders without such access). Such opportunities would not require the transfer of land but would be based on more traditional contracting and outgrower schemes (Cotula 2010; Vermeulen and Goad 2006).

Third, if payments for land are made or if advantageous opportunities exist for nonagricultural employment, small farmers, especially those with limited management skills or access to capital, may increase their welfare by renting their land to an investor. A land rental payment can be computed that, for a given (exogenous) wage rate, would leave a small landowner indifferent between self-cultivation and renting out the land and working for wages on a large farm. In many cases, the land rents to be paid would be large, implying that investors may prefer to engage in contract farming rather than acquire land.

rental fees leave local communities better off than would self-cultivation. The most appropriate arrangement will depend on local contexts (see box 1.4 for an example).

If rights are well defined, if land markets function competitively, and if information is accessible to all, land prices should ensure that a mutually satisfying outcome is achieved. In this context, entrepreneurs can earn rents by bringing technology to improve productivity on land that is currently used less intensively (and thus available at fairly low prices). Land rights holders can in theory capture some of this rent through well-informed negotiations. The situations in which this can occur and land can be transferred at an adequate price are described in more detail in box 1.5.

Box 1.4 Options for Engaging Small Farmers

Although compensation for land is only one way for local populations to benefit from large-scale investment (in addition to employment and access to markets or technology), it will be critical in many situations. Case studies illustrate that there are a number of options in the way in which land compensation can be provided. For example, in Sarawak, Malaysia, four options have been analyzed.

- A smallholder model tied to a nuclear estate
- A joint venture model in which local people with customary rights to the land receive an equity share in a plantation run as a single operation by a company
- A fixed land-lease model based on an annual rental payment
- A purely private company operation, with government providing the land through a concession without compensation to communities.

As it helps to overcome smallholders' limited access to technology and capital, the joint venture model almost doubles total benefits per hectare compared to lower-yielding smallholder-managed fields (box figure 1.4). Still, unless ways are found to share the benefits, it would be rational for smallholders to self-cultivate.

Box Figure 1.4   Distribution of Benefits from Oil Palm in Sarawak, Malaysia

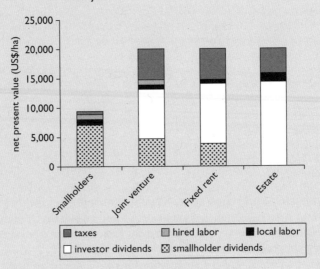

Source: Authors based on Cramb and Ferraro 2010.

Box 1.5 What Is the Right Price for Land?

Conceptually, the sale value of a land plot should be the discounted value of all net future income streams associated with the plot of land. The lease price should be the net return to land after all other factors (labor, capital, and management) have been properly remunerated.

The reasoning is simple: if prices were lower, demand for land plots would increase because potential buyers would gain from buying the land and putting it to better use. If prices were higher, land supply would increase because sellers would be better off selling the land rather than farming it themselves. These responses in supply and demand ensure equality between the net present value of income streams and the price of land that prevails on the land market.

If buyers and sellers have different characteristics (for instance, if a potential investor has a technological advantage or better access to capital or product markets), a mutually advantageous transaction can in theory make both agents better off and increase economic efficiency. For such a transaction to occur, the agreed price needs to be set between the net present value of income streams under present ownership and under the planned investment.

In practice, future income streams depend on the characteristics of the land, particularly its agro-ecological potential, which thus needs to be assessed by both parties. If the party selling the land rights is not well informed of the potential use of the land, it can enter transactions that will appear ex post to have squandered land assets.

Another important characteristic associated with location is transportation costs, which if low can increase the profitability of any investment and result in higher land values. If major infrastructure investments are expected in the future, investors will factor the investments into negotiations. The potential for irrigation will also increase the value of a land parcel. However, not all parameters that contribute to the value of the land are known with certainty. On the contrary, there can be much uncertainty (and asymmetric information) about future input and output prices, the future development of the land, and the best timing for a land use change.

To estimate the "right price" for a lease or land sale, three cases can be distinguished. Where land markets are active and transactions are open, observed prices for land transactions should reflect the economic fundamentals. Many governments and real estate agents publish prices of land transactions to provide better information to potential market participants. In areas with no established land markets, where land is made available to investors directly by the government or a government body, practices such as auctioning the land through a competitive bidding process can ensure that the host country is able to at least partially extract some of the surplus created by the project. Where no such auction mechanism exists, or where it is necessary to determine a starting value for an auction, it will be useful to

(continued)

Box 1.5 (Continued)

consider the value of profits from (planned or actual) production. As a rule of thumb, data from the United States indicate that leases are a relatively constant portion of crop value (35 percent to 40 percent of gross crop value from corn and 45 percent to 50 percent of gross crop value from soybeans).

Source: Authors.

With decentralized contracting, market imperfections due, for example, to limited access to markets or lack of access to technology, that affect potential returns from landowners' self-cultivation will weaken the bargaining position of small producers and the returns they can obtain from their land. The potential impact of such imperfections is illustrated in Ukraine, where high transaction costs in input and output markets and lack of competition in land markets reduce land rents to only a fraction of what is obtained in Argentina, even though the productive capacity of the land is very similar. This implies that there is an important role for the public sector to ensure access to information and a level playing field for all. The public sector needs to be involved only to ensure that no negative external effects on others or the environment are imposed so that land users can make informed and independent decisions.

There Can Be Considerable Potential for Employment Generation

How much local populations can benefit will be determined to a large extent by the employment intensity of potential investments. Employment generation is often a key avenue for local people to benefit from outside investment because for bulk commodities, it is at the production, rather than the processing stage that employment is generated. In many developing economies, the ability of the agricultural sector to absorb labor and provide gainful employment provides a key safety net. Labor requirements for production vary greatly among crops and production systems so that crop choice and organization of production will have far-reaching impacts on the scope for agricultural growth to reduce poverty.[8]

The crops of interest to large investors differ widely in their labor requirements. Oil palm and (manual) sugarcane generate between 10 and 30 times more jobs per hectare than does large-scale mechanized grain farming (table 1.6), generating large amounts of employment. The reason is that, for tree crops and perennials, the scope to substitute capital for labor is more limited than in grains and annuals. In the former, key operations, especially harvesting, are thus usually manual regardless of farm size and labor intensity varies little between production systems. In fact, large oil palm

Table 1.6 Key Factor Ratios in Case Studies of Large-Scale Investments

Commodity	Jobs per 1,000 ha	Investment US$/ha	Investment US$/job
Grains	10	450	45,000
Jatropha	420	1,000	2,400
Oil palm	350	4,000	11,400
Forestry	20	7,000	360,000
Rubber	420	1,500	3,600
Sorghum	53	900	17,000
Soybean	18	3,600	200,000
Sugarcane-ethanol[a]	153	5,150	33,600
Sugarcane-ethanol[b]	150	15,500	105,000
Sugarcane-ethanol[c]	700	14,000	20,000
Wheat-soybean	16	6,000	375,000

Source: Authors based on business plans for investments covered in case studies undertaken for this report.
a. Rainfed, one-third mechanized harvest (Brazil).
b. Irrigated, mechanized harvest (Mozambique).
c. Irrigated, manual harvest (Tanzania).

plantations may employ more labor per hectare than smallholder-operated ones. By contrast, the ease of mechanizing grain production leads to vast differences between small and large operations. For example, a smallholder using animal power and manual labor in Cameroon is estimated to require 40 days to produce a hectare of maize; a large, fully mechanized farm will use 2 days of labor but higher amounts of capital to achieve the same result (World Bank 2009a).

If land is plentiful and neither in-migration nor need for employment is envisaged, mechanized large-scale farming of grains can be appropriate. If it is not, crops with higher labor intensity could provide greater benefits and may need to be actively promoted.

Proper Valuation Is Critical to Determine Compensation for Land

How land values are determined may also largely determine the benefits that local people may derive from investments. The price paid for land is clearly a central parameter. It is thus useful to consider ways to determine it in a "fair" way that can then serve as a point of reference in negotiations. Legitimate users and occupants of the land should be offered compensation by investors that reflects the value of the land, either through profit shares or through direct compensation for the transfer of land rights. Compensation may occur in several ways, either through the provision of equivalent land, the creation of a community fund to provide public services, or monetary transfers (including the payment of a land rent). But to determine the fair level of these compensations, it is necessary to be able to assess the value of the land used by the investor.

Assessing land values this way appears to be what is happening in Argentina, where companies determine residual returns to land based on expected yields, prices, and input levels and then use these returns as a basis for negotiating land rentals. The process is highly competitive, as landowners have the option of leasing their land to a different operator if they are not satisfied with the price on offer (Manciana, Trucco, and Pineiro 2009). Mutually beneficial outcomes are possible because, despite higher expenses for management, costs on farms operated by large operators are some 10 percent below those on smaller farms. With competitive land markets and land rents of US$250–US$300, a landowner of 50 ha would net more than US$10,000/year from renting.

In many of the countries where land is relatively plentiful, land markets are either absent or do not function well. In the absence of markets, an upper bound for land values can be provided by the imputed residual return to land after all other factors have been remunerated. Inspection of the land expectation value (LEV), which captures the residual return to land based on actual ventures (table 1.7), suggests that returns to land close to infrastructure can be very high.[9] For irrigated sugarcane, the up-front investment may be US$6,000/ha. As short-term rental is not a viable option in this case, the LEV provides a better measure of land values (Zinkhan and Cubbage 2003). Although adjustments for risk and a proper return to entrepreneurial initiative would significantly reduce the amounts that could be obtained in a market setting, LEVs for perennial crops suggest scope for raising significant revenue by selling or leasing currently unused land to investors, especially if such land has fairly good access to infrastructure and water (Cubbage and others forthcoming). For example, based on an existing (optimistic) business plan, the sugarcane-ethanol investment in Mozambique yields a LEV of US$9,800 per hectare, significantly more than the net present value of the annual US$0.60 rental fee investors are charged for cropland.

Profits from agricultural cultivation and implicit values of land can be high in areas with good infrastructure access and for crops with readily available technology and markets but in practice the compensation received by original rights holders is often limited. The scope for land payments—which can provide an avenue for all rights holders to benefit—may thus not always be fully utilized. Although investors are of course justified in requiring a return for the risks they assume, at the same time, comparisons of these returns to land with the levels of official payment required in some countries—which may not be collected or fully accrue to local people—suggest scope to negotiate deals that provide higher benefits for local communities. For such scope to be feasible, local communities need to have their customary land rights recognized and be able to transfer these rights in a credible way based on a consensus that will not be challenged in the future.[10]

Table 1.7 Land Expectation Values for Perennial Crops	
Commodity and country	Land expectation value (US$/ha)
Oil palm	
Indonesia	4,800
Plantation forestry	
Argentina	3,125
Brazil	5,250–8,300
Colombia	5,400
South Africa	2,900
Uruguay	750–1,400
Sugar	
Brazil	3,750
Kenya	8,000
Mozambique	9,750
Tanzania	11,000
Zambia	18,500

Source: Authors based on Marques 2009 and World Bank 2009a for Brazil; World Bank 2009a for Zambia; Mitchell 2010 for Kenya; Locke 2009 for Mozambique; Mitchell 2010 for Tanzania; Fairhurst and McLaughlin 2009 (adjusted) for Indonesia; and Cubbage and others forthcoming for plantation forestry everywhere.

Note: Values for all countries except Brazil are imputed. For Mozambique, sugarcane-ethanol is irrigated and (optimistic) yields are from the business plan. For Tanzania, sugar is irrigated. For Indonesia, the figure is based on palm oil price of US$600/t. For Uruguay, production is targeted at marginal lands. For Brazil, market rental rate is paid in kind converted at 8 percent. For Kenya, sugar is rainfed; high prices due to import protection. For Zambia, sugar is irrigated, high prices due to European Union access.

CONCLUSION

A broad review of experience with expansion of cultivated area illustrates not only that land expansion has happened in the past, but also that buoyant demand for agricultural produce provides opportunities that relatively land-abundant countries can use to foster social and economic development. Experience suggests that the ability of investors large or small to capitalize on these opportunities will be affected by availability of public goods. It highlights how technology and infrastructure can be instrumental in facilitating a strong supply response, a nondistortive policy environment can help to create a supportive investment climate, and well-defined property rights can allow the emergence of factor markets.

How property rights were assigned or could be acquired had a critical impact in several ways. While requiring self-cultivation or productive use may make sense, requiring forest clearance as a precondition for gaining property rights, as in Brazil, can lead to potentially wasteful processes of area expansion with high social and environmental costs and only limited benefits. Brazil also suggests that identification of protected areas will be critical to prevent encroachment on these areas and avoid negative social and environmental impacts. In Indonesia, limited ability to uphold local rights, together with free provision of land to large investors, led to processes of area expansion that caused immense social disruption and environmental damage. Such land price subsidies have encouraged speculative landholding and displacement of traditional land users.

The nature and profitability of any investment will be affected by the availability of infrastructure and technology. Public investment in R&D underpinned most successful smallholder expansions as well as the expansion of production in the Brazilian cerrado. For perennials, the private sector may invest in R&D, for example, for oil palm, sugarcane-ethanol, and eucalyptus. Investment in infrastructure was also critical as the basis for the supply response in Thailand. Where such investment is not available, private operators can to some extent substitute by establishing networks of their own. But proper regulation will be needed to prevent monopolistic abuse.

Price distortions and subsidies affected land investment and area expansion processes in specific countries. On one hand, policies discriminating against (export) agriculture have long stymied private investment in Africa. In Brazil's cerrado, on the other hand, capital subsidies led to the emergence of a highly capital-intensive mode of production with very limited poverty impacts. A history of subsidies helped to entrench very large units of production in Eastern Europe, providing them with a head start in an environment characterized by significant market imperfections. The export growth witnessed in countries such as Vietnam, Thailand, and Peru following a clarification of the property rights system illustrates the importance of secure property rights. It also suggests that, in a favorable policy environment, providing investment incentives to existing smallholders can be highly effective in fostering commercialization. This then implies that large-scale investment is not the only option and that it should complement and support local dwellers rather than trying to substitute for their efforts. The definition of property rights also affects how factor markets work and thus how factors can transmit signals about economic opportunities to the private sector and allow producers to insure against risks.

With the exception of plantations, owner-operated farms were the main model of production to respond to increased demand, with increases in farm sizes mirroring the emergence of the nonagricultural sector. While a number of technological and economic developments may have weakened the advantage of owner-operated farms, they did not undermine it. In fact, very large operations as observed in a number of countries appear to have emerged mainly to overcome imperfections in other markets (such as those for output, finance, and insurance). This means that there is no reason to abandon the model of smallholder agriculture as the main pillar of poverty-reducing agricultural growth. At the same time, the gaps in public good provision characteristic of many of the more land-abundant countries considered here may well provide a competitive edge to large operations. Policies to promote smallholder involvement and sharing of benefits with local populations can help to fully unleash this potential.

NOTES

1. Both the magnitude and the type of land conversion have large impacts on greenhouse gas emissions. Estimates based on satellite data suggest that 59 percent of agricultural land expansion in the tropics has been at the expense of forests, and 25 percent, disturbed forests, with the highest share in Latin America. Forests, particularly tropical ones, also provide other environmental services such as increasing biodiversity and protecting watersheds.

2. Hertel, Tyner, and Birur (2010) estimate that U.S. and European Union mandates indirectly increase cropland by 11.3 percent in Canada (4.4 percent from pastureland, 6.0 percent from forests, and 0.9 percent other) and 14.2 percent in Brazil (11.0 percent from pastures, 1.7 from forests, and 1.5 percent other).

3. These feedstocks present major advantages over first-generation feedstocks in environmental impacts because using the entire plant for energy production allows much greater efficiency than conventional starch and oilseed feedstocks (FAO 2008). The availability of such technology will not ease the pressure on land, but will shift it toward more marginal areas, where competition with conventional crops is less intense (Melillo and others 2009).

4. Brazil's cerrado is an extensive area of about 200 million ha, of which about 125 million ha can be made suitable for agriculture with significant investment in soil improvement. It is largely made up of savanna, shrubs, and dry forests with low timber value but high biodiversity.

5. Eight of the 25 largest agricultural production-based global companies identified in the 2009 *World Investment Report* have major interests in oil palm (UNCTAD 2009). Some very large global companies control 200,000–600,000 ha of oil palm.

6. According to Salih (1987, p. 112) "It is estimated that 80 percent of the 350,000 pastoralists and agropastoralists of Southern Kordofan province are seriously affected by the expansion of large-scale mechanized schemes. This is mainly because the owners of the schemes do not abide by the agricultural practices devised by the Mechanized Farming Corporation. They have in many cases cultivated even the animal tracks specified by the Corporation. [There is] continuous conflict between the owners of the large-scale mechanized schemes and the pastoralists . . . pastoral nomads are driven out of the best areas of their traditional pasture to places which are not favorable to their herd growth, and agropastoralists are being subjected to various socioeconomic pressures to abandon one of the two activities and change over to agricultural laborers with lower standards of living." In some states, combatants reported that the expansion of mechanized agricultural schemes onto their land had precipitated the fighting, which had then escalated and coalesced with the north-south political conflict (Saeed 2008).

7. Under constant technical returns to scale and with perfect markets for land, capital, and labor, the ownership distribution of land would be irrelevant for production

and affect only the distribution of income. Landowners would either rent the necessary factors of production (labor and capital) and make zero profits operating their own holding or, if there were transaction costs in the labor market, rent in or rent out land to equalize the size of their operational holdings.

8. Processing and other upstream activities are highly capital-intensive for all crops.

9. The land equivalent value is the maximum an investor could pay for land for use, given a risk-free return from the investment in perpetuity.

10. In practice, customary rights are often not recognized and land under customary tenure is often considered to be "owned" by the government, which may be prone to divest it without compensating the users as documented in chapter 4. The divestiture of public land has traditionally been considered one of the most common forms of land grabbing. It has involved many high-profile cases of bad governance; outright corruption (bribing government officials to obtain public land at a fraction of market value); and squandering public assets that deprived original land users or the broader public of resources and created tenure insecurity for a large number of subsequent land transactions.

REFERENCES

Agri Benchmark. 2008. "Cash Crop Report 2008: Benchmarking Farming Systems Worldwide." Frankfurt, Germany.

Allen, D., and D. Lueck. 1998. "The Nature of the Farm." *Journal of Law and Economics* 41 (2): 343–86.

Al-Riffai, P., B. Dimaranan, and D. Laborde. 2010. "Global Trade and Environmental Impact Study of the EU Biofuels Mandate." International Food Policy Research Institute, Washington, DC.

Andrae, G., and B. Beckman. 1985. *The Wheat Trap: Bread and Underdevelopment in Nigeria.* Uppsala, Sweden, and London, U.K.; Scandinavian Institute for African Studies and Zed Books Ltd.

Bacha, C. J. C. 2008. "Analise da Evolucao do Reflorestamento no Brasil." *Revista de Economia Agricola* 55 (1): 5–24.

Barr, C., A. Dermawan, H. Purnomo, and others. 2010. "Financial Governance and Indonesia's Reforestation Fund during the Socharto and Post-Socharto Periods 1989–2009." Occasional Paper 52, Center for International Forestry Research, Bogor, Indonesia.

Binswanger, H. P., and M. R. Rosenzweig. 1986. "Behavioural and Material Determinants of Production Relations in Agriculture." *Journal of Development Studies* 22 (3): 503–39.

Binswanger, H. P., and K. Deininger. 1997. "Explaining Agricultural and Agrarian Policies in Developing Countries." *Journal of Economic Literature* 35 (4): 1958–2005.

Bitswanger, H. P., K. Deininger, and G. Feder. 1995. "Power, Distortions, Revolt, and Reform in Agricultural Land Relations." In *Handbook of Development Economics*, ed. T. Behrman and T. N. Srinivasan. North Holland; Elsevier.

BNDES (Banco Nacional de Desenvolvimento Econômico e Social). 2008. *Sugarcane-based Bioethanol Energy for Sustainable Development.* Rio de Janeiro: BNDES.

Brookfield Agriculture Group. 2010. "Farmland Investment Thesis: Why Brazilian Farmland Will Outperform." New York: Brookfield Asset Management Inc.

Butler, R. A., and W. F. Laurance. 2009. "Is Oil Palm the Next Emerging Threat to the Amazon?" *Tropical Conservation Science* 2 (1): 1–10.

Bruinsma, J. 2009. "The Resource Outlook to 2050: By How Much Do Land, Water Use and Crop Yields Need to Increase by 2050?" Paper presented at the Expert Meeting on How to Feed the World in 2050, Food and Agriculture Organization of the United Nations, Rome.

Carle, J., and P. Holmgren. 2008. "Wood from Planted Forests: A Global Outlook 2005-2030." *Forest Products Journal* 58 (12): 6–18.

Chavas, J. P. 2001. "Structural Change in Agricultural Production: Economics, Technology and Policy." *Handbook of Agricultural Economics*, ed. B. Gardner and G. C. Rausser. North Holland: Elsevier.

Colchester, M., N. Jirwan, Andiko, M. A. Sirait, A. Y. Firdaus, A. Surambo, and H. Pane. 2006. "Promised Land: Palm Oil and Land Acquisition in Indonesia: Implications for Local Communities and Indigenous Peoples." London, U.K., and Bogor, Indonesia: Forest Peoples Programme, World Agroforestry Centre, Perkumpulan Sawit Watch, and HuMa.

Collier, P., and S. Dercon. 2009. "African Agriculture in 50 Years: Smallholders in a Rapidly Changing World." Paper presented at the Expert Meeting on How to Feed the World in 2050, Food and Agriculture Organization of the United Nations, Rome.

Cossalter, C., and C. Pye-Smith. 2003. *Fast-Wood Forestry: Myths and Realities.* Bogor, Indonesia: Center for International Forestry Research.

Cotula, L. 2010. "Investment Contracts and Sustainable Development: How to Make Contracts for Fairer and More Sustainable Natural Resource Investments." London: International Institute for Environment and Development.

Cramb, R. A., and D. Ferraro. 2010. "Custom and Capital: A Financial Appraisal of Alternative Arrangements for Large-scale Oil Palm Development on Customary Land in Sarawak, Malaysia." Paper presented at the 54th Annual Conference of the Australian Agricultural and Resource Economics Society, Adelaide, February 10–12.

Cubbage F. W., S. Kosebandana, P. M. Donagh, R. Rubilar, G. Balmelli, V. M. Olmos, and others. forthcoming. "Global Timber Investments, Wood Costs, Regulation, and Risk." *Biomass and Bioenergy.*

de Souza, C. M., S. Haiashy, and A. Verissimo. 2010. "Deforestation Alerts for Forest Law Enforcement: The Case of Mato Grosso, Brazil." In *Innovations in Land Rights Recognition, Administration, and Governance*, ed. K. Deininger, C. Augustinus, S. Enemark, and P. Munro-Faure. Washington, DC: World Bank.

Do , Q. T., and L. Iyer. 2008. "Land Titling and Rural Transition in Vietnam." *Economic Development and Cultural Change* 56 (3): 531–79.

Doughty, R. W. 2000. *The Eucalyptus: A Natural and Commercial History of the Gum Tree.* Baltimore: Johns Hopkins University Press.

Eastwood, R., M. Lipton, and A. Newell. 2010. "Farm Size." In *Handbook of Agricultural Economics*, vol. 4, ed. P. L. Pingali and R. E. Evenson. North Holland: Elsevier.

Eickhout, B., H. van Meijl, A. Tabeau, and E. Stehfest. 2009. "The Impact of Environmental and Climate Constraints on Global Food Supply." In *Economic Analysis of Land Use in Global Climate Change Policy*, ed. T. W. Hertel, S. Rose, and R. S. J. Tol. London: Routledge.

Ekasingh, B., C. Sungkapitux, J. Kitchaicharoen, and P. Suebpongsang. 2007. "Competitive Commercial Agriculture in the Northeast of Thailand." Background paper for the Competitive Commercial Agriculture in Sub-Saharan Africa Study, World Bank, Washington, DC.

Fairhurst, T., and D. McLaughlin. 2009. "Sustainable Oil Palm Development on Degraded Land in Kalimantan." World Wildlife Fund, Washington, DC.

FAO (Food and Agriculture Organization of the United Nations). 2008. "The State of Food and Agriculture Biofuels: Prospects, Risks, and Opportunities." FAO, Rome.

———. 2009. http://www.faostat.fao.org, accessed April 15, 2010.

Fargione, J., J. Hill, D. Tilman, S. Polasky, and P. Hawthorne. 2008. "Land Clearing and the Biofuel Carbon Debt." *Science* 319 (5867): 1235–38.

Fearnside, P. M. 2001. "Land-Tenure Issues as Factors in Environmental Destruction in Brazilian Amazonia: The Case of Southern Para." *World Development* 29 (8): 1361–72.

Feder, G., and R. Slade. 1985. "The Role of Public Policy in the Diffusion of Improved Agricultural Technology." *American Journal of Agricultural Economics* 67 (2): 423–28.

French Inter-Ministerial Food Security Group (GISA). 2010. "Large-Scale Land Acquisition and Responsible Agricultural Investment: For an Approach Respecting Human Rights, Food Security, and Sustainable Development." GISA, Paris.

Fuglie, K. O. 2008. "Is a Slowdown in Agricultural Productivity Growth Contributing to the Rise in Commodity Prices ?" *Agricultural Economics* 39 (3): 431–41.

Gardner, B. L. 2002. *American Agriculture in the Twentieth Century: How It Flourished and What It Cost.* Cambridge, MA: Harvard University Press.

Global Exchange for Social Investment. 2008. "Global Market Study on Jatropha: Final Report." World Wildlife Fund and GEXSI, London and Berlin.

Government of Sudan. 2009. "Study of the Sustainable Development of Semi-mechanized Rainfed Farming." Ministry of Agriculture and Forestry, Khartoum.

Hayami, Y. 2010. "Plantation Agriculture." In *Handbook of Agricultural Economics*, ed. P. L. Pingali and R. E. Evenson. North Holland: Elsevier.

Hertel, T. W., W. E. Tyner, and D. K. Birur. 2010. "The Global Impacts of Biofuel Mandates." *Energy Journal* 31 (1): 75–100.

Johnson, D. H. 2003. *The Root Causes of Sudan's Civil Wars.* Bloomington, IN: Indiana University Press.

Keeney, R., and T. W. Hertel. 2009. "The Indirect Land Use Impacts of U.S. Biofuel Policies: The Importance of Acreage, Yield, and Bilateral Trade Responses." *American Journal of Agricultural Economics* 91 (4): 895–909.

Koh, L. P., and D. S. Wilcove. 2008. "Is Palm Oil Agriculture Really Destroying Tropical Biodiversity?" *Conservation Letters* 1 (2): 66–64.

Lane, C., and J. N. Pretty. 1991. "Displaced Pastoralists and Transferred Wheat Technology in Tanzania." Gatekeeper Series No. 20. International Institute for Environment and Development, London.

Liefert, W., E. Serova, and O. Liefert. 2009. "The Big Players of the Former Soviet Union and World Agriculture: Issues and Outlook." Paper presented at 27th International Association of Agricultural Economists Conference, Beijing.

Lipton, M. 2009. *Land Reform in Developing Countries: Property Rights and Property Wrongs.* New York: Routledge.

Lissitsa, A. 2010. "The Emergence of Large Scale Agricultural Production in Ukraine: Lessons and Perspectives." Paper presented at the Annual Bank Conference on Land Policy and Administration, Washington, DC, April 26–27.

Locke, A. 2009. "Economic and Financial Analysis of Large-Scale Land Acquisition for Agricultural Production in Mozambique." Draft paper, World Bank, Washington, DC.

Maertens, M., and J. F. M. Swinnen. 2009. "Trade, Standards, and Poverty: Evidence from Senegal." *World Development* 37 (1): 161–78.

Manciana, E., M. Trucco, and M. Pineiro. 2009. "Large-Scale Acquisition of Land Rights for Agricultural or Natural Resource-Based Use: Argentina." World Bank, Buenos Aires.

Marques, P. V. 2009. "Custo de producao Agricola e industrial de acucar no Brasil na safra 2007/08." Universidade de Sao Paolo Escola Superior de Agricultura, Sao Paolo.

Martin, S. M. 2003. *The UP (United Plantations) Saga*. Copenhagen: Nordic Institute for Asian Studies Press.

Melillo, J. M., J. M. Reilly, D. W. Kicklighter, and others. 2009. "Indirect Emissions from Biofuels: How Important?" *Science* 326 (5958): 1397–99.

Mitchell, D. 2010. "Biofuels in Africa: Prospects for Sustainable Development." Africa Region, World Bank, Washington, DC.

Morton, D. C., R. S. DeFries, Y. E. Shimabukuro, L. O. Anderson, E. Arai, F. D. Espirito-Santo, R. Freitas, and J. Morisette. 2006. "Cropland Expansion Changes Deforestation Dynamics in the Southern Brazilian Amazon." *Proceedings of the National Academy of Sciences of the United States of America* 103 (39): 14637–41.

Nelson, G. C. and others. 2009. "Climate Change: Impact on Agriculture and Costs of Adaptation." Food Policy Report, International Food Policy Research Institute, Washington, DC.

OECD (Organisation for Economic Co-operation and Development) and FAO (Food and Agriculture Organization). 2010. *Agricultural Outlook*. Paris and Rome: OECD and FAO.

Pacheco, P. 2009. "Agrarian Reform in the Brazilian Amazon: Its Implications for Land Distribution and Deforestation." *World Development* 37 (8): 1337–47.

Pantuliano, S. 2007. "The Land Question: Sudan's Peace Nemesis." Humanitarian Policy Group Working Paper, Overseas Development Institute, London.

Pingali, P. L., and V. T. Xuan. 1992. "Vietnam: Decollectivization and Rice Productivity Growth." *Economic Development and Cultural Change* 40 (4): 697–718.

Poulton, C., G. Tyler, P. Hazell, A. Dorward, J. Kydd, and M. Stockbridge. 2008. "All-Africa Review of Experiences with Commercial Agriculture: Lesson from Success and Failure." Background paper for the Competitive Commercial Agriculture in Sub-Saharan Africa Study, World Bank, Washington, DC.

Rasiah, R. 2006. "Explaining Malaysia's Export Expansion in Oil Palm and Related Products." In *The How and the Why of Technology Development in Developing Countries*, ed. V. Chandra. Washington, DC: World Bank.

Regunaga, M. 2010. "The Soybean Chain in Argentina." Implications of the organization of the commodity production and processing industry case studies, Latin America and the Caribbean Chief Economist Office, World Bank. Washington, DC.

Renewable Fuels Agency. 2008. "The Gallagher Review of the Indirect Effects of Biofuels Production." UK Renewable Fuels Agency, St. Leonards-on-sea.

Rezende, G. C. de. 2005. "Politicas trabalhista e fundiaria e seus efeitos adversos sobre o emprego agricoloa, a etrutura agraria e o desenvolvimento territorial rural no Brasil." Texto para discussao No 1108. Rio de Janeiro: Instituto de Pesquisa Economica Aplicada.

Rist, L., L. Feintrenie, and P. Levang. 2010. "The Livelihood Impacts of Oil Palm: Smallholders in Indonesia." *Biodiversity and Conservation* 19 (4): 1009–24.

Rogers, P. J. 2004. "Saskatoon on the Savanna: Discursive Dependency, Canadian-guided Agricultural Development and the Hanang Wheat Complex." Paper presented at the 45th Annual International Studies Association Conference, Montreal, Quebec, March 17.

Saeed, A. 2008. *Post-Conflict Peace Building and Socio-Economic Integration Issues in Southwest Kordofan*. Bergen, Norway: Chr. Michelsen Institute.

Salih, M. A. 1987. "The Tractor and the Plough: The Sociological Dimension." In *Agrarian Change in the Central Rangelands*, ed. M. A. Salih, 108–28. Uppsala, Sweden: Scandinavian Institute for African Studies.

Searchinger, T., R. Heimlich, R. A. Houghton, F. Dong, A. Elobeid, J. Fabiosa, S. Tokgoz, D. Hayes, and T. H. Yu. 2008. "Use of U.S. Croplands for Biofuels Increases Greenhouse Gases Through Emissions from Land-Use Change." *Science* 319 (5867): 1238–40.

Stiglitz, J. E., and A. Weiss. 1981. "Credit Rationing in Markets with Imperfect Information." *American Economic Review* 71 (3): 393–410.

Swinnen, J. F. M. 2009. "Reforms, Globalization, and Endogenous Agricultural Structures." *Agricultural Economics* 40: 719–32.

UNCTAD. 2009. *World Investment Report 2009: Transnational Corporations, Agricultural Production, and Development*. New York and Geneva: United Nations.

UNEP (United Nations Environment Programme). 2007. "Sudan: Post Conflict Environment Assessment." UNEP, Khartoum.

———. 2009. "Towards Sustainable Production and Use of Resources Assessing Biofuels." UNEP, Paris.

Vermeulen, S., and N. Goad. 2006. "Toward Better Practice in Smallholder Palm Oil Production." International Institute for Environment and Development, London.

Winter-Nelson, A., and E. Aggrey-Finn. 2008. "Identifying Opportunities in Ghana's Agriculture." International Food Policy Research Institute, Washington, DC.

World Bank. 2008. "Cameroon Aricultural Value Chain Competitiveness Study." Africa Region, World Bank, Washington, DC.

———. 2009a. "Awakening Africa's Sleeping Giant: Prospects for Competitive Commercial Agriclulture in the Guinea Savannah Zone and Beyond." World Bank, Washington, DC.

———. 2009b. "Environmental, Economic, and Social Impacts of Oil Palm in Indonesia: A Synthesis of Opportunities and Challenges." Draft Paper, Indonesia Country Office, World Bank, Jakarta.

Zinkhan, F. C., and F. W. Cubbage. 2003. "Financial Analysis of Timber Investments." In *Forests in a Market Economy*, ed. E. O. Sills and K. L. Abt. North Holland: Kluwer.

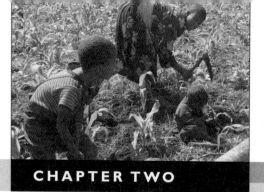

CHAPTER TWO

Is the Recent "Land Rush" Different?

As chapter 1 highlighted, the expansion of cultivated areas through markets continues to be important in many regions. The jump in investment following the 2008 food price hike also affected countries not traditionally considered viable targets. To understand this "land rush" and the factors shaping it, we used three methods.

- To characterize the demand for land from potential investors that may not (yet) have resulted in projects on the ground, we coded press reports on agreed or contemplated private investments. We find that putative investments have a strong focus on Africa, most of them have not started any work on the ground, and having weak land governance and poor recognition of local land rights is associated with increased investor interest in a country as evidenced by press reports.
- To assess what is happening on the ground and governments' awareness, we use official inventories of land transactions for 14 countries that featured prominently in press reports. Procedurally, we find that unclear responsibilities, lack of staff and capacity (and little outsourcing), poor land records, low payments (for example, for land and/or taxes), and limited emphasis on consultation, economic viability, and social and environmental criteria all reduce target countries' ability to regulate investments and protect local property rights. These imply large implementation gaps and lower than expected generation of assets and employment. While local investors are

more prevalent than foreign ones, policy is a main determinant of the volume of transactions.

- To determine how actual livelihoods are affected, we conducted case studies of 19 projects in the field. We find that in many of the countries affected, public agencies lack the tools and capacity necessary to implement regulations or to monitor compliance. Negative impacts arise if local land and resource rights are unclear, if investors' lack of capacity or unrealistic expectations lead to nonviable projects, and if responsibilities agreed to in consultations are not recorded and enforced. Case studies also demonstrate that well-executed projects can generate large benefits, which can then be shared with local people through provision of public goods, employment, access to markets and technology, or taxes paid by investors to local or national governments.

EVIDENCE FROM MEDIA REPORTS

While media reports do not capture actual land allocations or implementation on the ground, they can illustrate the nature and magnitude of investor intentions. The nongovernmental organization GRAIN deserves credit for having recognized that, without information, it will be impossible to either understand the phenomenon of land acquisition or to take action to improve outcomes. To provide such data, GRAIN launched an open blog for global surveillance of large-scale land acquisition.[1] Although both media coverage and postings by users are likely to impart an upward bias and independent monitoring of the phenomenon would be highly desirable, cross-checking the information from media reports against official inventories in the field suggests that, for projects that moved forward, information from the blog was in line with the facts.[2] Moreover, this is the only source that can claim global coverage. It has been used by research institutions (Braun and Meinzen-Dick 2009), think tanks (Centre d'Analyse Stratégique 2010), and donors (Diallo and Mushinzimana 2009; Centre d'Analyse Stratégique 2010; Niasse and Taylor 2010; Uellenberg 2009) to make inferences on the size of the "land rush." We use it to identify investment characteristics, provide descriptive evidence on reported investor intentions, and conduct an econometric assessment of the factors that increase a country's attractiveness as a target for such investment.

Descriptive Evidence

Plotting prices for rice, wheat, and maize as well as the number of media reports on foreign land acquisitions as a 5-month moving average since July 2005, figure 2.1 illustrates that media interest in this topic started to take off in the wake of the 2007–08 commodity price boom. However, while commodity prices soon declined, reports about land acquisition continued to increase to peak in end of 2009 and have since ticked up again.

Figure 2.1 Key Commodity Prices and Number of Media Reports on Foreign Land Acquisition

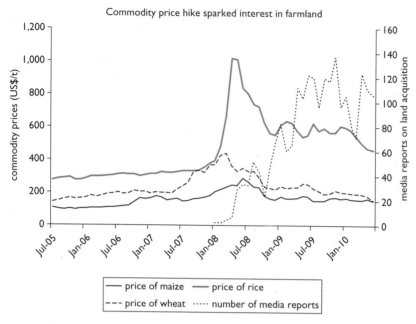

Commodity price hike sparked interest in farmland

— price of maize — price of rice
--- price of wheat ····· number of media reports

Source: Authors based on Food and Agriculture Organization of the United Nations data media reports posted on the GRAIN Web site (http://www.grain.org) and IMF (3-month moving average).

To bring the evidence into a form amenable to quantitative analysis, we coded implementation status, area of investment, commodity group, target and origin countries, and type of investor for all the information posted on the blog between October 1, 2008, and 31 August 31, 2009. This provides us with a database of 464 projects, with 203 including area information that totals 56.6 million hectares (ha). Although projects target 81 countries, 48 percent of projects covering some two-thirds of the total area (39.7 million ha) involve Sub-Saharan Africa, followed by East and South Asia (8.3 million ha), Europe and Central Asia (4.3 million ha), and Latin America and the Caribbean (3.2 million ha) (figure 2.2).

With a median project size of 40,000 ha, reports highlight the scale of investor ambition. In fact, a quarter of all projects involve more than 200,000 ha and only a quarter involve less than 10,000 ha. Of the 405 projects with commodity data, 37 percent focus on food crops, 21 percent on industrial or cash crops, and 21 percent on biofuels, with the remainder distributed among conservation and game reserves, livestock, and plantation forestry (figure 2.3).[3]

In sharp contrast to reported intentions, according to media reports most of the projects listed have either not acquired land or fail to use the land they

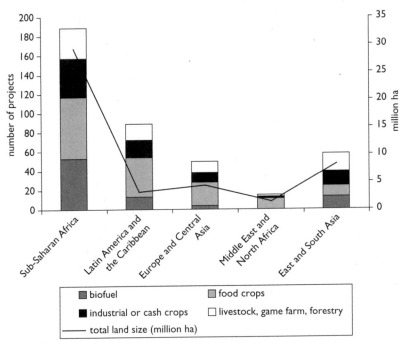

Source: Media reports posted on the GRAIN Web site (http://www.grain.org) between October 1, 2008, and August 31, 2009.
Note: The histogram for the frequency of projects is drawn for the 405 projects for which the purpose and the destination region are known. The total areas are computed based on the 202 projects for which the size is known.

acquired as intended. In fact, almost 30 percent are still in an exploratory stage; 18 percent have been approved but have not started yet; more than 30 percent are at initial development stages; and only 21 percent have initiated begun actual farming, often on a scale much smaller than intended. No clear pattern across commodities is evident for projects that have started implementation.

Putative demand focuses on Sudan, Ethiopia, Nigeria, Ghana, and Mozambique in Sub-Saharan Africa, which together account for more than 23 percent of projects worldwide. Twenty-one percent of projects are in Latin America and the Caribbean (mainly in Brazil and Argentina), 11 percent in Europe and Central Asia (mainly in Kazakhstan, the Russian Federation, and Ukraine), and 10 percent in Southeast Asia (the Philippines, Cambodia, Indonesia, and the Lao People's Democratic Republic). A larger share of food crops relative to industrial or cash crops and a focus on investments for biofuels are evident in Sub-Saharan Africa and Latin America and the Caribbean.

Figure 2.3 Share of Projects by Commodity and Production Status of Capital

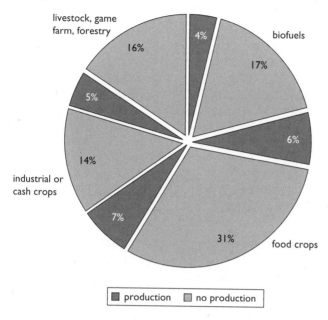

Source: Media reports on the GRAIN Web site (http://www.grain.org) October 1, 2008, to August 31, 2009.

Press reports allow identification of source countries without complicated searches in the company registry. Although part of this may reflect reporting bias or strategic use of press reports by some types of investors, most of the projects in the database originate from a few countries. These include China, the Gulf States, (Saudi Arabia, United Arab Emirates, Qatar, Kuwait, and Bahrain), North Africa (Libya and the Arab Republic of Egypt), Russia, and such developed economies as the United Kingdom and the United States.[4] Across countries, there are marked differences in the share of projects that have started activities on the ground, with the gap between intent and implementation particularly high for Libya, India, the Gulf States, and the United Kingdom.

Agribusiness and industry account for the largest share of investors, with agribusiness more specialized on food crops and industry on biofuels. Although few sovereign wealth funds appear directly as the origin of investments, investment funds are key players. Funds from the Middle East and North Africa are far more specialized in food crops than funds outside the region, suggesting that part of the demand for land from the Middle East is internal demand for food.

Econometric Analysis: Determinants of Country-Level Demand

Complementing data on planned agricultural investment projects with country-level information allows us to identify factors that make it more likely for a country to be targeted by investors interested in acquiring land on a large scale. Key independent variables include the amount of unused agricultural land based on analysis of spatial data, which distinguishes between forest and non-forest land, the yield gap on cultivated land (as measured by the fraction of the production potential achieved), and two measures of governance, one for investment protection and one for land tenure security.[5]

Four results are of interest (table 2.1). First, investors featuring in media reports are more likely to target countries with abundant non-forested but not forested land. Second, in contrast to standard results on general foreign direct investment, rule of law and a favorable investment climate as proxied by the Doing Business rank for investor protection has only a weak effect on planned

Table 2.1 Estimated Probability that a Country Is Targeted by Investments

	Probability of attracting investment interest		Probability of attracting implemented investment
	Coefficient		
Dependent variable	Model 1	Model 2	Model 2
Nonforest noncultivated suitable land	0.3049**	0.2987**	0.3916***
Forest noncultivated suitable land	0.0503	0.0396	0.0770
Yield gap (in percent)	−0.3635	−0.2774	−1.7457**
Rural land tenure recognition[a]	−0.5117***	−0.6906***	−0.3416*
Investment protection rank[b]		−0.0058*	0.0033
Number of countries	104	102	102
Pseudo R-squared	0.311	0.339	0.268

Source: Arezki, Deininger, and Selod 2010.
Note: Significant at *** = 1%; ** = 5%; * = 10%. Estimation with robust standard errors. Constant estimated but not shown.
a. Variable B6091 from the 2009 Institutional Profiles Database measuring the share of the population in rural areas whose land rights are recognized. Countries where rural land tenure is recognized are attractive if the coefficient is significantly positive.
b. Doing Business 2009 classification of investment protection. The countries protecting investments are attractive if the coefficient is significantly negative.

and none on implemented investment. Third, the impact of rural land tenure recognition is negative, strongly significant for intended investment, and still significant at 10 percent for implemented projects. This finding is robust to alternative measures, in particular a principal component index of all variables of rural land governance and tenure recognition, included in the database we used. It suggests that lower recognition of land rights increases a country's attractiveness for land acquisition. For implemented investments (column 3), the coefficient on recognition of rural land rights, though still negative, is only half the magnitude of what is observed in the other regressions and is of marginal significance. This could either mean that, in these environments, more challenges need to be overcome to successfully implement projects or imply that these countries attract investors who are less able or willing (for example, because they are interested more in speculative land acquisition) to put together projects that can actually be implemented on the ground. Finally, the yield gap is not relevant to explain interest in large-scale land acquisition, but is negatively associated with implemented investments, consistent with the notion that technical feasibility is not a major determinant of investor interest and that, in countries with low productivity, investors need to overcome more challenges to successfully implement investments, everything else equal.

As countries that failed to formally recognize land rights were more attractive for foreigners in search of land in the wake of the 2008 commodity price hike, even after accounting for other factors, they may become a target if commodity prices were to increase again. This has three implications for policy makers.

- The focus of investor interest on countries with weak land governance increases the risk that investors acquire the land essentially for free and in neglect of local rights, with potentially far-reaching negative consequences. Such failure to value land at its true opportunity cost could result in projects that, while desirable from the investors' point of view, may not yield social benefits.

- In areas where land demand for agricultural investment is evident or expected to materialize in the near future, measures to record rights, educate communities about their rights and ways to interact with investors, engage in local land use planning, and make arrangements for consultation and monitoring of agreements will be critical. There is ample scope for South-South exchanges to promote wider application of successful experiences as implemented, for example, in Latin America and the Caribbean (see chapter 4).

- To the extent that overall institutions are weak, civil society will have an important role in educating local communities and monitoring outcomes as a watchdog. Equally, the corporate sector can help by demonstrating its commitment to performance standards through voluntarily disclosure of information, such as social and environmental impact assessments, as well as minutes of agreements reached in community consultations.

EVIDENCE FROM COUNTRY INVENTORIES

Despite global attention to large-scale land acquisitions for agricultural invest-ment, available information is often not validated officially. To overcome this, official data on actual and pending land transfers in 2004–09 were compiled by local collaborators in 14 countries from land administration officials and other key informants, including ministries of agriculture and land or investment promotion agencies.[6] Following the lead of earlier studies (Cotula and others 2009), we aimed to obtain information on key aspects of each project or proposal.

These aspects include the following:

- Commodity and main market (processed/raw, domestic/export)
- Type of investor (public/private, domestic/foreign)
- Planned capital contribution and employment to be generated by the investment
- Date of first filing for approval and stage in the process of obtaining approval or, if approval had been obtained, the actual progress of the investment
- The area and nature of land rights transferred (land sale/lease or land use rights through contract farming/outgrowers)
- The extent of the social and environmental impact assessment completed during the application process
- The geographic coordinates of the investment.

Because government capacity to record land transactions varies widely across the study countries, information from government departments was cross-checked as far as possible through interviews with key informants, such as investors, government officials not directly involved in data, and non-governmental organizations monitoring these issues.

We find that deficiencies in the processes to award land and the lack of capacity of the institutions implementing these processes make it more difficult to screen investments with good potential and undermine efforts to protect local rights. Instead, they increase transaction costs, reduce tenure security—and thus the investment incentives for investors—and reduce social and envi-ronmental sustainability. Projects struggle to get off the ground, fail to generate employment and investment at the envisaged scale, and often end up neglecting both local rights and established social and environmental norms.

Administrative Processes

We recognized from the start that reporting processes and the data collected were likely to differ across countries. We hoped that using a structured ques-tionnaire, collecting information on the legal and regulatory environment, and collaborating with relevant local institutions would nevertheless provide a reasonably complete picture. It thus emerged as somewhat surprising that the amount of information collected from investors before and especially after approval of the investment was quite limited, that coordination between different agencies and levels of government was lacking, and that, in many cases, details such as the investment's location or implementation status, were either not available or of questionable provenance. Key administrative gaps relate to the following:

- Unclear assignment or duplication of institutional responsibility
- Limited capacity to implement or monitor environmental or social safeguards
- Rudimentary boundary descriptions for investment properties
- Low, if any, payments for land, which are often not collected
- Deficient approval processes, with gaps relating specifically to assessments of economic viability.

Together these gaps reduce tenure security and investment incentives, make it more difficult for projects to quickly initiate production, increase transaction cost and the likelihood of conflict, and complicate efforts by public institutions to collect land taxes and monitor project progress (table 2.2). Detailed experiences are described in appendix 2.

Assignment of institutional responsibilities is often unclear. The resulting lack of clarity about who can make final decisions and failures to (satisfactorily) conduct essential regulatory functions creates an environment with ample space for discretionary decisions and high transaction costs. Competition between investment promotion agencies and line ministries and confused authority for approval and record keeping at local, state, and national agencies are related to the policy framework. The discretionary implementation of regulations is a practical issue that can be discovered only through case studies (box 2.1).

Despite the potentially far-reaching environmental and social impacts of many projects, implementation of environmental and social impact assessments is deficient in many settings. Even where they are required by law, environmental and social impact assessments are often not conducted. In Ethiopia, few agricultural investment projects had an environmental impact assessment (EIA) as required by law. Key reasons were a lack of capacity and a rush to approve projects by the investment authority that precluded sectoral agencies from performing due diligence. In Zambia, where an EIA is required for land clearance to establish large-scale agriculture, only 15 percent of projects in the inventory had EIAs. In Nigeria, by contrast, about 85 percent of the projects in the inventory performed such assessments. Even where they are conducted, however, compliance is rarely if ever monitored. This increases the risk that standards or agreed actions will not be adhered to and the likelihood that negative external effects may materialize.

Table 2.2 Challenges Encountered in Collecting Inventory Data

Country	Data obtained	Issues
Cambodia	Government inventory of concessions up to 2006 produced in response to intense international pressure about the process of awarding concessions	Government had committed to updating the data base in 2009 but did not do so. Issues with internal consistency of data and interpretation of global positioning system coordinates. Interviews confirm that large concessions continue to be granted despite a sub decree aiming to limit this practice.
Congo, Dem. Rep.	National inventory for concessions above 500 ha; up data collection in selected districts of five provinces	Multiple concessions for grants up to 1,000 ha to the same investor to circumvent national concession approval process. Few awards in forested provinces or for Reducing Emissions from Deforestation and Forest Degradation in Developing Countries.
Ethiopia	406 projects in five regions from national and regional governments total 1.19 million ha	Data from different regions are not in a standardized format. Regional investment authorities can authorize awards below 5,000 ha without consulting other agencies; no process for central data sharing. Possibility of conflict of interest in award process.
Indonesia	Failed to obtain data despite widespread concessions for plantations and a field visit to East Kalimantan province	Limited information at the provincial level may be related to delayed approval of provincial spatial plan, which has prevented allocation of land for new concessions
Liberia	Complete data from central government sources on new and old concessions that were cancelled and renegotiated	Information on land area awarded, rents, and tax payments is official and complete, but investment data (including cultivated area) relate to plans rather than actual values. Mismatch to cultivated area as concessions fell into disuse during the war or were never used in the first place.
Lao, PDR	Data on 1,143 concessions covering 248,846 ha, including at least 398 for foreign investors	Fragmentation, lack of upstream reporting, and lines of accountability led to underreporting. Limited data on implementation progress.
Mozambique	All concessions more than 1,000 ha from government sources for a total of 259 approved projects (more than 1 million ha) and 117 proposals involving more than 1.27 million ha	No implementation data collected by government, so no project received definitive rights, which requires demarcation and demonstrated implementation. Projects < 1,000 ha do not enter national approval processes.

Nigeria	State level data collection in 26 of 36 states, cross-checked with federal institutions (Ministry of Agriculture; Forestry Research Institute)	All land allocations are decentralized to the state level. But state-level data are not standardized, making it difficult to draw conclusions. Many investments approvals lack even basic information, such as the year of approval.
Pakistan	Political sensitivities surrounding land ownership did not allow data collection; relied instead on field trips.	Field trips to cross-check the projects cited in media reports cataloged on the GRAIN blog. In none of these cases could evidence of any investments be found.
Paraguay	Registration and census data were examined to explore patterns of large-scale land ownership. Census data provided information on overall land concentration	Data from census and cadastre provide some information on ownership and farm size, but exploring data from the registry proved difficult due to low registration rate and considerable overlaps between parcels. Inaccuracies are greater in active land markets.
Peru	Auctions of public land: data on both land size and value publicly available Private land transactions: not available	Concessions for forestry and agriculture are processed by separate agencies with different processes. Agriculture concessions processed through public auctions; forestry concessions allocated through bidding. Concern over agricultural cultivation on former forest concessions that were cleared of vegetation.
Sudan	Data on 132 land use licenses from the national Ministry of Agriculture and from investment commissions in nine states.	Data beyond land size limited; nothing on implementation. Data quality suffered as a result of the transfer of responsibilities for land allocation and investment approval between ministries and investment commissions.
Ukraine	Land transactions between individual owners and investors. Interviews with all 2,984 operators of > 2,000 ha	No central database; basic data (land area, location, crops, rental) obtained through phone interviews.
Zambia	Data on projects > 500 ha from Ministry of Lands (100 projects), Zambia Development Agency (20) and Patents and Companies Registration Office (10)	Only 10 projects for agricultural investments; the 20 Zambia Development Agency projects are mostly tourism and game farms. Underreporting may be an issue. Very limited implementation throughout.

Source: Authors.

In the Lao People's Democratic Republic, land concessions are negotiated, awarded, and managed haphazardly, with no systematic or unified monitoring and evaluation procedures. The result is a loss of valuable natural resources and the marginalization of vulnerable populations. Failure to integrate concessions into the regular land administration system leads to corruption, speculation, and a parallel land market characterized by a lack of security. Such tendencies are reinforced by unclear assignment of responsibility to relevant institutions. This situation leads to incorrect interpretations and uneven application of laws and regulations, abuses of public powers to support private developments, and failure to provide compensation to local communities. Addressing these issues, and the many underperforming or poorly performing concessions that have resulted from them, requires better communication with investors and a more reliable land information system.

Source: Authors based on Schoenweger 2010; World Bank 2010.

The technical and economic viability of investments are critical to ensure that local people benefit from outside investment. Also, verifiable quantitative targets with respect to, for example, investment, employment generation, and tax payments are critical for anybody to monitor project progress against plans. Investors may not always have the knowledge or incentive to correctly represent economic viability. Still, in most countries it is implicitly presumed that investors will have the right incentive and be the best qualified to assess economic viability. As a result, reporting requirements or arrangements for monitoring are at best rudimentary. In Ethiopia, many project proposals, even in regions with more advanced governance, only vaguely indicate intended land uses and lack key information, such as the value of the investment and the type of production. Moreover, checks on economic viability do not exist. In Sudan, no economic analysis is conducted and limited attention to identifying existing rights reportedly led to entire villages being transferred to investors. The irreversibility of investment decisions, high transaction costs for making or canceling investments, and the often large external effects (such as those on the environment) imply that greater attention to economic viability and measureable performance indicators are needed.

Even if the land transferred to investors is quite valuable, many countries devote little attention to administrative records, particularly the geographical description of boundaries for land allocations.[7] Potential negative consequences include the double allocation of land to different parties, the inability to unambiguously ascertain who has rights to a given piece of land without costly field investigation, and boundary disputes that undermine local rights. This inability to determine the uniqueness of land rights is therefore likely to also reduce investors' ability to use the land as collateral for credit. Even where concession boundaries are mapped (in Liberia and Mozambique, for example), little ground-checking for potential overlaps with other land uses, including community lands, is done, which leads to potentially large risks. Only about 12 percent of communities in Mozambique have their land demarcated. However, the total area over which land use titles given to investors overlapped areas previously delimited in the name of communities amounted to 1.4 million ha in 418 cases (about 20 percent of the total), raising concern about potential future conflicts (see appendix 4, map A4.2.1). In Zambia, cross-checking of coordinates for concessions awarded since 1995 against recent satellite imagery reveals defects. Many of the areas awarded as concessions were apparently used by shifting cultivators, boundaries were often drawn schematically rather than according to natural (physical) features, and in many cases cultivation had not yet started.

Regulations in some countries, including Indonesia, Liberia, and Mozambique, make land allocation contingent on compliance with requirements that may include implementation of business plans, land demarcation, compliance with the stipulations of social or environmental impact assessments, and rental payments. The effectiveness of such rules is, however, reduced by weak monitoring of compliance and the fact that channels to lodge complaints are difficult to access or entirely absent. Public access to information about the modalities of land transfers, including investors' business and investment plans, could be a basis for independent monitoring and third party verification, thus providing stronger incentives for compliance. This could strengthen capacity in the public sector and allow it to focus on essential regulatory functions (for example, EIAs).

Incidence and Characteristics of Large-Scale Land Acquisitions

While weak administrative processes may be cause for concern, the outcomes in terms of productivity and distribution of benefits are even more important. Available data point to several observations:

- Amounts of land transferred differ widely across countries as a function of policy.
- Domestic investors appear to be more prevalent than foreign ones in most contexts.
- Land policies are key determinants of the size and nature of land transactions.
- Most projects are smaller than those reported in the media, though the distribution is skewed.[8]
- Amounts of new employment and physical investment are often well below expectations.

Inventory data from six countries with fairly reliable information highlight that the amount of land transferred can be large and that there is wide variation across countries depending on the policy context. Total transfers in 2004–09 amounted to 4.0 million ha in Sudan, 2.7 million in Mozambique, 1.6 million in Liberia (many were renegotiations of existing agreements), and 1.2 million in Ethiopia (table 2.3; appendix 2, table A2.1).The median transaction is generally much lower than in the media reports, except for Liberia, where there were only a few projects, but two were very large.

Generally, the volume and average size of officially recorded deals are well below those asserted in media reports. Policy is also a decisive factor. In Tanzania, where land rights are firmly vested with local villages, fewer than 50,000 ha were transferred between January 2004 and June 2009. In Mexico, most investors enter joint ventures with communities because of legal restrictions that preclude land transfers beyond a certain size to outsiders and a 10-year program to systematically recognize and demarcate local land rights and establish clear structures to represent communities. By contrast, over the same period, 2.7 million ha were acquired by investors in Mozambique. A 2009 land audit found that, from a sample of projects, more than 50 percent of projects had either not started any activity (34 percent of the total) or lagged significantly behind their development plan. In Peru, auctions of 235,500 ha along the coast over the last 15 years brought in almost US$50 million in investment, generating large numbers of jobs and underpinning the country's emergence as a major force in high-value agro-exports.

For most projects, size is well below the large areas mentioned in press reports. At the same time, the distribution of project sizes is skewed, with a few often accounting for a large share of the area. In Ethiopia, only 23 of the 406 projects (5.7 percent) involve foreign investors, and more than half of projects are less than 1,000 ha in size. Still, five large projects make up half the area leased out by the government. In Mozambique, where we considered only projects involving more than 1,000 ha, the median size is 1,500 ha (1,000 ha

Table 2.3 Large Land Acquisitions in Selected Countries, 2004–09

Country	Number of projects	Area (thousand ha)	Median size (ha)	Domestic share of area (%)
Cambodia	61	958	8,985	70
Ethiopia	406	1,190	700	49
Liberia	17	1,602	59,374	7
Mozambique	405	2,670	2,225	53
Nigeria	115	793	1,500	97
Sudan	132	3,965	7,980	78

Source: Country inventories collected for this study.

for domestic and 3,500 ha for foreign investors), and two-thirds of land use requests involve Mozambican investors. The 8 percent of projects involving more than 15,000 ha account for 50 percent of the total land area.[9] In Sudan, the total area for 132 approved projects amounts to almost 4 million ha, with a median size of 8,000 ha; the largest project covers more than half a million ha. Of these 132 projects, 42 (32 percent) involve foreigners, including 39 Middle Eastern investors, and 90 (68 percent) were approved for Sudanese investors, possibly jointly with foreigners. In Sudan, the largest single country of investor origin is Saudi Arabia, with 19 projects totaling 376,000 ha, slightly less than half the total of all approved foreign investments in the country (879,000 ha).

Notwithstanding the fact that investment sizes are smaller than reported in press reports, in many of the cases studied, investors acquired land in quantities much larger than they could use, at least initially. Many saw this tactic as motivated by a desire to lock in very favorable terms of land access and eliminate future competition. In settings where either the technology or investor capacity is unproven, the acquisition of land in larger quantities than an investor can reasonably operate involves significant risks. Especially in areas where land values are expected to appreciate and no effective mechanisms for land taxation are in place, large land allocations to investors with little experience are risky. Wherever feasible, it will thus be desirable to give land to a larger number of entrepreneurs in smaller lots and provide them with the option of acquiring more land in the future once they have proven their capacity to use the land effectively. Such an approach would also reduce the danger of creating local monopolies in input and output markets, an issue that will be of relevance if land users continue to depend on land-based livelihoods. Given the evidence that investors do not always live up to their promises, greater scrutiny of investment proposals' viability and use of deposits to ensure investment is actually made are now widely recognized as necessary to screen investors.

Contrary to the image of a neocolonial foreign scramble for land that often emerges from media reports, acquisitions recorded by official inventories are dominated by local individuals or companies. Domestic investors account for more than 90 percent of the area allocated in Nigeria and half or more in Cambodia, Ethiopia, Mozambique, and Sudan.[10] Also contrary to media reports, Sudan is the only country where the majority of foreign projects are from the Middle East. The share of investors of domestic origin is much higher, reflecting the smaller size of domestic projects. But as local businesses may act as fronts for foreigners, the share of land acquired by foreigners may be larger than reported.

Given the central nature of asset and employment generation through planned investments, the level and recording of information on planned (temporary or permanent) employment and physical investment is surprisingly limited. The patchy data that are available suggest that investments create far fewer jobs than are often expected (or promised, as discussed later) and that their capital intensity varies widely. For example, projected job creation ranges from less than 0.01 jobs/ha (for a 10,000 ha maize plantation) to 0.351 jobs/ha (for an outgrower-based sugarcane plantation) in the Democratic Republic of Congo. Expected job creation in Ethiopia is similarly limited, with an average of 0.005 jobs/ha for cases where figures are given. Planned capital investments also vary widely, from US$27/ha for mixed livestock farming to US$21,000/ha for sugarcane. Some are unbelievably low (for example, US$5/ha for an oil palm plantation in Nigeria). Given the importance of capital investment and job creation for the viability of ventures and the sharing of benefits, more attention would be warranted not only to recording these figures but to giving them greater weight in project evaluation and monitoring. Measures to ensure that plans are complied with may be warranted also (for example, the requirement of a substantial share of planned investment to be deposited upfront, as in Peru).

EVIDENCE FROM PROJECT CASE STUDIES

Case studies allow us to understand how aggregate phenomena reported in inventories affect local livelihoods, identify potential unintended consequences, and formulate hypotheses that can then be tested through quantitative methods. Key insights from each case study are presented in table 2.4 and elaborated further in appendix 2, table A2.2. We thus draw on case studies to assess how large-scale investment affects local livelihoods and identify factors that may not be obvious from aggregate data. We conducted 19 case studies on individual investment projects in seven countries.

Countries were chosen based on investor interest and media attention as indicated by press reports and on a review of social risks, vulnerable groups and recent policy reforms that might hold lessons for other countries. A team with at least one social analysis specialist then visited each project and interviewed stakeholders. Where available, they also examined project documents, such as environmental impact assessments. Appendix 2, table A2.2 explains why each case study country was chosen. The sample can be considered to represent the projects that were in operation and where investors did not refuse access.[11] If anything, these projects are likely to be the ones that are more successful and that will provide larger benefits to local people. The fact that in many of these cases outcomes and processes left much to be desired suggests that there is an urgent need to monitor outcomes on the ground and to publicize both good and bad examples to draw lessons for policy.

Investments can affect local livelihoods and food security by generating jobs, providing social services, increasing knowledge, and improving the asset base of the local population by, for example, providing it with a stake in a joint venture or compensation for land and resources lost. Case studies point to high

Table 2.4 Key Insights from Case Studies

Country	Cases selected	Key insights
Congo, Dem. Rep.	**Maize** (10,000 ha given, 2,000 ha planted)	Project design changed from sugar to maize in response to provincial drive for food self-sufficiency. Local cultivators were pushed off into a national park.
	Mixed (24,000 ha obtained; planted 4,000 ha rubber; 150 ha coffee, 95 ha cacao)	Rubber project employs 1,282 workers and provides them with social benefits. Workers receive variable wages of some US$3–US$5 per week. Some forest clearance for new rubber.
Liberia	**Rice** (14,999 ha)	Investor encroached illegally on fertile wetlands, displaced 30 percent of the population (1,000 people). Unskilled jobs created but often filled with foreigners willing to work for lower wages. Silting of swamp.
	Timber (119,240 ha)	Investment restricted local access to forest products in context of increasing population and decreasing farmland.
	Rubber (32,540 ha)	Dispute about investor's right to expand beyond originally cultivated area exacerbated by the age of the grant (from 1960s); lack of consultation and compensation
Mexico	**Maize** Chiapas (3,066 ha), **Maize** Jalisco (2,070 ha)	Both public and private sector actors involved in improving smallholder access to maize markets. *Ejido* members and peasants often maintain ownership and receive technical assistance, financing from suppliers.
	Rubber (2,970 ha)	Key private sector companies support project by guaranteeing harvest sales. 300 jobs created.
Mozambique	**Sugarcane for ethanol** (30,000 ha)	Job creation significantly lower than anticipated; salary insufficient to compensate for lost livelihoods
	Forestry (26,000 ha)	Investors damage nonrenewable natural resources (water) without compensation, disadvantaging women who are responsible for gathering it.
	Sugarcane for ethanol (20,000 ha)	Lack of agreed boundaries of concessions led to displacement from agricultural and grazing lands. Consultations did not include vulnerable groups, who were disadvantaged by land transfers to investors.

(continued)

Table 2.4 (Continued)

Country	Cases selected	Key insights
Tanzania	**Teak** (28,132 ha awarded, 7,800 planted) **Livestock and jatropha** (4,455 ha at present but investor targets 18,211 ha) **Multiuse** (5,000 ha) **Rice** (5,818 ha)	Investors create local benefits through employment and social infrastructure projects; some concern about in-migration. Investors often circumvent legal land acquisition procedures, such as by soliciting land directly from villages. Land conflicts with local agriculturalists, bee keepers, other investors have damaged public relations. Potentially negative impacts on pastoralist communities' access to grazing land, firewood, and water Some EIAs completed but most environmental impacts still hypothetical Many recent investments involve public-private partnerships and/or foreign investors.
Ukraine	**Multiple crops and pigs** (9,477 ha) **Multiple crops** (150,000 ha) **Multiple crops** (300,000 ha)	Profitable companies employ local people at competitive rates, use modern production methods, and train workers. Community relations were improved through social infrastructure and regular communication with and training of local people. Land rentals are low; investors try to lock these in for the long term.
Zambia	**Export-oriented crops** (155,000 ha) **Sugar** (17,838 ha estate + 13,860 ha outgrowers; smallholder + commercial) **Jatropha** (250 ha nucleus, only 65 ha planted, + outgrowers)	No progress toward implementing government farm block program; investors appear uninterested in this land Negative impacts included displacement, loss of access to natural resources, and land clearing for cultivation. Outgrower sugar scheme results in average wages lower than alternative smallholder cropping options. Outgrower schemes not subject to environmental impact assessment, even large farms often do not complete EIA Sugar contract pricing mechanism works against smallholders; local people encouraged to cede land rights to company. Environmental concerns include eutrophication from agricultural chemical runoff, sedimentation, and pollution. Smallholders reluctant to join jatropha outgrower scheme due to unproven technology and poor plantation results

Source: Authors, based on case study reports.

expectations in employment generation, which, at least in some cases, do not seem to be commensurate with the investment or the qualifications of the local populace. The extent to which assets are provided or local people gain access to knowledge and technology varies widely across investments. Most successful investments provide social services and encouragement for local entrepreneurship. As many of the projects considered began only recently, few positive impacts have yet materialized. Careful future monitoring as well as attention to the time profile of benefits and the distribution of risks will be important.

Implementation Status and Viability

One key finding from the case studies is that, especially for investments started recently, progress with implementation is surprisingly limited, in part because many were approved during the 2008 boom. In Mozambique, Tanzania, and Zambia, it was difficult to identify any projects operating on the ground. Among the projects that had started, the areas in operation were typically much smaller than those allocated. This lag in implementation was normally attributed to unanticipated technical difficulties, reduced profitability, changed market conditions, or tensions with local communities. A large share of operating projects involved either the transfer of ongoing concerns—rather than the establishment of new ones—or contract farming ventures. Investors may thus have underestimated the complexity of agricultural operations, particularly the challenges associated with clearing land, establishing internal infrastructure, and linking to markets. It could also mean that the approval criteria applied may not have been sufficiently rigorous in situations where government is involved in screening projects and transferring land.

Many projects in the biofuel sector experienced financial problems or were cancelled entirely due to lower oil prices. For example, none of the biofuel operations in Mozambique were operating at the envisaged scale and all of them reported delays of at least three to five years. While the financial implications are unknown, liquidity problems and the difficulty of raising additional funds led some projects to change plans. In Katanga province in the Democratic Republic of Congo, for example, one project shifted its planned 10,000 ha of sugarcane to maize for food consumption, partly in response to government subsidies. Similarly, a much-hyped Chinese interest in 3 million ha of Congolese rainforest for oil palm has so far made little progress.

Beyond economic and technical challenges, tensions with local communities have often stymied implementation and could give rise to a downward spiral of conflict. Land allocated without prior consultation or agreement on the amount and type of compensation and a lack of local involvement in the concession led to significant tension that affected project operations in Liberia. In a number of cases, including Ukraine, such conflict required costly restructuring of plans or court action that could possibly have been avoided if projects had been better conceptualized and local residents had been consulted. In

Liberia, Mozambique, and Zambia, conflict, in one case involving the killing of a senior company representative, ensued after the government transferred land that communities considered theirs without effective consultation. In Liberia, such conflict escalated to the highest political levels, with undesirable impacts for all involved.

Socioeconomic Impacts

Even projects that are not fully implemented can seriously undermine local livelihoods. Project proposals not implemented have often affected patterns of resource access and shifted the local balance of power. Expressions or expectations of outside interest in agricultural land did in some cases set in motion "land grabbing" by local elites with undesirable social impacts that could deprive vulnerable people of their livelihoods. In several cases, investors aimed to strategically influence public opinion and exploit coordination gaps within the public sector by circulating rumors. This created the impression that the investments had been finalized and had already been approved at a higher level, either strengthening the investor's negotiating position or allowing the investor to strategically co-opt local leaders. In some instances, implementation delays reduced negative impacts on local communities. In other cases, investors restricted access to land (including common property resources) in a way that negatively affected local livelihoods and then failed to use the land productively.[12]

Provision of public goods by investors was in many cases a more direct way to share benefits, including schools, transport (maintenance of access paths and local roads), and social activities as well as activities to complement local resources (for example, water) and productive activities (by providing access to inputs or output markets, for example). It was particularly effective in doing so where local input was sought through local governments (as in Ukraine) or user groups (as in Liberia, Mexico, and Tanzania). Such input helped in making decisions on the type of goods to be provided and often led to dialogue between the investor and the local population.

Employment is a key factor for transmitting effects. Local people often identified jobs as the most important and immediate benefits of the investments. Communities in Liberia, Mexico, Mozambique, and Ukraine very much appreciate employment generated by investments and believe that such employment contributes to their well-being. In Ukraine, one company employs 5,000 workers, almost all of them local residents, at wages some 50 percent higher than the average. The company also trains workers to operate and maintain expensive equipment. Infrastructure construction can also create additional (temporary) jobs. In Liberia, observers interviewed for one case study linked the creation of full-time jobs for 400 unskilled workers, mostly ex-combatants, to reductions in crime and prostitution. But high expectations for employment gains may not always be realized. The most frequent reason for such a failure was that projects were not viable economically and/or progress with implementation was lagging. For example, one biofuels project in Mozambique had planned to hire 2,650 workers, but at the time of this study only 35–40 people were employed full-time in addition to some 30 seasonal workers.

Moreover, given that jobs will naturally benefit those with better skills and higher levels of education, even the creation of large numbers of jobs may not always be perceived as an unmitigated benefit. This was particularly pronounced in cases where jobs were expected to provide compensation for land and where vulnerable groups lost access to some livelihood resources but did not benefit in terms of jobs. Attention to distributional impacts, possibly by complementing jobs (and market access, which also favors those with skills) with support to social infrastructure that will benefit all local people, helped in some cases to counteract such possible bias against vulnerable groups.

Local peoples' appreciation for job-related benefits may also be reduced if these jobs are only seasonal or if they are taken up by migrants. Seasonality has been an issue in a project in Mozambique where 280 local people (56 of them women) are employed to plant and weed. Investors bringing in migrants from elsewhere was a frequently cited social issue particularly in Liberia, Indonesia, and Ukraine. While in-migration should not be a problem as long as land rights are compensated independently, in many instances jobs were supposed to partly compensate for loss of access to local resources. The fact that these jobs failed to materialize or were taken by outsiders led to conflict and accusations of cheating. A lack of records made it difficult to substantiate such claims.

Where smallholder cultivation is already practiced, large-scale investment can generate large benefits by providing access to markets and technology. In Mexico, some large investors (Nestlé, Bimbo, Maseca, Comercial Mexicana, Monsanto, and Pepsi) increased access to technical packages and markets through partnerships with local groups. As a result, participating communities' livelihoods improved, as evidenced by the increase in the incomes of maize producers and the decline in out-migration. Large-scale investment also significantly reduced farmers' risk by providing a secure outlet for produce. All these investments involved continuing cultivation of land by local *ejidatarios* (farmers). In contrast, a 2,000 ha rubber project in Chiapas relies on land rented from local people. The company provides *ejidatarios* with technical assistance and supervision as well as a secure market for their produce. In Ukraine, a (local) investor brought in technology to dramatically raise yields, provides machinery services, and shares technical advice with local people in regular town hall meetings. In Paraguay, an outside investor uses strong community involvement to help overcome a legacy of violence and conflict, generate opportunities for local entrepreneurs, and provide inputs for local farmers.

Many of the projects studied had strong negative gender effects, either by directly affecting women's land-based livelihoods or, where common property resources were involved, by increasing the time required of women to gather water or firewood and take care of household food security. In many cases, it was presumed that land rights were in the name of men only, and consultations were limited to males in the community, leaving women without a voice. Bargaining power within the household was affected in unpredictable ways.

In some cases, negative distributional and gender impacts arose because consultation, if conducted at all, had very narrow outreach. Vulnerable groups, such as pastoralists and internally displaced people, were excluded from consultations in an effort to override or negate their claims. Without proper safeguards, they then became aware of pending land use changes too late to be able to voice concerns. Females and other vulnerable groups are also less likely to obtain employment from investors or be included in decisionmaking processes surrounding the investment. Even if land was fairly abundant, reduced access to land and associated natural resources was a frequent concern. Potential distributional impacts on food security were also raised as some people lost control over food production and acquisition.

Consultation was particularly critical if land rights were not formalized. Documenting rights to communal areas prior to investment can help to prevent conflict that can otherwise arise easily, especially if contractual arrangements are fuzzy. In Tanzania for example, written records from comprehensive land use plans conducted before investors arrived in an area were invaluable as a means of documenting claims. Where such documents were unavailable, conflict often arose regarding the precise location of the land, the terms of transfer, the type and quantity of other resources (for example, water or nontimber forest products) transferred with the land, and the scope and modalities for making modifications to earlier contracts. Where land was maintained by original owners, issues familiar from the contract farming debate—terms of payment for produce, scope for side-selling, terms of credit, and monopsonistic behavior by processers with a de facto local monopoly on buying produce—emerged in Indonesia, Liberia, Mexico, Mozambique, and Tanzania.

CONCLUSION

Media reports suggest that the recent wave of investment differs from the past trends described in chapter 1. Recent investment involves new types of investors and focuses mainly on African countries that did not appear to be attractive targets earlier and have very weak land governance. As a consequence, the new wave of investments creates risks beyond those present in more traditional investments: investors may lack the necessary experience, countries' institutional infrastructure may be ill-equipped to handle an upsurge in investor interest, and weak protection of land rights may lead to uncompensated land loss by existing land users or land being given away well below its true social value. This could lead to a large divergence between financial and economic benefits and an illusion of profitability even for projects that are undesirable from the country perspective.

Compilation of inventories based on official government data and case studies of a select set of projects confirm that in many instances these are real dangers that need to be addressed if the potential benefits from such investments are to be realized. Public institutions in target countries not only lack the capacity to handle the upsurge in investor interest but are also not geared toward attracting viable investments. Approval processes are often ill-defined, centralized, and discretionary, with different parts of the same government often at odds with each other. In some cases investors can benefit more from trying to navigate the system than from trying to design investments that generate jobs and increase productivity. Consultation with local right holders is in many cases superficial, with a lack of prior information and no written agreements that would clearly specify different parties' responsibilities and thus could be used to provide a basis for redress in case agreements are not adhered to. Land boundaries (and rights) are often ill-defined, and environmental and social safeguards can be neglected. Government capacity to monitor compliance is severely limited. But instead of relying on publicity of relevant documents and independent third-party verification, agreements are surrounded by an air of secrecy that makes public reporting and monitoring near impossible.

In light of these deficiencies, it should not come as a surprise that many investments, not always by foreigners, failed to live up to expectations and, instead of generating sustainable benefits, contributed to asset loss and left local people worse off than they would have been without the investment. In fact, even though an effort was made to cover a wide spectrum of situations, case studies confirm that in many cases benefits were lower than anticipated or did not materialize at all. At the same time, successful cases also highlight that, if projects were economically viable and existing rights enjoyed recognition and protection, local land owners could benefit significantly. There are four main channels through which benefits can materialize:

- Provision of public goods and social services, often through community development funds into which part or all of the compensation for land is deposited
- Job generation and indirect employment due to the project
- Access to technology and markets for existing smallholder producers
- Payment of taxes to local or central government.

The most appropriate way for ensuring that benefits are in line with local ambitions will depend on the capacity, cohesiveness, and entrepreneurial aspirations of local communities as well as the level of economic activity, public goods available, and capacity of local governments.

NOTES

1. *Land acquisition* as defined involves not only traditional purchases but also leasing. Many countries, especially lower income ones, have highly regulated land markets, often maintain residual public ownership, and place restrictions on possible land ownership by foreigners (Hodgson, Cullinan, and Campbell 1999). In many cases, especially in Africa, transactions thus involve long-term leases of use rights through the public sector rather than outright ownership. Modalities differ widely, particularly the extent to which such transactions extinguish preexisting claims (de jure or de facto), whether subleasing is allowed, in the lease conditions and the way they are monitored, as well as the remedial measures (including procedures for revoking the lease in case of noncompliance). Although they will be discussed in detail later, two critical elements in this context are the clarity of framing regulations and assigning responsibility for monitoring and the capacity of the relevant institutions to do so. See http://farmlandgrab.org. The authors are grateful to Charlotte Coutand for helping with the coding.

2. Not all projects mentioned in the blog could be identified in official inventories. For projects that did match, details given in press articles were in most cases close to what was documented in official data.

3. Percentages are calculated for the 454 projects for which the purpose and implementation status are known (excluding rejected or withdrawn projects).

4. Identifying an investor's country of origin for a specific project can be problematic given the complicated business structures that may be involved. It is less problematic when analyzing media reports, because the investor origin is usually investigated and mentioned by journalists.

5. We used the Doing Business 2009 classification of investment protection as a measure of governance meaningful for such investments. Our measure of land tenure security is an ordered variable extracted from the 2009 Institutional Profiles Database (variable B6091) jointly published by the Agence Française de Développement and the French Ministry of Economy, Finance, and Industry describing the share of the rural population with formally recognized land tenure.

6. Countries include Cambodia, the Democratic Republic of Congo, Ethiopia, Indonesia, Lao PDR, Liberia Mozambique, Nigeria, Pakistan, Paraguay, Peru, Sudan, Ukraine, and Zambia.

7. Countries in the sample in which the spatial reference is either nonexistent or incomprehensible include Cambodia, the Democratic Republic of Congo, Ethiopia (some regions), Ghana, and Sudan.

8. In many cases, the information given by the press on specific projects that could be identified in inventories was consistent with inventory data.

9. Several of these large projects are game farms for safari hunting and have not yet been approved.

10. The exception is Liberia where the inventory is made up of renegotiation of huge concessions, many awarded in the 1960s, with a median more than 80 times that in Ethiopia.

11. In countries where an inventory or list of large investments was available (Ukraine, Mozambique, Zambia), the list was used to select projects for case studies. In many cases, the projects originally selected turned out to be nonoperational, and in some cases private investors opposed being included in the study and refused researchers access to the premises. These projects had to be replaced by others where production had started or where investors were willing to have local populations and

workers interviewed. In countries where no public list of projects was available, consultants used interviews with officials at national and provincial levels to put together a list from which to select projects. Given the large number of investments that were not operational, our methodology for project selection implies that the results obtained here can be considered representative of operational and projects where cooperation was obtained.

12. In at least one case, it appears that an investment project was not economically viable because the land identified was not suitable for cultivation. Confronted with this reality, investors encroached on more fertile land cultivated by local communities, creating conflict.

REFERENCES

Arezki, R., K. Deininger, and H. Selod. 2010. "Interest in Large-Scale Land Acquisition for Agribusiness Investment: Extent and Determinants and the 'Global Land Grab.'" Policy Research Working Paper, World Bank, Washington, DC.

Braun, J. von, and R. Meinzen-Dick. 2009. "'Land Grabbing' by Foreign Investors in Developing Countries: Risks and Opportunities." Policy Brief 13, International Food Policy Research Institute, Washington, DC.

Centre d'Analyse Stratégique. 2010. "Les Cessions d'Actifs Agricoles dans les Pays en Développement. Diagnostic et Recommandations." Report 29, presided by Michel Clavé and coordinated by Dominique Auverlot. La Documentation Française, Paris, France.

Cotula, L., S. Vermeulen, R. Leonard, and J. Keeley. 2009. "Land Grab or Development Opportunity? Agricultural Investment and International Deals in Africa." International Institute for Environment and Development, Food and Agricultural Organization of the United Nations, and International Fund for Agricultural Development, London and Rome.

Diallo, A., and G. Mushinzimana. 2009. "Foreign Direct Investment (FDI) in Land in Mali." German Society for Technical Cooperation (GTZ) on behalf of the German Federal Ministry for Economic Cooperation and Development, Eschborn, Germany.

Hodgson, S., C. Cullinan, and K. Campbell. 1999. "Land Ownership and Foreigners: A Comparative Analysis of Regulatory Approaches to the Acquisition and Use of Land by Foreigners." Legal Papers Online, Food and Agriculture Organization of the United Nations, Rome.

Niasse, M., and M. Taylor. 2010. "Building an Informed and Inclusive Response to the Global Rush for Land." Paper presented at the Annual Bank Conference on Land Policy and Administration, Washington, DC, April 26–27.

Schoenweger, O. 2010. "Establishing a Concession Inventory: The Case of Laos." Paper presented at the Annual Bank Conference on Land Policy and Administration, World Bank, Washington DC, April 26–27.

Uellenberg, A. 2009. "Foreign Direct Investment (FDI) in Land in Madagascar." German Society for Technical Cooperation (GTZ) on behalf of the German Federal Ministry for Economic Cooperation and Development, Eschborn, Germany.

World Bank. 2010. "Lao PDR: Investment and Access to Land and Natural Resources: Challenges in Promoting Sustainable Development." Washington, DC.

CHAPTER THREE

The Scope for and Desirability of Land Expansion

For an accurate assessment of future trends in land use, it is important to look at supply as well as demand (Hertel 2010). By focusing only on demand, many analyses of large land acquisition to date are investor-centric rather than country-oriented. This risks creating the impression that large land acquisition is inevitable or an end in itself rather than exploring how investments can help countries achieve their development goals most effectively. A country-level assessment of rainfed land resources available, the effectiveness with which these are used, and ways to move closer to utilizing the productive potential of these resources, has three advantages:

- It highlights that large-scale land acquisition is only one of many options, the desirability of which has to be weighed against that of alternatives to increase output and improve smallholder welfare.
- It highlights that, even if unused land is available, investors are likely to make socially optimal land use decisions only if current uses are appropriately compensated and if external effects are considered.
- Having an independent assessment of land suitability to identify hotspots where investor interest may materialize in the future will allow countries to take measures in anticipation of such interest and can also provide a yardstick to assess whether investors do indeed focus on the most productive land.

Of course, even currently noncultivated land that is identified as "suitable" for rainfed cultivation by these criteria will normally be subject to existing claims that investors will have to recognize and compensate even if they are not formalized.

To identify the potential supply of land suitable for rainfed cultivation at the country level, we use agro-ecological modeling to simulate, for every pixel on the global map, the potential output from rainfed cultivation of five major crops. Linking this to current land use, population density, infrastructure access, and other variables allows us to determine the land that might be suitable for expansion of these crops using rainfed cultivation given the current climate.

At the country level, this approach allows us to quantify the scope for expansion of rainfed cultivated area and intensification on land already cultivated as the two main sources of higher output. The first is done by identifying currently noncultivated areas with different attributes that could be suitable for rainfed cultivation of main crops. The second is done by quantifying the gap between actual and potential yield for currently cultivated areas. This provides useful insights in several respects:

- The largest amount of land potentially suitable for rainfed agriculture is in Sub-Saharan Africa, followed by Latin America and the Caribbean. It is concentrated in a limited number of countries. In many of these countries, the ratio of land that is potentially suitable for rainfed agriculture to what is currently cultivated is large, highlighting the possibly far-reaching social impacts of outside investment. Where yield gaps are high, it will be important to explore options for increasing smallholder yields prior to or simultaneously with those for expanding the cultivated area and to ensure that investment addresses market, infrastructure, or technology constraints faced by existing producers.

- In the aggregate, there is no need to expand into forest to cope with projected increases in demand for agricultural commodities and land. However, we can identify countries where the presence of large tracts of forest that could be converted to agriculture together with little suitable nonforested land for potential area expansion is likely to generate pressure for conversion. Raising countries' and local populations' awareness of this is a precondition for putting in place more forceful efforts and innovative approaches for protecting such critical areas and monitoring their use more intensively to allow action before potentially irreversible changes have occurred.

- The magnitude and spatial concentration of land suitable for expansion of rainfed cultivation, and the fact that such land is often located far from infrastructure or in environments that lack technology, highlights that rainfed cultivated area expansion through large-scale investment faces numerous challenges. To overcome these challenges, a strategic approach and partnerships between private and public sectors in infrastructure investment and technology transfer will be needed. In many cases, such actions can also help smallholders increase their productivity and close the yield gap.

- A typology based on country yield gaps and the potential for expansion of rainfed cultivation allows comparison of the scope for area expansion with

that for intensification to identify ways in which investment at the country level can most effectively support broader development efforts. Using this information strategically can help countries set rules for the parameters of investments and engage more proactively with investors to ensure they contribute to development.

METHODOLOGY AND POTENTIAL AVAILABILITY OF LAND FOR RAINFED CROP PRODUCTION

To provide the basis for identifying yield gaps and thus the scope for raising productivity on existing farmland as well as aggregate area potentially suitable for rainfed cultivation, and to allow more specific identification of potential hotspots of investor interest, we assess the potential revenue from cultivation of five main crops (sugarcane, wheat, maize, oil palm, and soybean) under rainfed conditions and apply prices to determine the one with the highest value of output. Doing so allows us to identify three types of land:

- Land currently cultivated where comparing potential to actual yield provides a basis for estimating the "yield gap"—the amount by which output could be increased under best practice management and production technologies.[1]
- Land not cultivated, not forested, and not protected with low levels of population density that could potentially be suitable for rainfed agricultural production.
- Land currently forested in unprotected areas with low population density that are potentially suitable for rainfed crop production.

To be relevant for actual decisions, such an assessment will need to be complemented with data on other types of relevant land uses (for example, biodiversity), which, if at all, are available only at the country level. As long as their shortcomings are borne in mind, global data can, however, provide a first approximation. They point toward the availability of some 445 million hectares (ha) of currently uncultivated, nonforested land that would be ecologically suitable for rainfed cultivation in areas with less than 25 persons/square kilometer (km^2). This implies that projected future demands could in principle be satisfied without cutting down forests. Much of this land is concentrated in a limited number of countries, many in Africa, and some of it is far from infrastructure. Although transport cost will reduce economic land rents depending on the market for which output is produced, potential output values in many of these areas are likely to be far above what is obtained from the land under its current use. As it is imperative that any transfer of land to large-scale investors be voluntary, we can identify the areas where such voluntary land transfers would be an option in principle.

Methodology

The starting point for any assessment of the potential supply of land for rainfed cultivation is an assessment of potential yields that can be achieved on a given plot based on simulation of plant growth, which depends on agro-ecological factors, such as soil, temperature, precipitation, elevation, and other terrain factors.[2] We use the agro-ecological zoning (AEZ) methodology developed by the International Institute for Applied Systems Analysis (IIASA) for five main rainfed crops. It predicts potential yield for rainfed cultivation of five key crops based on a large array of environmental factors summarized in land use types globally at a very high resolution (Fischer and others 2002; Shah and others 2008). Together with assumptions on management and input intensity, this can be used to identify suitability and potential yields for different crops in each cell.[3] Applying a price vector then allows the determination of the crop that produces the highest revenue and the construction of a surface of output values. In other words, this information highlights the maximum potential value of output that can be produced from one of the five crops in our set at a given pixel based on current climate and prices. To illustrate the concept, the resulting output value surfaces (in 2000 U.S. dollars) for Europe, the Middle East and North Africa, Asia, Oceania, Latin America and the Caribbean, and Sub-Saharan Africa are shown in appendix 4.

To make these data useful for policy, we link agro-ecological potential for rainfed cultivation to information on current land use (for example, whether an area is protected or forested), population density, and infrastructure access. Overlays with protected areas currently under forest with high biodiversity value, for example, can identify areas where better enforcement of protection will be needed because the value of current and future social and environmental benefits from forest use exceeds that of potential cultivation for agriculture. For cultivated cells, the difference between potential and actual yield provides an estimate of the yield gap. For noncultivated cells, the map identifies the crop that would generate the highest monetary output under rainfed cultivation. All this information can then be used as an input into local land use planning. Such planning, especially if combined with identification and mapping of rights, can help identify both underused potential and subsequent measures to better use it, such as by attracting capable investors to directly farm, to contract local farmers, or to construct complementary infrastructure. Aggregation at the country level then provides information that can feed into policy formulation, classification of priority areas for identification and demarcation of land rights, and monitoring efforts.

Global Availability of Suitable Land

We use the AEZ methodology to identify regions and countries within regions where nonforested, unprotected, and currently noncultivated land suitable for rainfed cultivation of at least one of five key crops (wheat, sugarcane, oil palm, maize, and soybean) is available in areas with less than 5, 10, or 25 persons/km^2, implying availability of 100, 50, or 20 ha per household. Very little, if any, of this land will be free of existing claims that will have to be recognized by any potential investment, even if they are not formalized. But case studies suggest that, at such low levels of population density, voluntary land transfers that make everybody better off are possible. To highlight that in many cases effective use of such land may require addition of infrastructure, we classify land based on the travel time to the next city with a population of at least 50,000 inhabitants using the most common means of transport with a cutoff of six hours to market.

Results suggest that the nonforested noncultivated area suitable for rainfed cultivation of at least one of the crops considered here amounts to some 445 million ha, less than a third of the currently cultivated area of just over 1,500 million ha (table 3.1 and appendix 2, table A2.6). Depending on the cutoff in population density, the amount of nonforested and unprotected area suitable to cultivate the five crops considered here varies between 198 million ha and 446 million ha. As one moves toward successively lower levels of population density, the share of this area located within six hours of the next market is reduced from 59 percent to 51 percent and 44 percent, respectively, for the three levels considered here. In all cases, though, the largest total area available for rainfed cultivation is in Africa (202 million ha, 128 million ha, and 68 million ha corresponding to 45, 42, and 34 percent of the total, respectively), followed by Latin America. The concentration of currently uncultivated but potentially suitable land for rainfed cultivation illustrates that availability of such land in the rest of the world (namely, Eastern Europe, East and South Asia, Middle East and North Africa, and all other countries together) is less than what is available in Latin America and the Caribbean alone.

Even within regions, land not currently cultivated but potentially suitable for rainfed cultivation is concentrated in a few countries. Using the 25 persons/km^2 cutoff, the seven countries with the largest amount of land available (Sudan, Brazil, Australia, the Russian Federation, Argentina, Mozambique, and Democratic Republic of Congo, in that order) account for 224 million ha, or

Table 3.1 Potential Supply of Land for Rainfed Cultivation in Different Regions (thousand ha)

	Total area	Area < 6 hours	Area > 6 hours
Sub-Saharan Africa	201,540	94,919	106,621
Latin America and the Caribbean	123,342	93,957	29,385
Eastern Europe and Central Asia	52,387	43,734	8,653
East and South Asia	14,341	3,320	11,021
Middle East and North Africa	3,043	2,647	396
Rest of world	50,971	24,554	26,417
Total	**445,624**	**263,131**	**182,493**

Source: Fischer and Shah 2010.

more than half of global availability. The 32 countries with more than 3 million ha of land each account for more than 90 percent of available land. Of these, 16 are in Sub-Saharan Africa, 8 in Latin America and the Caribbean, 3 in Eastern Europe and Central Asia, and 5 in the rest of the world. Many of the countries with ample land available have only limited amounts of land under cultivation. Currently uncultivated land suitable for cultivation is more than double what is currently cultivated in 11 countries and more than triple the currently cultivated area in 6 countries.[4]

Using 2005 prices to determine output-maximizing crops and focusing on areas not currently cultivated, not forested, and within six hours to the next market, we find some interesting patterns (table 3.2 and appendix 2, table A2.7).[5] First, for the total area of 263 million ha, just under a third is suited for maize and soybean (some 83 million ha each), followed by about a fourth for wheat (71 million ha), a little less than a tenth for sugarcane (22 million ha), and less than a fiftieth for oil palm. Comparing the potential for area expansion with what is currently cultivated suggests that the potential area for expansion close to markets is significantly below what is currently cultivated for wheat, maize, and oil palm, and about equal to the area currently cropped for maize and sugarcane.

Table 3.2 Potential Area of Nonforested, Nonprotected Land Close to Market Most Suitable for Different Crops under Rainfed Cultivation, (thousand ha)

	5 crop total	Maize	Soybean	Wheat	Sugarcane	Oil palm
Sub-Saharan Africa	94,919	44,868	38,993	3,840	6,023	1,194
Latin America and the Caribbean	93,957	28,385	37,716	11,043	15,021	1,793
Europe and Central Asia	43,734	3,851	419	39,464	0	0
East and South Asia	3,320	465	443	1,045	500	867
Middle East and North Africa	2,647	0	10	2,637	0	0
Rest of World	24,554	5,741	5,289	12,747	722	55
Total < 6 hours to market	263,131	83,310	82,870	70,776	22,266	3,909
Total	445,624	156,828	137,711	88,149	41,176	21,760
Total cultivated 2008	520,411	161,017	96,870	223,564	24,375	14,585

Source: Fischer and Shah 2010.
Note: Assessments are based on fewer than 25 persons/km² and less than six hours to market. 2005 output prices are used to determine gross revenue.

RISING GLOBAL INTEREST IN FARMLAND

The large amounts of nonforested areas with potential for rainfed production in areas with a low population density imply that there is no need, in principle, to draw on currently forested areas to satisfy demand for agricultural commodities in the future. As logging can generate large rents that could be further enhanced for land suitable for rainfed agricultural cultivation, it will be important to identify currently nonprotected forested areas suitable for agricultural cultivation to identify potential hotspots and help governments and other stakeholders take necessary precautions. Doing so reveals that most of these forests are in the Amazon, the Congo Basin, and the outer islands of Indonesia. Brazil has the largest area of unprotected forested land with high rainfed cultivation potential (some 131 million ha[6]), followed closely by Russia at 129 million ha. Other countries, including Colombia, the Democratic Republic of Congo, Gabon, Guyana, Peru, Suriname, and Zambia, have suitable nonprotected forested areas several times the size of their currently cultivated area. Cutting down such forests can result in the loss of a wide range of social and environmental benefits. Methods to value these benefits (box 3.1) will be important as a basis for decisions on how to compensate users for social benefits they provide, whether or not to protect these areas, and how to enforce such protection.

Comparing actual to potential physical yields for each cultivated pixel provides an estimate of the maximum potential output that can establish a benchmark for the scope of increasing output on currently cultivated areas. Aggregate results from doing so at the crop and regional level point to clear regional and cross-commodity differences (table 3.3). Oceania is close to realizing its full potential, followed by North America (0.89), Europe (0.81), and South America (0.65). By contrast, with only 20 percent of potential production realized, Sub-Saharan Africa offers large potential for increasing yields on currently cultivated areas.

To illustrate this concept, attaining 80 percent of potential yield—the level usually considered to be economical (Fischer and others 2009)—would quadruple maize output in Sub-Saharan Africa. This would be equivalent to a potential area expansion of 90 million ha—more than the total global area suitable for maize expansion within six hours of market. Such increases would provide significant benefits to local populations while involving lower risks—and often significantly lower cost—than area expansion. Countries with large areas of land potentially suitable for rainfed production and large yield gaps will thus need to strategically assess how to combine intensification with area expansion. They will also need to identify public and private investments and the incentives required to attract private investors accordingly.

While aggregate results from applying the AEZ methodology demonstrate the methodology's potential, its application at the country level can yield highly relevant policy insights. To do so, a first step is often to better organize existing information or to complement it with additional layers, such as data on land rights, to add value. Complementing global with country level analysis could, in particular, expand the analysis in three ways.

Box 3.1 Assessing and Valuing Indirect Impacts of Land Cover Change

Land characteristics (soils, slope) and vegetative cover (crops, pasture, forests, woodlands, grasslands) are linked to ecosystem services such as carbon sequestration, surface and groundwater flows, and biodiversity niches with implications far beyond an individual parcel. Converting land use from natural state to intensive use will have immediate and longer-term impacts on hydrology, carbon stocks, and biodiversity that often provide important livelihood support and safety nets for poor and landless people. Although these are at present mostly neglected, finding ways to quantify and value such impacts is an important challenge for research that has immediate policy implications.

To address this challenge, tools and decision support systems to provide stakeholders (local communities, local governments, and policy makers) with timely and spatially relevant information and projections of land and water use and interacting climate change are being developed in a number of contexts. One such model that many countries are currently using to assess impacts of infrastructure development, large-scale farming, and land cover changes, among others, is the Variable Infiltration Capacity (VIC) model (Richey and Fernandes 2007). The basic idea is to simulate the hydrometeorological cycle by building on layers of meteorological forcing (land surface climatology of daily precipitation, minimum and maximum temperature, and winds), vegetation attributes by vegetation class, a river network derived from a digital elevation model, and river discharge history at select stations. But these models can provide the basis for a wide range of applications, including prediction of the impact of climate change or deforestation. To apply them in practice, it will be important to bring these models to a sufficiently localized level where they can inform policy decisions and resource valuations.

Source: Richey and Fernandes 2007.

Table 3.3 Current Yield Relative to Estimated Potential Yield

Region	Maize	Oil palm	Soybean	Sugarcane
Asia (excluding West Asia)	0.62	0.74	0.47	0.68
Europe	0.81	n.a.	0.84	n.a.
North Africa and West Asia	0.62	n.a.	0.91	0.95
North America	0.89	n.a.	0.77	0.72
Oceania	1.02	0.6	1.05	0.91
South America	0.65	0.87	0.67	0.93
Sub-Saharan Africa	0.20	0.32	0.32	0.54

Source: Fischer and Shah 2010.
Note: n.a. = not applicable.

- First, it would allow adjusting for input costs to compute net profit rather than gross revenue. Computing net profit would allow us to impute the implicit market value or Ricardian rent for every grid cell on the surface. These implicit land values could be an important input into land valuation and land price negotiations.
- Second, apart from considering the time to market, use of the cost of transporting inputs and outputs on a cost per ton-km basis, for example, could help obtain more realistic estimates of profit and, more interestingly, simulate potential impacts of investment in transport infrastructure on land prices and potential local welfare.
- Third, the model is static and does not include investment costs, risk, or price changes due to shifts in global supply and demand. However, climate projections under different climate change scenarios can, for example, be used to simulate crop output in a way that incorporates long-run impacts of climate change on countries' potential.

ADOPTING A COMMODITY PERSPECTIVE

To explore the implications for policy, the potential for expanding currently cultivated area needs to be compared with that for increasing output and productivity on areas already cultivated. Making this comparison will identify how private investment in agriculture—badly needed in many circumstances—can improve smallholder productivity as the central pillar of a pro-poor development strategy.

Wheat

Food security concerns have led to a surge in investments for wheat, often originating in Middle Eastern countries. Compared with a total cultivated area of 223 million ha, our analysis points to availability of an additional 88, 56, or 38 million ha in areas with fewer than 25, 10, and 5 persons/km^2, respectively (appendix 2, table A2.8). The suitable uncultivated area is largest in Argentina (6 million ha compared with 4.2 million ha used) and Russia (36 million ha compared with 26 million ha). For many countries with expansion potential, and for some large producers, the scope for increasing yields is considerable. Kazakhstan cultivates 13 million ha of wheat, with an additional 2.8 million ha potentially available for expansion. Yields, however, are less than 1 t/ha. If productivity on currently cultivated land were to increase to the regional average, the associated increase in output would be more than 10 times the 2.8 million tons from bringing all of the suitable area under rainfed cultivation at current yields. Interestingly, with the exception of Ethiopia, none of the African countries that have recently been the targets of large-scale investment have much potential for wheat cultivation, suggesting that efforts to cultivate wheat in Africa on a large scale must overcome a number of agro-ecological challenges.

Maize

The total area for maize expansion is almost equal to the 161 million ha already under the crop. There is considerable potential for expansion in countries that have recently attracted investor interest. Well-established producers in Latin America and the Caribbean, mainly Argentina and Brazil, already achieve rather high yields (6.5 and 4.1 t/ha) and have the potential of adding some 20 million ha to the 3.5 and 14 million ha currently cultivated, respectively. Depending on land prices, they appear to provide the most immediate potential for area expansion.

A second group is made up of countries that cultivate more than 1 million ha of the crop (Angola, the Democratic Republic of Congo, Ethiopia, Kenya, Mozambique, and Tanzania) but with low yields. In this situation, any efforts at area expansion will need to be combined with efforts to improve output by existing smallholders. Mozambique could add 7.1 million ha of maize (3.1 million ha in areas close to markets) to the 1.4 million ha it already cultivates. With current yields of 0.92 t/ha (less than a tenth of potential yields), however, this land is far from reaching its productive potential. Infrastructure access is also a major issue, as only 4 million ha are within six hours from the next market. Infrastructure access differs markedly across countries: Zambia has some 13 million ha available for maize, more than 80 percent of which is located within six hours of a market town. In Ethiopia, on the other hand, virtually all of the 3.6 million ha suitable for rainfed maize production is located far from infrastructure.

A third group of countries has large potential for area expansion but currently has little area under production. This group includes Sudan (32 million ha), Chad (9), Madagascar (7), República Bolivariana de Venezuela (5), Angola (4), Bolivia (2.5), Mali (2.4), and Burkina Faso (2.3), among others. Madagascar's maize yields are slightly higher (1.5 t/ha) than Mozambique's, but very little maize (0.25 million ha) is grown. In this context, the requirements of establishing the infrastructure, for example technology, markets, processing, and regulatory infrastructure, are much higher. To realize them, significant investment is likely required. A fourth group is made up of countries that cultivate large areas of maize such as India, Malawi, Nigeria, and Zimbabwe. Even though the uncultivated area for expansion is limited, the potential for increasing yields is significant (appendix 2, table A2.9).

Soybean

While soybean is currently grown on some 97 million ha, AEZ calculations point toward an estimated 138 million ha of noncultivated nonprotected area with a population density of fewer than 25 persons/km^2 that have high suitability for rainfed cultivation of this crop. Countries with large amounts of suitable but currently uncultivated area fall in three groups:

- Current producers, many with high yields and a history of past area expansion
- Current producers with potential for yield increases as well as area expansion
- Countries with potential for expansion but no experience with the crop.

In the first group, Brazil is not only the largest producer with the highest yields but also has 22 million ha of uncultivated land available to double its cultivated area. Argentina's capacity to add to its 16 million ha under the crop is more limited, with some 10 million ha of additional suitable land. However, Uruguay, Paraguay, and Bolivia, all countries into which Brazilian and Argentine firms have already expanded heavily, have another 10 million ha of suitable area, thus accounting for almost a third of the area potentially available for expansion globally. This contrasts sharply with the third group made up of many African countries with considerable potential but little current cultivation. This includes Sudan (14 million ha), the Democratic Republic of Congo (9), Mozambique (7), Chad, Madagascar, Zambia (6), Angola (5), and Tanzania (4), as highlighted in appendix 2, table A2.10. Realizing this potential is challenging in terms of establishing an industry almost from scratch similar to that discussed for maize.

Sugarcane

Countries with more than 1 million ha of cultivated area account for some three-fourths of total area (19 of 24 million ha) and 83 percent of the expansion potential (34 of 41 million ha), as illustrated in appendix 2, table A2.11. More than two-thirds (70 percent) of the area with expansion potential is in South America, mainly Brazil (9 million ha) and Argentina (4), followed by Sub-Saharan Africa (24 percent), mainly the Democratic Republic of Congo (7 million ha) and Madagascar (2.1). Discrepancies in infrastructure access are pronounced. For example, Argentina and the Democratic Republic of Congo have almost an equivalent amount of suitable area available (some 6.5 million ha each), but most of this area is reasonably close to markets in Argentina and very far from them in the Democratic Republic of Congo. Yields in Argentina (84 t/ha) are more than twice those in the Democratic Republic of Congo (39 t/ha). Thus, the extent to which sugarcane for biofuels as recently established in many Sub-Saharan African countries will be globally competitive remains to be seen.

Oil Palm

Establishing oil palm on forested areas will be associated with greenhouse gas emissions and can lead to considerable loss of biodiversity. Appendix 2, table A2.12, points toward large productivity differences on already cultivated areas. Nigeria cultivated 3.2 million ha of oil palm in 2008, accounting for 20–25 percent of the global area under the crop. But it achieved yields of only 2.66 t/ha—less than half the yield in Ghana (6.33 t/ha) and just one-eighth that achieved in Malaysia (21.3 t/ha). In light of expected strong demand for palm oil, yield increases or expansion into degraded lands could relieve pressure on valuable intact forest lands elsewhere.

TOWARD A COUNTRY TYPOLOGY

To explore the potential tradeoff between intensification and expansion of the rainfed cultivated area at the country level, we plot, for each country, the yield gap (that is, the amount that actual yields, on either irrigated or rainfed areas, fall short of potential production) and the ratio of nonforested, noncultivated area suitable for rainfed production relative to what is actually cultivated (appendix 3, figures A3.1 through A3.5). This typology, which will be of interest from a country perspective, can be complemented by plotting absolute amounts of suitable noncultivated and nonprotected land in areas with low population density as in appendix 2, table A2.6. As figure 3.1 illustrates, classifying countries depending on whether they are above or below the mean yield gap (0.6) or relative land availability (a log value of –2), allows us to define a

Figure 3.1   Yield Gaps and Relative Land Availability for Different Countries

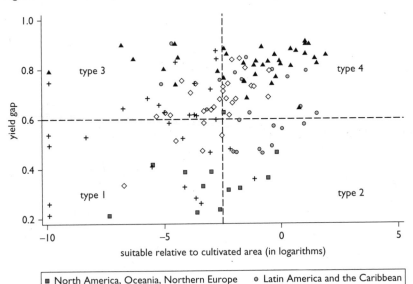

Source: Authors based on Fischer and Shah 2010.

RISING GLOBAL INTEREST IN FARMLAND

typology that can provide insights as to the options open to different countries to use investor interest to promote their development agenda as well as the types of investors that may help them to do so most effectively. The global picture clearly points toward large differences across countries and regions in land availability and productivity levels.

Type 1: Little Land for Expansion, Low Yield Gap

This group includes Asian countries with high population density, such as China, Vietnam, Malaysia, the Republic of Korea, and Japan, Western European countries, and some countries in the Middle East and North Africa with limited land suitable for rainfed production, such as the Arab Republic of Egypt and Jordan (figure 3.2). Agricultural growth has been, and will continue to be, led by highly productive smallholders. To meet expanding demand for horticultural and livestock products, private investors increasingly provide capital, technology, and access to markets through contract farming. As some of these countries reach declining agricultural population due to rural-urban migration, land consolidation—largely by entrepreneurial farmers leasing or buying plots from neighbors—will gradually increase farm sizes. Well-functioning land markets that allow such processes will thus be of

Figure 3.2 Yield Gaps and Relative Land Availability for South Asia, East Asia and Pacific, and the Middle East and North Africa

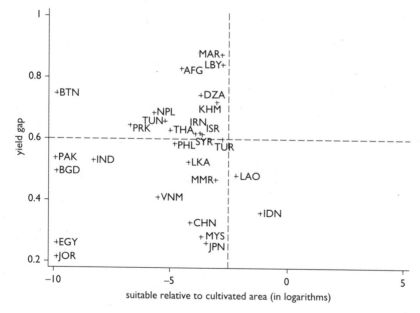

Source: Authors based on Fischer and Shah 2010.

Figure 3.3 Yield Gaps and Relative Land Availability for Latin America and the Caribbean

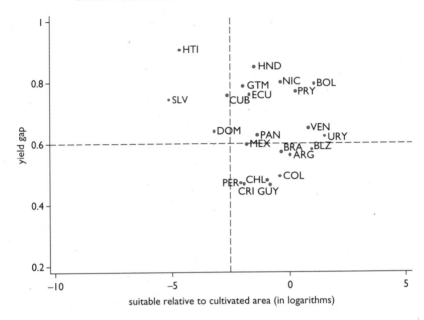

Source: Authors based on Fischer and Shah 2010.

increasing importance. The growing need for land for nonfarm industries, urban expansion, and infrastructure also implies a need for good governance of land and related natural resources in facilitating the transition.

Type 2: Suitable Land Available, Low Yield Gap

This group includes countries where land with reasonably well-defined property rights and where infrastructure access is fairly abundant and technology advanced, mainly in Latin America (Argentina, Uruguay, and central Brazil) and Eastern Europe (figure 3.3). It is here where savvy investors have exploited opportunities for cropland expansion. In many of these cases, past investment in technology, infrastructure, institutions, and human capital have helped increase productivity. If property rights are secure, markets function well, and areas with high social or environmental value are protected effectively (possibly using market mechanisms, such as payments for environmental services) the public sector's role is mainly regulatory. The public sector takes care of environmental externalities and allows markets, including those for land, to function smoothly and to encourage expansion into low grade pastures or degraded forest rather than into areas already occupied or with high biodiversity value. But if land rights are insecure or ill-defined, large-scale land acquisition may threaten forests or lead to conflict with existing land users. Good institutions and land governance will thus be critical to ensure that the technical potential is realized sustainably.

Type 3: Little Land Available, High Yield Gap

This group includes the majority of developing countries, including relatively densely populated areas in highland Ethiopia, Kenya, Malawi, the Philippines, Ukraine, Cambodia, and Central American countries (such as El Salvador) with limited land availability as well as Middle Eastern and North African countries where water availability constrains the expansion of agricultural production. Although there is little land available, large numbers of smallholders may be locked into poverty because the area cultivated remains far below the yield potential.

Strategic options depend on the size and evolution of the nonagricultural sector. If it is small, higher agricultural productivity will be the only viable mechanism for rapid poverty reduction. This will require public investment in technology, infrastructure, and market development to raise smallholder productivity, following the example of the green revolution in Asia. If the land sector is well-governed, private investment—largely through contract farming—can promote diversification into high value crops, especially for export markets. There is, however, a danger that insecure property rights will allow large-scale land acquisitions to push people off the land. With limited nonagricultural employment, grave equity effects could result in social tensions.

The situation is different if incomes and employment in the nonagricultural sector grow rapidly, land markets work reasonably well, and population growth is low, as in parts of Eastern Europe where there is scope for faster land consolidation and the associated move to larger operational units (figure 3.4). Parties will more likely enter into mutually advantageous contracts if the transaction costs of doing so, particularly those of enforcing agreements, are low. Commodity and market characteristics are also in play: contract farming, where investors provide capital and technology, is easier for crops where the need for processing limits side-selling and makes enforcement easier, such as oilseeds or sugarcane. If the investment needed is larger—for example, for horticulture, perennials, and oil palm, or in cases with high up-front investment in irrigation—ownership of land, or at least long-term contracts, is more likely to be chosen.

Type 4: Suitable Land Available, High Yield Gap

This group includes sparsely populated countries—such as the Democratic Republic of Congo, Mozambique, Sudan, Tanzania, and Zambia—with large tracts of land suitable for rainfed cultivation (in areas of sufficient precipitation) but also a large portion of smallholders who only achieve a fraction of

Figure 3.4 Yield Gaps and Relative Land Availability for Eastern Europe and Central Asia

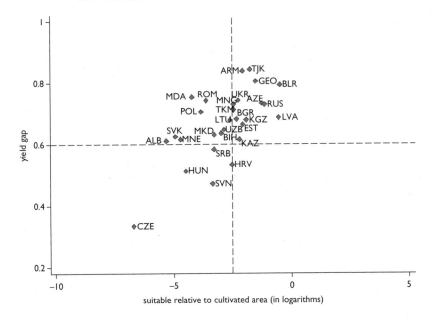

Source: Authors based on Fischer and Shah 2010.

potential productivity (figure 3.5). In some cases, such as Sudan, these areas are located in areas with political tensions and dispute. Labor supply often constrains expansion by smallholders, implying that not all potentially suitable land is used for crop production. The prospect of outside investment can help foster local development. If migration from other regions is inelastic in the medium term, as is often the case, intensification will require larger farm sizes, and labor-saving mechanization may be the most attractive short-term option. In some cases, the investment needed for this transition can be generated locally. However, if it requires the introduction of new crops and farming systems, large investments in processing, or links to export markets, the amounts of skill and capital available locally may not be sufficient, and outside investors can have a role. In these cases, bringing institutional arrangements, technology, and infrastructure together could thus provide a basis for mutually beneficial and agreed on land transfers.

It is this context that defines most of the recent upsurge in investor interest and where there is scope for the private sector to contribute technology, capital, and skills to increase productivity and output in the short to medium term. The most effective way of doing so will depend on local conditions.

Figure 3.5 Yield Gaps and Relative Land Availability for Sub-Saharan Africa

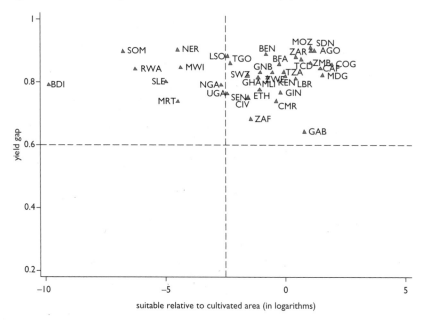

Source: Authors based on Fischer and Shah 2010.

Capital-intensive activities with low labor absorption, such as annual crops using fully mechanized production, will be appropriate only if population density is low, the likelihood of in-migration is limited, and a vibrant nonagricultural sector can absorb expected future growth of the labor force. Even then, expected changes in the long term, due for example to population growth or climate change, need to be considered as the transition from large-scale mechanized to smallholder farming has not been observed historically. Many countries in this group have weak institutional frameworks for land governance that can create challenges for reigning in opportunistic behavior by local or foreign elites, for example, by ensuring adequate consultation with local and indigenous populations.

To maximize benefits and ensure they are broadly shared, institutional arrangements must include recognition and respect for existing land rights. They must also identify the channels that will allow local people to benefit—employment generation, social benefits, access to markets and technology, or taxes—and technically and economically viable business models. Clear articulation of what is expected from investors, open processes, public disclosure of contractual arrangements, and the extent to which these arrangements are complied with over time will be critical to help realize the potential benefits inherent in such situations.

CONCLUSION

Complementing the focus on demand for land and associated natural resources that has long characterized the debate on this topic with an assessment of the potential supply of land suitable for rainfed production increases access to information for all involved. There is ample evidence to document that agro-ecological potential will be realized only in a supportive policy environment. However, assessing agro-ecological potential can help governments anticipate demand for agricultural land. It can also feed into development strategies and spatial planning to guide the provision of public goods (technology, infrastructure, property rights) to areas where they can complement and stimulate private investment to provide local benefits. Calculating agro-ecological potential can also help to assess the extent to which past land demand or actual transfers focused on areas with high potential. For communities, the ability to identify suitable land can help inform land use and local development planning, clarify visions of development, and take steps toward implementing them. And by determining the opportunity costs of a given piece of land, it can guide potential land price negotiations. For investors, reliable information about the potential supply of land can direct demand to areas that are economically viable and competitive and, especially if combined with information on rights, can reduce search costs.

Against this background, this chapter makes four substantive contributions. It highlights that, at the global level, there is enough nonforested, nonprotected land suitable for rainfed cultivation available to satisfy anticipated increases in demand for agricultural commodities for the foreseeable future. Africa has the most suitable land available, but access to infrastructure and technology are higher in Latin America and the Caribbean. Within countries, areas with the highest potential are clearly visible. In these areas, public investment to construct complementary infrastructure or educate local communities about their rights and take measures to document land rights on the ground may help increase the benefits of investment and reduce its risks. At the same time, in many of the countries with suitable land available, the potential for increasing output and welfare by narrowing high yield gaps on currently cultivated land rather than expanding cultivated area is very high. Tradeoffs and potential synergies between closing the yield gap and area expansion need to be carefully explored with a realistic assessment of the social, environmental, and financial costs of area expansion.

Aggregating data at the commodity level provides a global perspective. Doing so highlights that, with the exception of commodities more suited to temperate climates such as wheat, large amounts of land suitable for rainfed production are available in Sub-Saharan Africa. For each of these commodities, however, Latin America and the Caribbean also has suitable land that is in most cases closer to infrastructure than in Africa. The reason investor interest has recently shifted to Sub-Saharan Africa is because factors in

Latin America, such as infrastructure access and a large pool of readily available skilled manpower, have already been capitalized into land prices. In contrast, relatively cheap land in Sub-Saharan Africa appears to provide investors with potentially better deals. Still, any land transfers will need to be voluntary and negotiated to compensate current land users in a way that makes them better off than without the investment. It appears that opportunities exist at least in principle to use such investment to bring about increased productivity and equity by closing yield gaps on existing cultivated areas. We can compute the potential output increase from more fully using the available resource base.

Using the scope for area expansion with the magnitude of the yield gap to establish a typology of countries, the methodology highlights countries (and crops within countries) with small yield gaps where efforts to expand cultivated area can rely on available technology. In comparison, crops with large yield gaps will require up-front efforts to transfer and adapt technology. The latter is likely to require greater attention to the technical and managerial aspects of proposals and may disqualify passive investors. It does, however, provide considerable opportunities to pursue investment as a way to provide technology and market access to existing smallholder producers. The careful design and rigorous evaluation of business models to accomplish this outcome will thus be an important area for follow-up work.

NOTES

1. The *yield gap* is defined as the difference between attained and possible output on areas currently cultivated taking crop choice as given. Obviously, such a gap can come about for several reasons (distance to infrastructure, lack of access to markets and technology), a detailed analysis of which is beyond the scope of this study.

2. Cropped area yields are for 2008. Suitable area is not currently used for crop production, could attain at least 60 percent of the potential yield for this crop, is located in an area with population density less than 10 persons/km^2, and at 2005 prices will not yield higher gross revenues with any other of the five crops considered here (maize, soybean, sugarcane, oil palm, wheat). Close to infrastructure means a travel distance of less than six hours to the next market based on available transportation.

3. To keep things tractable, we use a 5' x 5' resolution that divides the world into 2.2 million grid cells but note that computation of output within each grid cell is based on far more disaggregated data.

4. Countries where the amount of suitable land is more than double what is currently cultivated include, in descending order, the Democratic Republic of Congo, Papua New Guinea, Madagascar, Uruguay, Central African Republic, Angola, Bolivia, Mozambique, Zambia, Sudan, and República Bolivariana de Venezuela).

5. To allow for the possibility that more than one crop is suitable for production on each grid cell, when aggregating at the country level we apply weights to each potential crop area based on the relative size to the available suitable area in that class for each country. This ensures that the sum of potential areas for all crops equals the total potential area.

6. This calculation does not account for two important factors that affect the total area of land potentially suitable for rainfed cultivation. Firstly, it does not consider Brazil's areas of permanent protection (APP) and legal reserve laws, which require that 20, 35 or 80 percent of an agricultural holding (depending on the biome) be set aside for conservation. The second factor that is not considered here is that areas with a declivity of more than 15 percent are not typically used for agricultural production for lack of ability to use mechanization.

REFERENCES

Fischer, G., H. Van Velthuizen, M. Shah, and F. Nachtergaele. 2002. *Global Agro-ecological Assessment for Agriculture in the 21st century: Methodology and Results.* Laxenburg and Rome: International Institute for Applied Systems Analysis and Food and Agriculture Organization of the United Nations.

Fischer, G., E. Hiznyik, S. Prieler, M. Shah, and H. Van Velthuizen. 2009. "Biofuels and Food Security." OPEC Fund for International Development and International Institute for Applied Systems Analysis, Vienna.

Fischer, G., and M. Shah. 2010. "Farmland Investments and Food Security: Statistical Annex." Report prepared under a World Bank and International Institute for Applied Systems Analysis contract, Laxenburg, Austria.

Hertel, T. W. 2010. "The Global Supply and Demand for Agricultural Land in 2050: A Perfect Storm in the Making?" Presidential address at the Annual Meeting of the Agriculture and Applied Economics Association, Denver, Colorado, July 25–27.

Richey, J., and E. C. M. Fernandes. 2007. "Towards Integrated Regional Models of Transboundary River Basins in Southeast Asia: Lessons Learned from Water and Watersheds." *Journal of Contemporary Water Research and Education* 136 (1): 28–36.

Shah, M., G. Fischer, and H. Velthuizen. 2008. "Food Security and Sustainable Agriculture: The Challenges of Climate Change in Sub-Saharan Africa: Proceedings Volume of Tenth African Economic Research Consortium." Senior Policy Seminar, African Economic Research Consortium, Addis Ababa, Ethiopia, April.

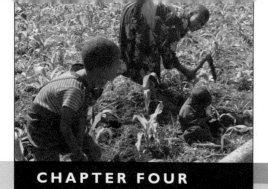

CHAPTER FOUR

The Policy, Legal, and Institutional Framework

The discussion thus far suggests that land potentially suitable for rain-fed agriculture (both currently cultivated and not) where investment could generate considerable benefits is available in some countries but also that such investment invariably entails high risks. Experience highlights that policies are needed to ensure that private sector decisions properly account for potential external effects. It also suggests that, therefore, the extent to which available potential will be realized—and the associated benefits accrue to local populations and contribute to poverty reduction—will depend on the policy and institutional environment.

A good policy, legal, and institutional framework can minimize risks and maximize benefits from large-scale investment involving land and related natural resources. It can help avoid involuntary permanent losses of rights that could have negative consequences, be instrumental in attracting technically competent investors able to generate significant economic benefits in line with a country's longer-term development strategy, and encourage the sharing of benefits with local land users who may lack capacity for negotiating with outsiders. But a good framework will also require adherence to social and environmental standards. A broad consensus exists that, to do so, it needs to facilitate recognition of rights, ensure voluntary land transfers, promote openness and broad access to relevant information, be technically and economically viable and in line with national strategies, and comply with minimum standards of environmental and social sustainability. There is broad agreement that an appropriate framework will, at a minimum, include the following elements:

- **Rights recognition:** For local people to benefit from investments, but also for investors to enjoy a level of tenure security that encourages them to make the needed long-term investments, rights to land and associated natural resources need to be recognized, clearly defined on the ground, and enforceable at low cost. This includes both ownership and user rights to lands that are managed in common areas, state lands, and protected areas.
- **Voluntary transfers:** Transfers of land rights should be based on users' voluntary and informed agreement, provide them with a fair level of proceeds, and not involve expropriation for private purposes.
- **Technical and economic viability:** For investments to provide local benefits, ways to ensure technical and economic viability need to be in place, consistency with local land use plans and taxation regimes be ensured, and effective ways to transfer assets of nonperforming projects be available.
- **Open and impartial processes:** Information on prices, contracts, rights, and ideally land use plans should be publicly available, with parties fully aware of and able to enforce any agreements they entered and with public agencies performing their functions effectively.
- **Environmental and social sustainability:** To prevent investments from generating negative externalities, areas not suitable for agricultural expansion need to be properly protected from encroachment, environmental policies clearly defined and adhered to, and social safeguards (including provisions on gender and worker welfare) defined and implemented.

To assess the extent and effectiveness of relevant country-level regulations in addressing these broad areas, we designed a structured questionnaire for assessment of the policy, legal, and institutional framework (PLIAF) that builds on the methodology of the World Bank's land governance framework (World Bank 2010) and used it in 14 countries.[1] A total of 42 dimensions of the policy, legal, and institutional framework for land-related investment were assessed in a multistakeholder process with three main steps:

- A country coordinator collected data necessary to rank each of the dimensions (indicators) and circulated this information to experts recruited to assess indicators grouped into panels.
- Panels of experts assessed individual dimensions based on the background data.
- The initial assessments made by the panels of experts were revised based on additional feedback and complementary information. The implementation of the PLIAF in Peru provides an illustrative example of how this tool was applied within the country context through a multi-stakeholder assessment (box 4.1).

Selection of experts. Taking into account that forestry sector governance regulations and institutions are significantly different from those in the agro-industrial sector, it did not seem feasible to organize a single panel to address the indicators from both perspectives. Consequently, two thematic sessions were organized, one for forestry and another for agribusiness. A total of 13 specialists met in the two sessions. The three government specialists were identified taking into account the relevance of their government agencies' involvement in the issues discussed by the respective panel. The ten private sector experts included lawyers, economists, engineers, and representatives from industry and nongovernmental organizations with a track record in this issue.

Preliminary work. Two preliminary documents compiled relevant data and information for the survey. One provided specific information on forestry and the other on agro-industrial activities. Both documents compiled data and information about institutions related to the promotion and follow-up of investments and their legal contexts. The services of two renowned consultants on forestry issues and large-scale land purchases were retained. Both experts reviewed the preliminary document, attended the panels' reunions, assisted in gathering complementary information and reviewed the final document.

Panel discussions. Panel participants were asked to rank each dimension. They were also asked to suggest ways to provide statistical or documentary support for each score as well as examples that would illustrate the situations described in their answers. Several panelists contributed specific sources of information that had been overlooked in preliminary surveys and that could be used by the study's coordinator to provide support for the indicators.

Feedback. To validate the discussions' findings, aide-mémoires for each session were drafted. The aide-mémoires summarized the debates' findings and posed specific questions to panelists as a complement to the information gathered in the panels. After the aide-mémoires had been circulated, we gathered complementary information and analyzed the findings under each dimension. This information was consolidated in a report circulated among panel members for their feedback.

Source: Authors, based on Endo 2010.

Doing so allowed us to identify good practice in some key areas but also points to wide variation across countries. It suggests that, in many of the countries reviewed, shortcomings in the legal and regulatory framework, together with weak capacity for implementation and enforcement, reduce the extent to which land-related investments provide local benefits and contribute to broader development. Instead, they foster conflict and reduce a country's attractiveness for serious investors.

Existing (informal) rights, especially to common property resources or fallow land, are often presumed to belong to "the state" rather than to local communities. This distinction makes it easy to appropriate or transfer common property areas to investors against the will of local rights holders or without proper consultation or compensation. Inability to determine existing rights holders—because rights are not recognized, not identifiable on the ground, not recorded, or contested—encourages processes that bypass formal channels entirely. These are often biased in favor of investors, difficult to monitor, and susceptible to corruption. Even where rights are recognized, processes to be followed by investors and criteria to be met for projects to be approved are often vague. Responsible institutions often lack the capacity to make informed decisions and monitor compliance and cannot ensure that standards are adhered to. These are often exacerbated by centralization, unclear delineation of responsibilities, limited interinstitutional coordination, and weak accountability. In many cases, addressing these gaps in well-sequenced steps will be both desirable and feasible.

RESPECT FOR EXISTING PROPERTY RIGHTS TO LAND AND ASSOCIATED NATURAL RESOURCES

Clearly defined rights to land and associated natural resources are important for a variety of reasons. First, investments seldom occur on a blank slate. In almost all cases, land and associated natural resources targeted for investment is subject to existing and often overlapping rights held by communities, individuals, the state, or some combination of the three. Understanding and respecting these rights is important if investments are to be socially legitimate and legally secure. Failure to do so can lead to conflict and strife that will negatively affect the economic viability of land-related investments.

Second, failure to map and record land rights, even if only at the community level, makes it difficult to identify boundaries and legitimate owners as a basis for engaging in mutually agreed to land transfers. Recording rights provides outside investors with "somebody to talk to," a legitimate and authorized partner to negotiate on the nature of investments and on compensation. A formal record is also very much in investors' interest as it reduces the scope for fraudulent transactions and the need for costly inquiry to prevent the surfacing of possible undisclosed prior claims or overriding interests (such as land use restrictions).

Finally, only if rights to cultivated land are recognized and demarcated on the ground will it be possible to identify protected areas and design strategies to prevent encroachment. This will be critical to help countries manage and preserve land that provides environmental benefits, such as forests, in a way that ensures continued provision of local or global environmental benefits.

Recognition of Long-Established Rights

In many areas recently of interest to investors, rural land is sparsely populated and outside demand for it has traditionally been low. Such areas have frequently been governed at the community level through customary arrangements that have uncertain official recognition at best. With higher values and thus greater demand for land and associated natural resources, the lack of legal recognition may make such rights vulnerable to challenges from outside the community or even from within it.

Historically, many countries have considered land and associated natural resources not formally registered as property of the state, which government could dispose of at will, often without considering the actual status of occupation. The tendency to neglect existing rights often derives from a legal framework inherited from colonial days—reinforced or more deeply entrenched postindependence—that presumes any unclaimed or unregistered land to be "empty" and thus available for transfer with few safeguards (Government of France 2008, 2010). This bias can take many forms, including the recognition of rights only to land currently cultivated (that is, excluding fallow land) or stipulations preventing registration of common property (Alden Wily 2010).

In Zambia, for example, customary rights of land and natural resources can be neither registered nor surveyed, and the law allows for registration only of individual rights. Thus, although most of the country's land is managed according to customary rules, the associated rights are impossible to register formally. In such a context, a gradual and organic evolution from communal to more individual rights is impossible. Such restrictions have tended to favor well-informed and well-connected individuals and, especially where land is appreciating, have given rise to land concentration and inequality. In Sudan, the 1970 Unregistered Land Act transferred all land not previously registered by landowners to the government by deeming it to have been registered in the government's name. Although this act was repealed in 1984, subsequent legislation upheld the de facto abolition of customary land rights and simultaneously prohibited judicial recourse against land allocation decisions by the government.

In Indonesia, about 70 percent of the country's land area is classified as "forest estate" (even if not covered by trees) and owned de jure by the state (represented by the Forest Department). The state can award concessions with little regard for those who have occupied or used such land. This legal distinction effectively eliminates the traditional land rights of indigenous and other local people who occupied these lands, possibly for generations. The ambiguous legal status of inhabitants on such land makes them vulnerable to displacement if policy makers decide to convert forest from customary to industrial plantation management by investors, something often done without proper consultation.

There is also significant legal debate in Liberia over whether customary lands enjoy formal recognition. The fact that many government officials and investors interpret the law in ways that deny customary land recognition facilitated the transfer of these lands to outsiders without compensation, with affected communities being notified only ex post.[2] Land assigned to companies was thus often occupied, causing violent clashes and conflicts. Similar issues continue to affect customary landholders in other parts of Sub-Saharan Africa and Asia, including Cambodia, Indonesia, and Madagascar.

Past decades have witnessed significant advances in the legal recognition of indigenous land rights and customary land tenure systems. Legal reforms in Benin, Indonesia, Mali, Mozambique, Niger, Tanzania, and Uganda, among others, led to recognition—or provision of ways to recognize—customary land rights that are of relevance to the majority of the population. Most of the relevant laws recognize that a community's relationship with land is more than just an aggregation of individual plots but extends to land-based resources used in common, such as pastures, forests, and water. Legal protection in principle thus extends beyond cultivated or inhabited parcels. But to make this effective, land rights will need to be documented.

Public Recording of Relevant Rights

In many countries with areas of low population density, rural land rights are recognized as existing independent of whether they are formally registered. This is important for ensuring that recognition of such rights will not depend on action by an often slow and inaccessible bureaucracy. But absence of written documentation can make it more difficult to defend such rights against challenges by outsiders or the state. In Cambodia, for example, rights over land exist by virtue of meeting occupancy criteria established in the law (essentially possession for a certain period of time). In practice, those with formal documents evidencing their rights have been better positioned to defend or transact those rights than those relying only on general statutory recognition. In Indonesia, where customary land ownership (*adat*) is recognized in principle, it is often not eligible for title in practice. Households in the state forest estate thus often lose rights to investment projects with few options for recourse.

Experts have long debated the pros and cons of registering land rights if customary systems still function relatively well. Titling and registration programs have tended to focus on defining and registering individual parcels and, not least because of their high cost, were often ill-equipped to capture the full range of rights land users may have by custom, including secondary rights and group rights to use common pool resources (Deininger 2003). If done poorly, formalization of land rights can indeed provide an opportunity for sophisticated and well-connected elites to grab land from those less well-equipped to navigate this process by asserting private control over forests and pastures that by custom were held in common.

Recent years have witnessed the emergence of low-cost and participatory tools that allow the tailoring of registration to more faithfully reflect local perceptions of existing rights rather than impose outside conceptions of property rights. The purpose of doing so would not be the much-vaunted ability to use land as a collateral to access credit—a possibility that will be beyond the reach of most rural areas in Sub-Saharan Africa for a long time. Rather, registration can be used to document and secure existing rights, often only by defining community boundaries rather than individual plots, and establish an accountable and representative structure for administering them locally. As land becomes more valuable, the need for such tools will increase.

To obtain the full benefits from one-time adjudication of rights through low-cost mechanisms, it will be important to ensure the following:

- It is possible to register group rights in a way that allows for community management of basic land administration processes (such as allocation of individual rights, updating of registries, and other internal affairs, according to given bylaws).
- Boundaries are recorded and a clear internal governance structure (with internal control structures) is established to allow interaction with outsiders.
- Records are integrated with those used in the regular land administration system to prevent double-allocation of land, to allow land users to enter into joint ventures with investors, or to allow groups to gradually individualize land rights if desired.
- Relevant secondary rights, including use rights to land and associated natural resources, such as those held by pastoralists, migrants, and forest dwellers, are recorded and protected, rather than eliminated or ignored, for example, by documenting them in land use plans that identify cattle tracks, seasonal grazing areas, and watering sources.

Some countries have made progress toward designing such registration systems. Tanzania's 1999 Village Land Act establishes local land management structures. Once villages agree on perimeter boundaries with neighboring villages and the boundaries have been demarcated and surveyed, villages receive a certificate of village land. This document in turn allows issuance of certificates of customary rights of ownership to individual landholders within the village on demand. The 1995 Land Policy in Mozambique recognizes customary land rights, and the 1997 Land Law extends the status of statutory rights to customary rights (held by 90 percent of the rural population) as well as to good faith occupation. The 1998 Regulations and Technical Annex provide voluntary mechanisms for registration of such rights and the issuance of land certificates (*direito de uso e aproveitamento da terra,* or DUATs) in the name of the community.

One advantage of registering community land at the group level is that, compared to individual titling, mechanisms to do so can quickly cover large areas, be tailored more flexibly to local needs, and be linked to local land use plans to provide documentary evidence of secondary rights. The potential impact is illustrated by Mexico, which in slightly more than a decade registered rights to more than 100 million hectares (ha) of rural *ejido* land, two-thirds of it managed by communities and one-third by individuals. Every household receives a certificate to three types of land: the house plot, one or more parcels of individually cultivated land (which can be transferred within the community but not to outsiders unless the whole ejido decides to join the private property regime), and a proportional share of communal land. This process also established an open and accountable internal structure for the ejido that entails a clear separation of powers, supervised by a specially formed office of the agrarian ombudsman.

Mexico's reforms demonstrate not only that it is possible to register property rights on a large scale and in a fairly rapid way, but also that doing so can help to resolve long-standing conflict on a massive scale. Moreover, there is evidence that doing so encouraged investment and provided a basis for joint ventures with outside entrepreneurs, with the government acting as a broker to provide investors with information on land access opportunities. To date, this has resulted in some 3,000 contracts, often with large firms (Gordillo 2010). In some cases, nongovernmental organizations (NGOs) help to manage contracts, facilitate input access, and provide technical assistance. Case studies of such arrangements in Chiapas point to very positive results, with maize yields of about 5 tons per ha, more than twice the state average.

By contrast, in many Sub-Saharan African countries innovative legal reforms have not yet been widely implemented on the ground, and local populations are often unaware of the content of such laws or of how to apply them. For example, more than a decade after passage of the Tanzania's Land Acts, only 753, or 7 percent, of the country's 10,397 registered villages have received a certificate of village land. Even where such certificates were issued, pastoralist rights continue to be neglected. In Mozambique, only some 12 percent of the 70 million ha estimated to be controlled by communities have been mapped, almost all with technical assistance from NGOs and donor financing. Investor interest, together with land demand from other sources (for example, environmental benefits), increases the urgency of adopting a systematic process to record land rights, making this a high priority for outside support.

Accountable and Representative Structures for Local Decision Making

Even if local rights are recognized and boundaries demarcated, local elites may try to capture the benefits from expected land appreciation and in some cases may even use efforts at land to strengthen their claims. To prevent this, structures are needed to make decisions about such rights in a way that is understood locally and represents the interests of all rights holders. Two options for doing so are through (ideally elected) local governments in a broader context of decentralization or through decision-making bodies that are specific to land, as for Mexican ejidos. The case of Mexico illustrates that, in addition to increasing clarity in demarcating boundaries, systematic delimitation of community land can help establish more accountable structures of local governance in rural areas. This is particularly remarkable because, before the 1992 reforms, ejidos were generally considered to be a highly politicized and often corrupt source of reliable votes for the ruling party (Zepeda 2000).

Mexico's *Procuraduría Agraria*, office of the agrarian ombudsman, has reduced widespread conflict. With representation in all states and at the local level, it legally represents agrarian subjects in court, promotes the conciliatory solution of disputes related to the agrarian law, monitors the observance of the agrarian law, provides legal counsel on legal and economic matters, and implements the program of land regularization and local land use planning. Support from the office has helped resolve a large number of land conflicts and jump-start local capacity building. Similar structures, including community assemblies or peasants' civil squads (*rondas campesinas*), administer justice for people too far from the formal system in Peru.

In contrast to the clearly demarcated rights and representative structures that govern ejido lands in Mexico, community lands in Mozambique can legally be transferred to investors by a quorum of just three to nine community members. This creates a risk that rights by less vocal groups, especially women, pastoralists, and internally displaced people, may be neglected. In one case study, communities in Gaza Province ceded to outside investors access to forest and water resources critical to the livelihoods of ex-combatants and women. Without having their rights documented or safeguards to ensure inclusive decision making, these groups could not make their concerns heard and, as a result, lost part or all of their traditional livelihoods.

Increasing land values and demand by outsiders can weaken customary leaders' accountability to their community and give rise to behavior inconsistent with their traditional obligations, such as the sale of community land for personal benefit. In Indonesia, there are many reports of custodians of customary natural resources (*ninik mamak*) making deals with companies that are well beyond the scope of their traditional authority and that contravene customary law (which prohibits selling of traditional lands). In Ghana, 80 percent of land is formally vested in traditional communities as allodial (absolute) owners, with chiefs or family heads who manage its use and allocate it on behalf of the community. Especially in areas with high investment potential and on the periphery of cities, chiefs have begun to perceive themselves as landowners in their own right, often reducing their subjects to lessees. Reports abound of chiefs striking deals with investors, in essence engaging in the privatization and sale of community lands that are by custom considered to be common property, fallows, or reserved for community expansion.

VOLUNTARY AND WELFARE-ENHANCING NATURE OF LAND TRANSFERS

Although involuntary means, in particular expropriation, are widely used to transfer land to investors, doing so suffers from three weaknesses:

- It is inappropriate conceptually and, by eliminating joint ventures from consideration outright, it unduly narrows the range of options for negotiation.
- In many of the countries of concern, regulations for implementing expropriation suffer from deficiencies (for example, lack of consultation or mechanisms for appeal).
- It implies a high level of centralization that is likely to divert attention from the technical determinants of viability, encourage rent seeking and political meddling, and create a temptation to impose below market values on communities without a clear justification or tangible benefits.

No Land Expropriation for Transfer to Private Interests

In some countries, including China, Ethiopia, Sudan, Tanzania, and Zambia, governments do not allow direct transactions between local people and investors without first having expropriated (or, if land is implicitly or explicitly considered state property, "taken back") the land. Purported advantages of this approach include the following:

- Compulsory acquisition, in theory, "cleanses" the land of existing rights and encumbrances, thus compensating for weaknesses of land administration systems that may be unable to provide conclusive information about the absence of competing claims.
- Compulsory acquisition allows the assembly of large land tracts to pass on in a single conveyance to the investor, possibly reducing transaction costs.
- By acting as an intermediary, the state may protect ill-informed landowners from predatory investors and negotiate on their behalf.

In each case, better and less draconian ways to achieve the objective exist, for example, by improving land administration, encouraging market-based transactions, or educating local groups about their rights. Conceptually, expropriation is justified only as a last resort against moral hazard and holdouts by private owners where the public good is at stake and alternatives are not available (a planned road, for example, cannot be built just anywhere). Its use centralizes decision making and may encourage corruption and rent-seeking. Moreover, even if it ensures the legality of land acquisitions, it cannot provide legitimacy for processes seen as contradicting local norms. Investors who acquire land that has been expropriated may see the viability of their investment jeopardized if they are unable to take possession of the land in question or find themselves exposed to a legacy of conflict due to long-standing disputes and unresolved claims.

Still, expropriation as a precondition for transferring land to investors remains widespread. In Ethiopia, more than a third of expropriations, not necessarily all for large-scale land acquisition, benefited private investments rather than the public. There are also concerns about conflicts of interest, as members of the executive who decide on expropriation also often sit on the commission that hears appeals to these transactions. Even if some compensation is paid, the fact that land cannot be sold implies that those who lost land will be unable to obtain land somewhere else even if monetary compensation is paid. Thus, the state may seriously undermine its authority by being seen as taking the side of one party, especially if amounts or modes of compensation are disputed.

The case of Peru illustrates that acquiring the land needed for a vibrant agricultural industry is not contingent on expropriation and may be easier without it. In this case, constitutional rules tightly circumscribe when expropriation can be used to prevent abuse of power by the state. Expropriations are void unless the state is the direct beneficiary. Public scrutiny and debate of individual expropriations are ensured by the requirement that every expropriation be authorized by the legislature in a law spelling out the future use of expropriated land. To ensure impartial and realistic valuation, property values have to be determined in a court proceeding. Expropriated owners can demand cash payment of the land's market value plus remedies for any damages.

Peru's process also has clear time limits; congressional expropriation orders automatically lapse after six months if the judiciary process has not started; and after 24 months if court proceedings are not concluded by then. Moreover, if within one year of the conclusion of the court process the expropriated property is not used for its planned purpose, it automatically reverts to the original owner. These strict limits have not inhibited agricultural growth—quite to the contrary. Peru's agro-exports have been expanding by about 8 percent a year, making it one of the largest exporters of agricultural produce in the world. More than 70 percent of the land used by the sector has been acquired through auction rather than expropriation, in many cases by investors with little experience in agriculture (Hernandez 2010).

The ability to appeal compulsory acquisition decisions varies widely across countries, and protection of local interests is often weak. In Nigeria and Sudan, the amount of compensation can be appealed but the expropriation decision itself cannot. Eviction orders are often given before a final judgment on appeals has been made and conflicts of interest are frequent, making it more difficult to uphold existing rights. So, even where complying with the letter of the law, expropriations may lack legitimacy, leaving investors open to what local people might consider justified acts of sabotage and pilfering that can significantly increase operating costs.

Procedural weaknesses and insufficient protection of existing rights are a concern in Tanzania, as well, given the country's long history of expropriation to acquire community land for subsequent transfer to private interests, often with delayed or insufficient compensation and in a highly regressive policy that is often perceived as pushing out poor indigenous landowners to provide land cheaply to the rich. This has led to concern about potential abuses of state power to transform unused village land into general land. At the same time, another concern of the concept of the "land bank" for transfer to investors, to be amassed by expropriating village land, is that it lacks provisions for joint ventures that would facilitate more active participation by villagers in the investment and provide an opportunity for transferring technology and skills.

Another disadvantage of relying on expropriation as the primary means of making land available to investors is that this makes land supply subject to capacity constraints in the public sector and runs the risk of embroiling investors in political disputes that may have little to do with the issues at stake.[3] As long as landowners can be identified and a regulatory framework to guide the process and uphold basic standards is in place, the private sector will often be able to negotiate more flexibly and quickly than the government. This can provide advantages if delays in the ability to put the land to productive use are costly financially. It will be advantageous to focus public sector efforts on creating the basic institutional framework, and to inform those affected of their rights, ensure fairness of the process, and create a level playing field.

Broad-Based and Effective Consultation

Consultation of affected populations is often required by law, especially if property rights are not formalized. However, laws are often insufficient for ensuring that consultation is meaningful and results in agreements that can be enforced. Even if consultations are mandatory, their usefulness may be limited by a lack of clarity about who must participate, what information needs to be made available beforehand, and whether the output of such meetings is formally recognized or enforceable. To be effective, consultations must be undertaken before approval, with clear rules on who has to attend, what type of information has to be available in advance, and how outcomes are to be recorded and enforced. To improve the chances of a meaningful process and resultant benefit sharing, local stakeholders need to enter consultations with a clear understanding of their legal rights, the issues at stake, and the rules of engagement.

In Mozambique, for example, the usefulness of consultations was limited by limited participation and lack of prior information about the nature of the investment (for example, a map identifying areas that would be planted) to allow local residents appreciate the potential impact on their livelihoods. Discussions were mostly general ("the investor will bring jobs" or "both sides hope that relations will be good") and the absence of district officials cast doubt on the procedural validity of many of these consultations. In many cases, investors had obtained approval before soliciting the views of the community, and their plans lacked detail or timelines that would have allowed monitoring. Not a single agreement was formally notarized or recognized in a way that could give it legal validity in a court should any party wish to pursue a claim. The government is now developing a manual of regulations to help address these deficits.

Access to legal information is often a key constraint. In some of the country studies, inability to see the texts of laws and regulations—even by lawyers and officials expected to adjudicate disputes at the local level—had a negative impact on communities' ability to understand the agreements they were about to enter. Innovative ways will be needed to bridge such gaps (for example, by ensuring that independent third-party advice will be available to potentially affected communities). In Liberia, stakeholder consultation is considered part of the implementation of a concession—that is, local communities are informed about decisions and presented with a *fait accompli* rather than asked for their input before the investment is shaped. In principle, requirements governing consultation in other sectors could be applied to land acquisition for agriculture.[4]

Given cultural and capacity gaps between investors and local communities, there is large scope for misunderstanding. For example, in Indonesia, *adat* (indigenous) communities on oil palm estates often interpreted money given as compensation for transfer of use rights only, whereas companies consider making payments to transfer ownership rights. In Liberia, investors in the forestry but not the agricultural sector are required to negotiate legally binding social agreements with affected communities. In some cases, such negotiations have provided considerable benefits to communities, including the right to 30 percent of the revenue from land rental fees plus fees for logs harvested, the construction of infrastructure (roads, concrete culverts, bridges, schools, and facilities), and employment opportunities.

If done well, consultation, both before project initiation and during implementation, can greatly increase the sustainability of investments by providing a space for seeking out mutually advantageous solutions. In one case from Mozambique, consultation about the rights of shifting cultivators resulted in a participatory mapping that allowed farmers to move their fields to an area outside the proposed concession in return for support in the form of inputs and assistance in land clearing. In Ukraine, investor interactions with local farmers, often intermediated by local government, provided a basis for identifying areas for technical and marketing support, as well as avenues for providing public goods that increase welfare and food security.

Fairness and Targeting of Proceeds from Land Transfers

Low valuation is common in situations where land either is state owned or has to be expropriated before it can be transferred to investors. This is despite the fact that the way in which loss of land, whether voluntary or involuntary, is compensated is critical for livelihood outcomes and the asset position of those affected. If they depend on land access for their income, compensation in land rather than cash to allow displaced owners to maintain their livelihoods at a comparable level is desirable. Compensation should, at a minimum, cover the loss of land, buildings, and other improvements, as well as the disturbance or loss to livelihoods. It should include not only owners but also those with secondary rights to these resources. Although this notion of compensation is often accepted in principle, implementation may not take these considerations into account. Compensation should ensure that those whose rights are affected benefit from the transaction or are at the very least not disadvantaged by it. This requires either a comprehensive valuation of affected people's current livelihoods/income streams or a voluntary decision (and market transaction) based on adequate information and their agreement to exchange their land in ways that protect their livelihoods and food security.

In Ethiopia, land-for-land compensation is available in some standard expropriation scenarios but not when investors who will gain access to the land are responsible for compensation. Although this arrangement reportedly facilitates timely payment of compensation, it has also contributed to landlessness of communities that find that they have few options to use the money they receive to purchase land elsewhere. Various approaches exist for regarding compensating customary rights in the countries studied. In most cases, however, especially where rights are not formalized, users receive little compensation. In Zambia, compensation is usually in the form of resettlement on alternative land, support through community projects, and inputs or compensation for dwellings and crops. In practice, such arrangements are often made without a clear and complete identification and understanding of the customary rights being displaced. As a result, some rights—especially those of groups that may not be considered part of the "community," such as pastoralists and migrants—are abrogated without compensation. In Tanzania, where pastoralism is an important rural livelihood strategy, compensation is paid only to landowners, not to holders of secondary rights, such as those related to grazing and access to forest products. There has also been concern that even registered village lands might be incorporated easily into urban expansion through processes that involve minimal compensation, calling into question the protective benefits of obtaining village land certificates.

Where land is leased and nominally state owned, rents charged are often set administratively with little regard to the land's potential and not transferred back to original landowners. Mozambique's lease payments for DUATs are symbolic (US$0.08/ha/year for livestock and game ranching; US$0.60/ha and year for rainfed agriculture). With weak information systems and limited capacity, the perceived costs of collection often exceed the benefits, especially as almost none of the lease payments are collected.[5] In Liberia, leases for agricultural concessions are US$0.50–US$2.00/ha a year subject to an inflation adjustment. In both countries, payments go to the central government as the *de facto* land owner. Local governments have no discretion in setting lease rates, which are either negotiated with the investor by the central government (as in Liberia) or set administratively (as in Mozambique and Ukraine). In Ukraine, where a moratorium on agricultural land sales prevented the development of a formal land market, the minimum land rental fee is set at 1.5 percent of the normative land value, or about US$20/ha, much lower than the rents paid on land with similar quality and infrastructure access in Argentina (some US$230/ha). Monopsonistic land markets (many landlords, each one with very small parcels of land, and few spatially concentrated operators who lease in land) depress land rents.

Undervaluation of land has not only negative distributional consequences, but also encourages projects that would otherwise not be viable, in addition to possibly fostering rent-seeking. As a result, land users may receive less than the benefits they derived from the land earlier, making them objectively worse off. This was reportedly the case in Tanzania, where compensation (some US$10/ha) paid by an outside investor was much less than the US$35/ha estimated to be the value of the annual harvest of nontraditional forest products (Sulle and Nelson 2009). In Ethiopia, some large investors not only received land and water free of charge, but also got tax benefits. This gave them an advantage over local small-holders who had to pay land taxes and various other fees but, to the extent that compensation is paid only for improvements rather than land itself, also consti-tuted a regressive subsidy from the poor to the rich.

ECONOMIC VIABILITY AND FOOD SECURITY

Economic viability is necessary but by no means sufficient for realizing posi-tive social impacts. Indeed, even if a project is viable, social impacts need not be positive if local land rights or livelihoods are disrupted, net employment generation is low, or if unequal distribution of benefits creates social tensions. At the same time, as it is impossible to find nonviable projects that generated sustainable social benefits, attention to the economic viability issue is critical.

Technical Feasibility and Economic Viability

Although the commercial risk associated with success or failure of specific proj-ects is an investor responsibility, an independent and rigorous check on eco-nomic feasibility could, in many cases, be appropriate. Why? Because of the high transaction costs involved in negotiating a deal; the irreversibility of many of the actions (for example, clearing natural vegetation); the fact that government often has a direct or indirect interest in the land involved; and the communities' limited capacity to evaluate the technical feasibility of proposed investments.

Recognition of the critical nature of economic viability prompted some governments to aim to evaluate the economic feasibility of investments, partly as an input into land price negotiations. While a positive first step, ensuring its effectiveness will require that reviews focus on substance rather than administrative details; that the implications (rejection or resubmission) are clearly laid out, and that responses can be monitored at the proposal and implementation stages.

Doing this effectively will in many cases require drawing in resources from outside government, such as investors with a proven track record of agricultural investment in other countries. Making results from such reviews publicly available could improve understanding of the opportunities and constraints to large-scale agricultural investment. It would also allow better assessment of the opportunities for transferring existing technology between countries.

Rather than focusing on projects that have been submitted by investors, rigorous and in-depth evaluation of "model projects" in line with the areas of interest to investors would be an ideal way of informing a country's broader investment strategy and establishing benchmarks that can then set the bar for subsequent investment proposals.

Competitive Processes for Approving Projects

As long as adherence to minimum technical requirements can be ensured, properly designed auctions are a low-cost mechanism to get agents to reveal their willingness to pay. In isolated cases, such as Peru, they have been applied to land with considerable success (box 4.2). Part of this impact is due to the fact that the auction process was complemented by a high-powered and independent technical committee comprising top executives from the private and the public sector. This example illustrates that, while there is no point in governments trying to second-guess private investors, attention to economic and technical viability, in addition to environmental and social viability, of proposals can be a very worthwhile investment even if it does not directly affect the price that can be charged for a piece of land.

Three aspects make the Peru case interesting. First, the requirement of a significant down payment eliminates speculators and ensures that only serious investors apply. Second, making business plans public generates positive externalities by quickly disseminating information on the profitability of agricultural ventures, information that can be very costly for potential applicants to acquire. Third, project proposals are reviewed by technical specialists from the private and the public sector, building capacity. Results are very encouraging: the mean payment for auctions realized since 1995 was some US$440/ha for land plus US$2,500/ha in investment.

Auctions have been effective in increasing public information and scrutiny in other cases, as well. In Ukraine, auctions were mandatory for leasing state land and an important mechanism for price discovery but were then abolished. Ethiopia's Amhara region had achieved positive results from a competitive process to allocate rural land to investors before more centralized mechanisms,

Box 4.2 Using Auctions To Transfer Public Land

Peru's national investment promotion agency, ProInversión, helps decentralized levels of governments attract investments. The mechanism to divest public lands for investment projects depends on whether the project is initiated by the government or by a potential investor seeking to buy land rights.

In the first case, a government agency (a ministry or a regional or local government) identifies the desirability of carrying out a project and asks ProInversión to start promoting the project. ProInversión then initiates a process of regularizing any land rights to determine the nature of preexisting claims that may need to be respected or cleared and the type of land rights that can be granted to the private investor. The intention to divest the land is then published in the official gazette, local and international newspapers, and a government Web site. The terms of bidding (that is, the minimum investment required and the minimum bid price for the land) are published for a minimum of 90 days (longer if the project is more complex).

Before the auction, bidders must prequalify by posting a bond amounting to at least 60 percent of the minimum bid price plus the intended amount of investment on the land. Bids are ranked by the price offered and the amount of projected investment, monetary offers are presented, and a winner is declared. Before the land is transferred through the signature of a contract, payment has to be made and a letter of credit covering the amount of the proposed investment deposited with the government.

In the second case, the potential investor is required to present a business plan that details the value of the proposed investment and the price for the land to a board composed of public and private sector specialists, including representatives of the responsible line ministries, especially if irrigation is involved. If the proposed project is considered viable and not in conflict with existing regulations, the proposal is published for a minimum of 90 days to allow other potential investors to present offers. If any investor comes forward, the public bidding process above is initiated (with the original investor receiving a discount equivalent to the cost of elaborating the proposal). If no other investor shows interest in the project during the 90-day publication period, the initial investor can proceed.

Source: Based on Endo 2010.

which in some respects were less clear, took its place. Public tendering and auctions are more advanced for concessions in the forestry sector, as in Liberia or Mozambique.

The auction mechanism also allows the incorporation of social concerns as part of the technical proposal. For example, the Piura regional government in Peru approved a US$32 million investment project for the production of ethanol on 10,800 ha of public land. As part of its obligations, the investor implemented a program to help local farmers switch from rice to sugarcane on 1,250 ha. The program, which included financing, technical assistance, and contracts to buy the smallholders' produce, had very positive outcomes for participating farmers.

Given the lack of information about the true value of a piece of land, the most appropriate technology to use on it, or the potential of infrastructure enhancing land values over time, flexibility to adjust contractual terms over time will be advantageous for communities. In Mexico, where short-term lease contracts allow adjustments over time, the parties either gain agricultural experience or move out of the sector. By contrast, many recently observed transfers are characterized by rather rigid conditions.

For example, 25-year lease contracts in annual agriculture, as in Ukraine, are likely to limit landowners' ability to adjust rents over time. Given that in some countries (including Liberia, Mozambique, and Sudan), large-scale leases have terms of at least 50 years, flexible contracts are even more crucial where public land is transferred to private use, potentially removing it from serving the public interest for generations. Although investors will want contracts to be long enough to allow realization of returns from fixed investments, ways exist for compromise (for example, by indexing rental fees to values of other lands). A one-time payment for land implies that any appreciation of the land will be captured by the investor. To prevent this, policy makers may prefer to contribute the land to a joint venture, as is generally done in Mexico.

Consistency with Local and National Visions for Development

Which agro-industrial activities are in line with existing opportunities and needs will depend on a country's endowments with different production factors and the size and speed of expansion by the nonagricultural sector. A strategy for promoting investment in large-scale agriculture based only on *ad hoc* decisions by often ill-informed investors may not correspond to a host locality's best interest in the long run. It may be advantageous to integrate such investments into a national strategy for agriculture or rural development. Such a strategic approach will be particularly important because providing complementary public services and infrastructure can significantly increase the benefits and attractiveness of such investment.

Adopting a well-reasoned national strategy for promoting investments also opens up the possibility of addressing food security by setting priorities for the expansion of particular land uses over others. Although many countries emphasize that investments need to be consistent with national objectives, the stated objectives are often not sufficiently operational and lack thresholds for approving or rejecting certain projects. Instead, they are formulated in generic terms ("job creation," "improved productivity") that make it difficult to determine whether specific projects should be approved or rejected. Earlier discussion suggests that, by setting minimum criteria and guidelines for private investment, local government can prevent priorities being set by investors *ad hoc* with poor consideration of broader goals.

Even in countries that lack elected local government structures, potential outside investment provides an opportunity to put in place structures that can institutionalize participation and create the preconditions for the emergence of democratic structures by creating revenue at the local level. The ability to collect taxes from local ventures has traditionally been a key mechanism to encourage local support to investments. Taxes on land and property are one of the best sources of self-sustaining local revenue.

Land taxation will be more attractive if local governments can retain a large part of the revenue they collect and if technical guidance is available. Local governments that benefit from taxation revenues will have a greater interest than outsiders in selecting investments that are profitable to the locality and generate tax proceeds that can be used to provide public goods (for example, physical and institutional infrastructure) that may improve the economic viability of these investments. Studies suggest that annual state and local revenues from the formal forestry sector in the Democratic Republic of Congo, which totaled just US$1.2 million in 2002, could increase to US$20 million to US$40 million over the next 5 years to 10 years (World Bank 2007), providing provincial authorities in the main forest provinces with some US$500,000 a year to support local development.

The ability to feed them into development planning at the local level is greatly enhanced if documents are public. While Liberia has made tremendous progress in improving land and forest governance, original concession agreements were often not publicly available, making it difficult to assess the potential impacts of plantation development or resolve border disputes. In the Democratic Republic of Congo, Indonesia, Liberia, and Mozambique, unclear and nonbinding contractual arrangements resulted in community disputes over concession boundaries and benefits.

The fiscal tool may also increase local governments' bargaining power in negotiations with investors and help them overcome informational imperfections (for example, by hiring consultants to advise on proper technology) and enforcement difficulties. In addition, it will provide the basis for localities to compete with one another in attracting economically viable investments, possibly enhancing the efficiency of project allocation across localities.

In thinking about the potential for local revenue generation, two potential problems must be avoided. First, unless local governments or beneficiary representatives are able to retain a significant share of tax receipts from outside investors, their incentives may be biased toward the short term. This bias could align local administrations' incentives with those of short-term investors rather than landowners or their broader constituents. Second, financial incentives such as tax rebates and exemptions established at the central level may significantly limit the revenue at the local level. In Ghana, far-reaching tax breaks imply that even profitable companies will pay almost no taxes, reducing the ability and incentive of local governments to provide complementary public goods.

Although establishing mechanisms for local taxation of land does not pose insurmountable technical challenges, the process may be resisted by parties who would be subject to significant taxation.[6] In the past, political considerations have often implied that the local fiscal instrument is not used to its full potential, encouraging speculation through, say, idle landholding in anticipation of large capital gains. The scope for speculation needs to be carefully considered when drafting country-specific regulations

IMPARTIAL, OPEN, AND COST-EFFECTIVE MECHANISMS TO IMPLEMENT INVESTMENTS

Governments can level the playing field and ensure that all parties, including local communities, have access to relevant information. Doing so requires that institutional responsibilities be clear, that administrative requirements be justified and enforceable at reasonable cost, and that reliable information be publicly available. A focus on the speed of completing processes or their cost should not distract from the need to focus on the quality of outcomes.

Assignment and Effective Performance of Institutional Responsibilities

In many countries, investment applications by foreigners have to go through an investment agency and a sector ministry. Objectives and processes between these institutions are often not fully aligned. Investment agencies try to increase outside investment, while line agencies aim to exercise due diligence in vetting proposals. Although the differing goals can give rise to constructive tension, if coordination remains ill-defined, it can create confusion and red tape that allows investors to play one agency against the other to ensure that proposals are approved, even if they do not fully meet legal requirements or comply with relevant safeguards.

Most target countries apply a graduated process of project review in which small projects can be reviewed locally while larger ones require ministerial, parliamentary, or presidential approval, usually depending on thresholds that vary. Requests for land allocations in Mozambique of 1,000 ha or less can be authorized by the provincial government, requests of 1,000–10,000 ha require Ministry of Agriculture approval, and land allocations of more than 10,000 ha require authorization from the Council of Ministers. In the Democratic Republic of Congo, investors wanting to acquire land must apply to provincial authorities before forwarding to the central administration for final approval at the ministerial level (for projects that exceed 1,000 ha), by a law (for projects that exceed 4,000 ha), or by the president (for projects that exceed 12,000 ha). In some cases, "bunching" of projects just below the cutoff point is observed.[7]

Although there may be room for scaling back unnecessary government approval processes that introduce opportunities for rent-seeking, great care should be taken to not cut out safeguards that are essential to ensure proper diligence, reduce risks, and inform all parties of their rights and obligations in a misguided desire to make property transfers "simple" and "easy." Such failure to apply due diligence may increase investment but come at a high cost in trying to unwind failed transactions that, with proper checking and safeguards, could have been avoided in the first place. In fact, in many countries the desire of central and local government agencies to attract investment is reported to have resulted in approvals of projects before the proper clearances (say, for environmental impacts) were obtained, signaling to investors that such regulations can be ignored with impunity.

Case studies suggest that the "urgency" of approving to avoid losing out on supposedly unique investments can lead to serious neglect of existing safeguards that can end up creating large damage in an environment of weak institutional capacity. Many countries establish time limits for certain administrative processes to make approval the default in cases where these procedures require additional time to complete. As this rushed approval process may well preclude due diligence assessments, hastily approved projects may abrogate local rights without proper safeguards and are thus not desirable.

In many cases, the transfer of rights to investors involves quasi-judicial processes that require public notice to provide an opportunity for interested parties to register claims. These processes are often designed more out of concern for investors than local people. In Sudan, if no objections are raised within 15 days, the local government authority issues a "free of rights" certificate, essentially transferring land to the investor. In the Democratic Republic of Congo, if processing a concession application takes more than six months, the regional authority can grant occupancy rights to the investor as requested in the application. The interests of both investors and landowners would be better served by instead taking measures to provide the capacity needed to ensure timely completion of the necessary review processes.

The absence of proper structures at the local level has led several countries to rely on highly centralized processes for project review. These processes rarely seriously consider whether the information needed for central decision makers to make informed decisions is available or how to strike a proper balance between local and central decisions and incentives. In Tanzania, all land transactions, regardless of size, require approval by the commissioner of lands (acting on behalf of the president) in the capital. Although it is unclear how much substantive improvement this step adds, it led to a large backlog of cases and significantly slowed the process.

A highly bureaucratic process also introduces incentives for investors to facilitate faster processing or to circumvent the established procedures entirely. For example, most investors in Tanzania either acquired land through informal transactions with local communities or previous investors or instead pursued an outgrower model (which is not possible according to legislation) thereby avoiding the land acquisition process altogether. District authorities in Liberia are typically excluded from investment screening and are informed by central government authorities about the investment after the fact. Such lack of participation complicates local development planning and prevents authorities from identifying opportunities for investment as well as potential conflicts with existing uses. But considerable capacity building may be needed to fully decentralize investment screening to the local level.

Enforcing Agreements and Contracts with Incentive Recipients

Many of the countries studied consider agricultural investment strategic and thus eligible for certain incentives and benefits in return for the social benefits it presumably provides. A danger in this context is the tendency, observed in several of the case study countries, to try and offload the cost of such subsidies to local landowners by providing land for free to investors without any compensation for the loss of existing rights to local communities. Instead, incentives should be simple, nondistortionary (that is, available to any investor), applied impartially, in line with prudent financial management, and linked to benefit provision as much as possible.

Some types of incentives may end up attracting speculative investment or undermining governance. This can happen if either of two conditions prevail: incentives are not given in return for provision of productive infrastructure or other goods that create positive externalities beyond the project area, or incentives are awarded in a discretionary process, with local rights holders rather than the general public bearing the associated cost of using public assets (that is, when land is given away). To benefit from incentives, the investor usually has to show that the project will create jobs, meet minimum levels of investment, and bring new technology. In Ethiopia, incentives for investors are clearly specified, but various privileges are often discretionary and thus may have negative impacts on the incentive scheme. In Sub-Saharan Africa, another drawback of incentives may be to attract projects that are not economically sound as many investors engaged in land-extensive projects indicate that subsidies and incentives play a major role in ensuring the viability of their ventures. In addition, because many of these incentives are given up-front (in the form of cheap land, for example) rather than *ex post*, there is very limited potential to enforce compliance with eligibility conditions.[8]

Public Disclosure of Relevant Information

In many contexts, the reliability and truthfulness of information provided by investors was identified as being open to doubt, and few countries have rigorous ways of assessing the aspects most relevant for future performance, especially those related to financial issues. Financial information from investors is often rudimentary, not checked, and not available to other parties or to the public. In Peru, 60 percent of the purchase price plus the value of anticipated investment has to be deposited at the time of making a bid. This simple mechanism seems to have screened out parties who lack the financial capacity for implementation.

Many countries are working to make information on potential land for investors available publicly as contemplated, for example, in Ghana and Tanzania. But public information rarely extends to information on key parameters of the investments, land prices paid, and other commitments by the parties. Making this information available publically could reduce mistrust, and gradually eliminate severe informational imperfections. For auction-based transfers of public land in Peru's Pacific coast, the fact that details on business plans and proposed payments for land are available from auction records can act as a price discovery mechanism in an environment where land markets do not exist. If business plans are published, the technical details in them can also point governments toward the need for private sector support in technology, market development, and other public goods that could increase the attractiveness of a location for outside investment.

In many cases, institutional fragmentation reduces the scope for data sharing and integration by different institutions. At best, fragmentation increases transaction costs for investors; at worst, it creates insecurity of property rights and may make successful investment applications subject to extortion by rent seekers. In virtually all the countries reviewed for this study, land information is scattered across various agencies and levels of government and kept in incompatible formats that make data sharing difficult.

In Zambia, for example, different and incomplete land information is collected by local authorities; land tribunals; the ministries of land, tourism, environment and natural resources; and other bodies. The data are maintained in different formats, of different scale, accuracy and extent; they are often damaged or missing; and they are kept in poor storage conditions with inadequate indexing. In postconflict settings, many records have been destroyed, and there is insufficient capacity to reconstruct the lost information. In the Democratic Republic of Congo, information on investments is held separately by all the institutions that have some authority over land and natural resources, and land titles are held only at the district level. The limited data sharing caused by these overlaps can be problematic when institutions grant licenses for exploitation of different resources without notifying one another.

In many countries, maps to identify land allocations are either unavailable or inaccurate. The limited ability to cross-check land allocations enables local chiefs or other people with privileged access to records to "sell" the same plot several times to different parties or to renege on earlier contracts—practices found in Ghana, Indonesia, and Liberia, for example.[9] Double allocation of the same land is also reported in Sudan, where foreign investors have in some cases been allocated land from local governments, the national Ministry of Finance and Planning, or local chiefs.

Monitoring Implementation

Monitoring is relevant for two reasons. First, it is not very effective to expend large amounts of resources in negotiating agreements without effective mechanisms to ensure that whatever was stipulated will indeed be adhered to. Second, even in the best of circumstances, investments of the type considered here will be risky and failure of at least a share of them can be expected. In order to not tie up potentially valuable resources, it will be critical to ensure that land assets of nonviable enterprises can be transferred to others who might be able to make effective use of them in an expeditious manner that does not create incentives for speculation. To guard against this risk, legal or contractual provisions often require putting land into use within a specified period and may prohibit subleasing or sale of the land to others.

Provisions that allow the cancellation of concessions that are not performing are expected to ensure that monitoring has real impact. For example, in Ethiopia, the government is entitled to cancel a concession if it is not implemented within six months. In the Democratic Republic of Congo, the concession must be occupied within six months of the contract's signing, and the land must be put to productive use within 18 months of signing. In Mozambique, an investor has 120 days after project authorization to start implementing the project and, according to the law, the provisional state land use right (DUAT) granted for investment purposes is nullified if the investment's business plan is not implemented after two years.[10]

In practice, however, such provisions lack bite because of three reasons. First, the public sector's capacity to monitor is severely limited. Second, criteria that could be monitored (for example, amounts of investment or job generation) are rarely laid down unambiguously or publicized. Finally, the processes that are envisaged to be used, for example to cancel concessions, are not well laid out and often cumbersome, implying that even if evidence on project performance were available, it would be difficult to quickly act upon it.

As a result, large amounts of what is often a country's most productive land may be unutilized. For example, in the Amhara region of Ethiopia, field visits confirmed that only 16 of 46 projects in the inventory of large-scale agriculture projects (see chapter 2) were used as intended (Tamrat 2010). In other projects, the land was either used for other purposes (such as forest clearance) or simply rented out to smallholders in explicit contravention of contract. In Mozambique, virtually all DUATs remain provisional, and a recent audit of a subsample of DUATs revealed that fewer than half complied with their investment plan. Similarly, although data are not available for agricultural concessions, a systematic review of forest concessions in the Democratic Republic of Congo pointed to extraordinarily high levels of noncompliance and led to the cancellation of 163 contracts that covered a total of 25.5 million ha. Moreover, the recent cancellation of a significant investment project in Mozambique suggests that effective monitoring can overcome strong vested interests and produce results.

There is also a need for publicity of investment details and public education. Given the barriers that a lack of information imposes on the ability to identify suitable technology, value land, and monitor performance, public access to basic information on land deals is likely to be one of the most effective ways to improve project quality, structure players' expectations, help understand business models, and facilitate a convergence of land values to a "fair" price. It can also dispel notions of secrecy and distrust surrounding this issue and, by allowing users to check the accuracy of their information, make it much easier to discover and possibly correct any gaps. And it can be combined with voluntary publication of such information by industry leaders and independent third-party verification. Competitive processes and performance bonds can thus significantly reduce the need to monitor and be combined with fiscal incentives.

Mechanisms for implementation will therefore need to be incentive-compatible, monitored at low cost, and subject to dispute resolution. Using recent satellite images to monitor investment implementation in Zambia reveals three interesting facts. First, land seems to have been allocated in an area already used by smallholders. Second, even though the image was taken four years after the land had been transferred, there is no visible sign of large-scale cultivation. Third, the land seems to have been given with scant attention to physical or other features.

A quick check of land use through satellite imagery, although informative, cannot substitute for local mechanisms to ensure compliance with agreements, especially for social and environmental issues. One way of jump-starting such local mechanisms adopted by some countries is establishing a community fund that would use all or part of the compensation obtained for land to provide social and other public services to benefit the entire community. Different forms for managing it exist, with the option of sharing responsibility among the local government, the investor, the representatives of those affected, and civil society, now being piloted in the Democratic Republic of Congo and Mozambique. Other efforts to ensure more effective monitoring include the recent publication of manuals and standardized checklists to allow local monitoring by provincial delegations of the investment authority.

ENVIRONMENTAL AND SOCIAL SUSTAINABILITY

Unless proper regulation is in place, negative social and environmental externalities arising from land transfers that are desirable for individual parties may outweigh or reduce the social benefits from such transactions to the point where they become undesirable. For example, transfers between parties may widen preexisting social inequalities, produce greenhouse gas emissions, or reduce local access to water because of toxic runoffs. In some cases, poor people displaced from their farms migrate to the frontier, where they cut down the forest to cultivate virgin land. Regulation at the national and project level will be needed to align the incentives of private agents with the public interest. Increased awareness of the importance of environmental issues has led to increased emphasis on environmental safeguards in national laws and in voluntary schemes promoted by industry associations (such as the Forest Stewardship Council).

Protection of Areas Unsuitable for Agricultural Expansion

Earlier analysis suggests that there is no need for area expansion into land that is currently being deforested. Still, such expansion continues apace in many countries, largely because the private benefits from such behavior can be high and existing mechanisms to identify or protect forest areas are ineffective.

In most of the reviewed countries, inventories of public land either do not exist at all or, if they do, not unambiguously identify boundaries of such land. Moreover, responsibility for managing public land is often dispersed among local authorities, sector ministries, and public agencies. The situation is complicated by fact that in many cases categorization of areas as public removes them from community ownership and management. Significant uncertainty prevails about boundaries of government land in Cambodia, Indonesia, Liberia, and Tanzania. Many countries have large swaths of their national territory under protection: 30 percent in Tanzania and 20 percent in Ethiopia. But lack of boundary demarcation often implies that it is difficult to enforce such protection on the ground. In Ethiopia alone, less than 10 percent of state forest boundaries have been mapped, and very few claims to rights over forestland have been identified and registered. This makes it difficult to protect public lands with high environmental value.

Having an inventory of economically valuable state-owned land that includes boundary identification and clear assignment of management responsibility is essential for proper asset management and enforcement. The absence of such an inventory provides opportunities for well-connected individuals to establish land rights through informal occupation and squatting, often with negative environmental impacts. In addition, information on revenues received from public lands—and costs to manage it—should be open to public scrutiny, requiring adequate staff capacity.

Legal frameworks also often encourage agricultural incursions. In much of Latin America and the Caribbean, land rights can be established by clearing forests and implementing "productive" use of the land, a doctrine that continues to have significant impacts on behavior. In the Brazilian Amazon, agriculturalists and ranchers take on large-scale squatting in the expectation that their occupancy will eventually be formalized. This occurs at the expense of both the forest and the indigenous communities. Recently, a law (11952/2009) regulated an estimated 67.4 million ha of land previously occupied (and deforested) by squatters with holdings of less than 1,500 ha before December 2004. Holdings of up to 300 ha (95.5 percent of the total) are to be regularized within three months and without physical inspection. Up to about 100 ha of land will be given for free; between 100 ha and 1,500 ha, a direct sale at highly subsidized rates and with credit will be undertaken; and above this will require returning some land. Sales are not allowed for a 10-year period for holdings below 300 ha and for four years for the remainder. Although the need to provide tenure security to encourage investment and reduce conflict is widely recognized, this law could encourage speculative land occupation and deforestation in expectation of future regularization. To prevent this and ensure that the land is not subject to traditional claims, the government issued Decree 9662/2009, which defines the procedures for registering land holdings in the land cadastre, including mandatory field verification for landholdings larger than 400 ha and prior consultation with environmental and indigenous agencies.

Although community land rights are recognized in Peru, a lack of boundary demarcation makes it difficult for communities to exercise their rights and defend them against settlers (colonos). These settlers can then illegally log the land and eventually apply to rezone the land, creating a loophole for large-scale agriculture in previously intact forests. Speculators and private firms are also said to "plant" settlers in areas identified for public investment, in areas where private investors received concessions, or as a strategy to deforest the area and have it adjudicated as agricultural land. This has led to loss of natural resources and serious violence.

Enforcement of Environmental Policies and Standards

The general picture from the case studies is a failure to articulate, implement, and enforce environmental regulations. This is possibly caused by stakeholders' desire not to let what is perceived as petty environmental concerns prevent them from capitalizing on what they view as a possibly short-lived bonanza of profitable investments. To avoid a race to the bottom—where eagerness to attract investors leads to neglect of essential regulations, consistently implemented national standards will be important.[11] This is particularly true regarding the lack of consideration given to indirect effects on the land, and the neglect of risks associated with standard agriculture projects.

In many cases, shortcomings in the application of environmental impact assessments (EIAs) or omissions of this requirement prevent effective implementation of environmental regulations and legal frameworks. In Mozambique, the investment and environment laws require investors to submit an EIA when seeking approval for their proposal. But few agricultural land applications had a comprehensive EIA, even if environmental issues were clearly at stake. This is attributed largely to the limited resources of public environmental agencies. EIAs in Ethiopia, though required, are often waived as sunset clauses for project approval. Although an EIA (which includes a social assessment) is required in Tanzania, only about half the required EIAs had been carried out according to the inventory of large-scale projects (see chapter 2). Even where EIAs were implemented, their quality was weak, and they were not publicly available. In Ghana, companies are registering their land at the Lands Commission before having acquired necessary environmental permits (Obidzinski and Chaudhury 2009).

Such problems are exacerbated if environmental agencies delegate functions to agencies in charge of investment promotion. In Ethiopia, the mandate of requiring or reviewing agricultural EIAs has been passed to the Ministry of Agriculture and Rural Development or respective regional bureaus, which lack the technical capacity and motivation to make compliance with EIA regulations a priority. Often the definition of situations that require environmental assessments is not clear or open to manipulation. And in cases such as Sudan, where insistence on far-reaching EIA requirements is justified,[12] it will also be important to think about ways in which their quality and implementation can actually be enforced in a resource-constrained environment.

In Latin America, some countries established a category of crimes against the environment, prosecuted by a separate entity. In Mexico, while the federal criminal law defines crimes against the environment, the institution specialized in investigating such crimes is part of the Attorney General's Office and replicated in the offices of the State Attorneys. A special agency, the Procuraduría Federal para la Protección al Ambiente (PROFEPA), receives and acts on any kind of claims, apparently quite successfully.[13] The environment law guarantees hearings (*audiencias*), which are becoming very important for land use changes, tourist developments in coastal ecosystems, the infrastructure of natural protected areas, and so on. With adjustments in implementation and disclosure, this could be a powerful tool.

Another mechanism for enforcing compliance is the prospect of legal action by affected groups, which under some national laws may publicize environmental violations. In Mexico, the environment legislation is the only type of legislation where the law allows a type of class action. This mechanism, which allows injunctions (*recurso de revisión*) to interrupt land use changes by any citizen, provides an incentive for investors to obtain local agreement before submitting the legally required documentation for the environmental impact assessment.

Adherence to Social Standards

Social issues arise in three areas: investors' failure to adhere to agreements that were entered into, distributional issues, and labor issues. All of these should be identified in social impact assessments or consultations.

Failure to adhere to social agreements, which can be caused by lack of economic success, can lead to significant negative direct and indirect social impacts. For example, in Liberia, a rice investor initially promised not to cultivate the fertile lowland areas that were crucial for local food production. However, after failing to develop the allocated lands, which were not as fertile, the investor reneged on the agreement and began cultivating the wetlands. This forced 1,000 farmers (30 percent of the local population) to relocate to nearby areas, and put a further 1,500 at risk of being displaced by continuing expansion.

Even when property rights are well defined, there may still be effects on third parties attributable to a project. To address this, Brazil has legal rules requiring the consultation of local people and protection of land tenure rights by indigenous people and *quilombola* communities (descendants of former slaves). Clear regulations respect secondary land tenure rights of occupants and rural laborers. And any economically significant investment project has to also comply with Brazilian labor legislation. These laws set maximum labor hours and minimum wages, weekly resting days, and yearly vacations, while guaranteeing collective representation and social security benefits and protecting against abuses of women's and child labor.

Distributional issues are likely to emerge if there is no correspondence between actual land users (which may involve secondary ones) and the property rights taken into account in investment-related decisions. For example, existing procedures for transferring the land may not take into account the full spectrum of rights (such as temporary rights by pastoralists). Or they may provide compensation to individuals who may not be the actual users of the resources (for example, men rather than women). When property rights are identified, this is less of an issue. But where investors have to make arbitrary judgments about the existence and legitimacy of claims, this can increase transaction costs and moral hazards significantly. A notable phenomenon in some of the case studies was for groups at the margins of affected communities (for example, charcoal producers in Mozambique) to be completely excluded from processes of local consultation—with potentially negative consequences for their livelihoods.

To ensure that all community members are involved in investment decisions and that investment results in durable benefits, participatory land use planning has been applied with success in some parts of Tanzania. Existing regulations, if implemented in a participatory way, could provide a basis to not only demarcate land rights by villages and their populations but also to recognize secondary rights by pastoralists. Similarly, Mozambique is planning to use recently passed regulations for the 2007 Territorial Planning Law, along with community land delimitation, to define rights and identify the suitability of specific types of land for investment. In 2008, the federal government in Brazil adapted the Ecological Economic Zoning framework to limit what can be planted to sugar in the state most affected by expansion. This is complemented by an industry-led boycott of all beef produced on pastures recently deforested, monitored with satellite imagery, following a Greenpeace campaign (Greenpeace 2009).

Finally, projects may not be socially sustainable if companies are perceived to treat employees, contract laborers, or contract farmers in ways that are illegal, inequitable, or do not conform to the original understanding of the contract on the part of the community. For example, a rubber plantation in Liberia employed most of its labor on a contract basis (day labor) with unclear terms and conditions. Considerable resentment was generated because different individuals received different levels and types of payment. By contrast, the formal employees received not only protected benefits but also free access to health and education services. Another issue frequently undermining relationships between communities and investors is the failure to deliver on initial expectations—either for employment or the provision of infrastructure or services. In Mozambique, communities gave up access to common property forest resources in the expectation that jobs and services would materialize—but this has not happened (and some of the "promises" were of dubious credibility). Clearer frameworks are needed for specifying standards, responsibilities (for communities and investors), and the mechanisms for monitoring and enforcing them.

In the case studies, there was a general lack of clarity about social standards applying to investors or public institutions involved in oversight. The country's overall framework of labor laws was in principle relevant, and in some countries procedures or norms had been established governing community consultation (such as the social agreements in the forest sector in Liberia and the more general provisions in Mozambique). But a range of significant social issues were generally not covered by any formal public standards—including all the key issues relating to livelihoods or equity. In no case was a dedicated social assessment carried out to provide detailed information on the impacts of the proposed investment on different social groups.

In 2004, to enforce labor regulation, the Ministry of Labor in Brazil created a national list of employers who have been convicted of using forced labor. Enterprises on this list, which is public and updated every six months by the ministry in collaboration with social organizations, cannot obtain public loans and other benefits. As an additional measure, Brazil launched the Pact for Eradication of Forced Labor as a public-private partnership in 2005. The pact now includes 250 companies, commercial associations, and social organizations that aim to avoid commercializing products and bar suppliers who used forced labor.

From the perspective of all the key stakeholders (including the investors), there would thus be considerable benefits to gathering a detailed understanding of the social and political context before designing details of the investment. Understanding the impacts by social group (including by gender, age group, ethnicity, and other significant fault lines) is critical to determining the social sustainability of operations and their distributional impacts. Strengthening practice in this area is therefore a major priority.

CONCLUSION

Review of key aspects of the legal, policy, and institutional environment suggests that a lack of success of a large number of investments can partly be attributed to the fact that the institutions tasked to process these ventures were ill-equipped and ill-prepared to deal with the sudden influx of interest. This points toward an urgent need to adjust processes as needed and build the capacity to implement them in practice. This is an important area for assistance by donors as well as investor countries.

Many of the policy measures needed to deal with the weaknesses in the institutional and policy framework can be addressed in the short term, with potentially significant multiplier effects. For countries with significant amounts of unused land, five steps are essential to move in this direction:

- Identify areas and crops where investment can provide the highest benefits (for example, by adapting the agro-ecological zoning methodology) and use this to establish parameters (for example, minimum size of investment and employment generation) to be included in any application by investors. Systematically map and document existing rights, and educate local populations about the opportunities available to use the land at their disposal, as well as the contractual options available to them (including model contracts and the amount of compensation based on potential land rental).
- Regulate consultation requirements, decentralizing them as much as possible, and ensure that participation and results are documented and widely publicized (including on the Internet) to allow enforcement and opportunities about learning for communities and investors alike.
- Take proper measures (including reviews by private sector experts or practitioners engaging in large-scale farming elsewhere) to scrutinize and publicize projects' technical viability and establish a competitive and incentive-compatible process with an up-front declaration of projected capital investment and job generation and a proportional deposit.
- Improve the public sector's capacity for processing of investment applications, reduce red tape, and ensure that subsidies, if deemed necessary, are clear and distributionally neutral (not in the form of an implicit subsidy on land), nondistortionary (that is, come in the form of public investment that will benefit all investors and be useful irrespectively of the success of any specific investment) and incentive-compatible (that is, focus on the start-up phase rather than on tax credits that may kick in once a project is up and running).
- Put in place a regulatory framework with appropriate mechanisms for enforcement to ensure that private or short-term benefits from any given investment will not be outweighed by negative externalities in terms of the environment, the way in which resources are distributed, or welfare of future generations.

NOTES

1. An assessment of the policy, legal, and institutional framework was carried out in Brazil, the Democratic Republic of Congo, Ethiopia, Indonesia, Liberia, Mexico, Mozambique, Nigeria, Pakistan, Peru, Sudan, Tanzania, Ukraine, and Zambia.

2. Although not required by law, recent land acquisitions in Liberia included provisions for compensation because companies had adopted Corporate Social Responsibility principles of their own.

3. One example that has received great publicity is the attempt to acquire land for building a Tata car factory in West Bengal. As expropriation proceedings became highly politicized, the project failed to materialize. Tight limits on expropriation in Peru are supported by entrepreneurs who prefer to directly negotiate with land users rather than having the public sector drag out the process.

4. The Democratic Republic of Congo's 2002 Forest Code, for example, provides a number of innovations regarding forestry concessions, including maintenance of all traditional use rights, including those held by indigenous people; establishment and implementation of forest management plans; the right for local communities to manage forests under customary rights; mandatory implementation of social responsibility contracts and consultation with local people before assigning a forest to conservation or production; publically open allocation of production forests; and stakeholder involvement in management decisions through national and provincial forest advisory councils that include the private sector and NGOs. Consultation for forestry projects needs to be accompanied by public information about the proposed concession in many forms and in the local language, so that the public can be fully informed about the project before it enters into consultation. The impact of this code remains to be seen, as it has been applied only rarely, and customary authorities are generally bypassed in the allocation of concessions.

5. Less than 30 percent of total taxes are collected with payments highest in tourism concessions (US$8.00 per hectare per year).

6. Provisions in this respect are often fairly well specified in forestry laws. For example, the Democratic Republic of Congo's Forest Code specifies how taxes and fees have to be shared in principle. Proceeds from the area fee (*la redevance de superficie concedée*) is split between administrations in the exploitation area (25 percent to the province and 15 percent to the local government, all to be used exclusively for basic infrastructure development) and the public treasury (60 percent). Proceeds from the felling tax are split 50/50 between a national forestry fund and the public treasury. All proceeds from export taxes go to the public treasury. Proceeds from the deforestation tax are split 50/50 between the national forestry fund and the public treasury. All proceeds from the reforestation tax go to the forestry fund.

7. In Mozambique, one forestry project involved simultaneous submission of six land applications for a total of 28,000 ha to avoid the need for authorization by the Council of Ministers. In the Democratic Republic of Congo, there have been reports of multiple land allocations of up to 1,000 ha each so as to meet the requirements of a single investor without obtaining the requisite approvals.

8. Indonesia requires that at least 75 percent of an investment be undertaken before any incentives can be claimed, but it provides large implicit subsidies for oil palm development by charging little if anything for forested land intended for oil palm development.

9. The government of Ghana has since recognized that the incomplete nature of acquisitions carried out several decades ago has left significant portions of land, and the people who live on that land, in a legal limbo that needs to be resolved.

10. The period can be extended by another 120 days by depositing 5 percent of total investment value, up to US$500,000.

11. Efforts to formulate and implement principles for agricultural investment can be justified by noting that similar arguments apply to competition for investment between countries.

12. The requirements include studying the implications of drainage systems for waterborne diseases, assuring that crop mix and rotations do not have detrimental effects on soils, and ensuring rational use of chemicals, among others.

13. According to PROFEPA's Web site (http://www.profepa.gob.mx), in 2008, 99.5 percent (8,111 of 8,149 complaints) regarding environmental matters were addressed, researched, and responded to. Of the total, 44 percent relate to irregular forestry exploitation, 12 percent to soil erosion, 11 percent to natural habitats, and the remaining 33 percent to flora deterioration, contamination, and other natural resource issues.

REFERENCES

Alden Wily, L. 2010. "Whose Lands Are You Giving Away, Mr. President?" Paper presented at the Annual Bank Conference on Land Policy and Administration, World Bank, Washington, DC, April 26–27.

Deininger, K. 2003. *Land Policies for Growth and Poverty Reduction.* World Bank Policy Research Report. New York and Oxford: World Bank and Oxford University Press.

Endo, V. 2010. "Applying the Land Governance Framework to Peru: Substantive Insights and Local Follow Up." Paper presented at the Annual Bank Conference on Land Policy and Administration, World Bank, Washington, DC, April 26–27.

Gordillo, G. 2010. "Analyis of the Policy, Legal, and Institutional Framework for Land Acquisition in Mexico." Report produced under World Bank contract, Mexico, D.F.

Government of France. 2008. Technical Committee: Land and Development. "Land Governance and Security of Tenure in Developing Countries. White Paper of the French Development Cooperation. Summary synthesis by Philippe Lavigne Delville and Alain Durand-Lasserve, Ministry of Foreign Affairs, Paris.

———. 2010. Technical Committee: Land and Development. "Large-Scale Land Appropriations. Analysis of the Phenomenon and Proposed Guidelines for Future Action." Synthesis by Michel Merlet and Mathieu Perdriault, AGTER. Ministry of Foreign Affairs, Paris.

Greenpeace International. 2009. *Slaughtering the Amazon.* Amsterdam: Greenpeace.

Hernandez, M. 2010. "Establishing a Framework for Transferring Public Land: Peru's Experience." Paper presented at the Annual Bank Conference on Land Policy and Administration, World Bank, Washington, DC, April 26–27.

Obidzinski, K., and M. Chaudhury. 2009. "Transition to Timber Plantation-Based Forestry in Indonesia: Toward a Feasible New Policy." *International Forestry Review* 11 (1): 79–87.

Sulle, E., and F. Nelson. 2009. "Biofuels, Land Access, and Rural Livelihoods in Tanzania." London: International Institute for Environment and Development.

Tamrat, I. 2010. "Governance of Large-Scale Agricultural Investments in Africa: The Case of Ethiopia." Paper presented at the Annual Bank Conference on Land Policy and Administration, Washington, DC, April 26–27.

World Bank. 2007. "Forests in Post-Conflict Recovery in the Democratic Republic of Congo: Analysis of a Priority Agenda." World Bank, Washington, DC.

————. 2010. "Towards Better Land Governance: Conceptual Basis and Pilot Applications of the Land Governance Assessment Framework." Agriculture and Rural Development Department, World Bank, Washington, DC.

Zepeda, G. 2000. "Transformación Agraria. Los Derechos de Propriedad en el Campo Mexicano bajo el Nuevo Marco Institucional." Central Independiente de Obreros Agricolas y Campesion, Mexico.

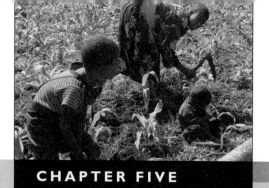

CHAPTER FIVE

Moving from Challenge to Opportunity

The previous chapters indicate that land acquisition and associated large-scale investment in countries that have not traditionally been targeted by such investment needs to overcome technical and economic challenges and that, in many instances, limited recognition of local rights, highly centralized approval processes, and gaps in institutional capacity further increase the associated risks. These challenges notwithstanding, host countries have an opportunity to use investor interest to help them utilize the resources at their disposal in a way that can increase smallholder productivity and improve local livelihoods. To do so, it will be necessary for different stakeholders to work together to not only address the risks described in more detail earlier in this report, but also to interact at the country level to create awareness of policy frameworks, monitor actual ventures, and adapt policies in light of new experience. This is important because policies need to be adapted to the specific reality of every country while being flexible enough to be able to respond to evolving experience and changes in the broader environment.

This chapter outlines ways in which different stakeholders can contribute to this objective. It also proposes efforts to improve land governance as a high priority. Roles and possible contributions of the different stakeholders can be described as follows:

- Governments in target countries now recognize that responses to the 2007–08 spike in land demand clearly failed to fully utilize the potential for these investments to contribute to poverty reduction and growth. Some have established moratoria on further transfers of land to investors pending the inclusion of such investment into their agricultural strategies and the creation of institutional preconditions to identify potentially suitable land and effectively process and monitor such investments. Many investing country governments realize that adherence to a set of key principles will be required to avoid jeopardizing the social, environmental, and economic sustainability of such investments. Tangible support to help target countries build the institutional capacity and strengthen the evidence base to make principles operational will thus benefit everybody.

- Investors in certain commodity sectors have established roundtables to formulate standards in order to guide expansion of their operations. While coverage, quality, and market acceptance vary, and the process is often time consuming, such standards can inform regulation and provide a platform for voluntary disclosure. A large number of financial institutions, the so-called "Equator Banks," have adopted principles that build on International Finance Corporation (IFC) performance standards to reduce social and environmental risks. With mechanisms for disclosure and the inclusion of investment and sovereign wealth funds, these initiatives could have a far-reaching effect on the implementation of projects on the ground.

- Civil society, producers' organizations, and academia demonstrate the ability to create awareness of this phenomenon and its repercussions. They provide input in several areas: (i) educating communities on their rights and helping them exercise these rights effectively (participatory mapping, land use planning, dispute resolution); (ii) assisting in designing, negotiating, and monitoring specific investment projects to make general principles operational; (iii) holding governments accountable for adherence to global standards and national legislation; and (iv) reviewing the impact of policies to foster policy debate.

- International institutions typically encounter the consequences of large-scale land acquisition on poverty and productivity in their regular work. This could give them an advantage in three areas, namely (i) serving as a catalyst to bring together stakeholders in support of common principles; (ii) supporting both high-quality analysis to make principles operational and monitoring to assess the impacts and potential unanticipated consequences of doing so; and (iii) providing technical and financial support to help countries build institutional capacity and infrastructure (for example, land registries, and roads) to facilitate market functioning.

KEY AREAS FOR ACTION BY GOVERNMENTS

Whether large-scale investment in agriculture or land acquisition will enhance opportunity and contribute to broader development will depend on a country's endowments and traditions, as well as its policy, legal, and institutional framework and its capacity to protect its resources and people. Our review suggests that in many of the countries that might be most affected by increased land demand, existing frameworks suffer from deficiencies that may increase risks and make it difficult to fully realize opportunities. To address these challenges, countries that may be subject to investor interest can act in three areas.

The first area is to assess available resources in light of global opportunities to determine comparative advantage. This will identify strategic priorities by commodity and link these to the processes of local planning. This process will ensure that investments can help achieve broader development objectives. Assessments would also provide inputs into policies and guidelines that deal proactively with investors (for example, in minimum amounts to be invested per ha or jobs created).

The debate on large-scale investment has often paid insufficient attention to the fact that such investment should ultimately facilitate equitable growth and poverty reduction in target countries and be linked to their broader development strategy. To inform such strategies, it is important to start with an assessment of whether such investment has the ability to contribute to employment generation, food security, regional development, and technology access. The agro-ecological zoning (AEZ) methodology, combined with growth projections, can help assess what type of investment—either in support of existing smallholders or through expansion of cultivated areas—will be desirable. While lack of infrastructure or technology may be a constraint to more effective land use, public investment could be used to increase the benefits from investments. It can also help to formulate criteria that investments should satisfy accordingly. By locating high potential areas, one can determine complementary public investment needed to make private investment attractive, for example, providing infrastructure, clarifying and securing local rights, improving administrative structures, and protecting critical natural resources. These can then be undertaken strategically and possibly in partnership between public and private sector, to increase the viability and sustainability of proposed investments as well as the opportunities for local producers to fully achieve their potential.

The best strategies will have little impact if local rights holders and investors are unaware of their rights and ways to enforce them. In addition to information campaigns drawing on media, local governments, and civil society, strategy formulation through a participatory policy dialogue is important. But information and knowledge must flow beyond the capital city and reach landowners and local governments in the field to educate them about existing rights. Model agreements, for example, can help structure expectations and thus reduce transaction costs for all participants. While incentives to promote outside investment are common in many countries, they are often not tailored to effectively achieve the intended benefits, such as jobs or capital investment. In worst case scenarios, poorly designed incentives may end up causing harm (for example, if land is transferred in neglect of local rights), or foster corruption.

Second, even if large-scale acquisition of land is not within a country's preferred set of strategies, increased demand for land implies a need to strengthen governance of land and associated natural resources more generally. As higher land values make control of this asset more desirable, existing rights must be protected and the governance of this asset adjusted to the changed situation. Achieving this effectively and on a nationwide scale will often involve policy and institutional reforms in the land sector with a 5-year to 10-year horizon. This is generally more cost-effective than addressing rights issues on a sporadic basis for areas where investor interest is likely to materialize. In the past, low land values and high implementation costs may have implied that the benefits from such efforts would have been below the costs. Higher land demand will increase reform benefits while new technologies can significantly reduce costs. Moreover, the fact that such reforms will be a precondition for attracting investment to generate economic benefits and to become eligible for payments in return for environmental services (for example, under REDD) can change the political economy of the issue and generate momentum in favor of change. Finally, although improving governance of land and associated natural resources is a long-term process and certain preconditions (such as a legal framework to recognize local rights) are required, implementation can be spread out over a longer time period, starting from hotspots where demand is already evident or about to materialize.

To improve governance along these lines, it is necessary to ensure the following:

- That existing rights to land and associated natural resources are recognized and ideally demarcated to allow users to defend them against challenges and engage in voluntary transfers
- That land use regulations help avoid negative externalities and land taxation contributes to effective decentralization and cost-effective provision of local public goods while discouraging land speculation
- That public land is clearly identified, managed transparently, and generates public rather than private benefits, with processes for acquisition of such land being tightly circumscribed and divestiture of such land done in an open and competitive process
- That landownership information provided by the public sector is comprehensive and reliable, with up-to-date information on landownership and relevant encumbrances maintained in a cost-effective way
- That legitimate and legally valid mechanisms to resolve disputes and manage conflict are accessible to most of the population and equipped to dispose of cases in a fair and expeditious manner (World Bank 2010).

Third, if large-scale investment can contribute to broader development, there is a need to build institutional capacity and improve procedures to manage the process. This will require emphasis on community consultation, coordinated processes for land transfer, analysis of economic and technical viability, land use planning, regulations to ensure environmental sustainability, and the monitoring and enforcement of contractual provisions. While the issues arising from this have been discussed in chapter 4 in a forward-looking perspective, it is important to note that few countries start with an entirely clean slate. Dealing effectively with investments that have been approved in the past but that may have ceased operation can, in some countries, pose significant challenges. In many instances, bankrupt investments have destroyed or degraded local resources but, with no resources available for dealing with this legacy, it is local communities who are left with the cost.

A number of key tasks appear to be relevant in this context. One relates to clarification of records and boundaries that may require attention to judicial or quasi-judicial processes of conflict resolution. Maintaining up-to-date data on land transfers are a precondition for monitoring investors' compliance with development conditions. It could also help generate data for policy purposes (such as land taxation) and allow local people to capture benefits.[1] Changes in legislation, together with new technology, now make it possible to conduct the required work much faster and at a lower cost than would have been possible even a decade ago. Still, it will be important to start with existing records and carefully assess readiness for expansion—in human, financial, and political resources—based on a phased approach.

A second area of concern, especially in countries where large amounts of land have been transferred but are not fully utilized, is the review and potential cancellation of past concessions. As land awards have often focused on areas with high agricultural productivity, this could make large amounts of land available to more productive uses.

Finally, in light of the outcomes they achieved on the ground, a careful audit of the processes and procedures that have been adopted to make land available for investments could be useful in providing relevant insights to policy makers. An audit of processes and contractual arrangements, for example, could generate important lessons at low cost.

INVESTORS

Responsible investors are well aware of the fact that large opportunities are often associated with a high level of risk and that ventures will produce sustainable benefits only if ways can be found to effectively address this risk. Building on more technical standards for product quality, some producers and processors throughout the supply chain for specific commodities have recently adopted principles and standards to protect them against business and reputational risk. These producers understand the importance of not being seen as supporting practices that are considered to have negative impacts on the environment (for example, biodiversity loss or greenhouse gas emissions) or the social well-being (for example, food security) of local populations. Major banks have signed up to the Equator Principles to protect against similar risks in the financial sector.

Commodity Standards

To address potential consumer concerns related to environmental and social outcomes, industry-driven initiatives to set standards and certify commodities in different parts of the value chain have recently multiplied. Among the earliest and best known standards are those of the Forest Stewardship Council (FSC) for forests and forest products, established after the 1992 Rio Earth Summit. Subsequent initiatives include the Roundtable on Sustainable Palm Oil (RSPO) in 2004, the Better Cotton Initiative in 2005, the Roundtable on Responsible Soy and the Better Sugarcane Initiative around 2006. Concerns surrounding sustainability of biofuels have recently given rise to standards and meta-standards, namely, general frameworks that benchmark existing standards, mainly by government agencies, to assess the social and environmental acceptability of biofuels. The latter include the Roundtable on Sustainable Biofuels (RSB), the Dutch Cramer criteria in 2007, and the meta-standard on sustainability reporting within the U.K. Renewable Transport Fuels Obligation (RTFO).[2] All of these initiatives involve negotiated trade-offs to reduce social and environmental risks to levels considered "acceptable" (de Man 2010). Review of this experience points to a number of lessons.

First, commercial viability of such efforts depends on either the ease of tracing produce and the willingness of consumers in target markets to pay premiums for sustainably sourced produce or, in the case of biofuel standards, the remit of regulatory authorities (such as European Union biofuels standards).[3] In Western retail markets for wood and associated products, certification by the Forest Stewardship Council has become a requirement, and the added cost of certification can be passed on to consumers. In the palm oil market, by contrast, demand in many new markets is highly price-elastic (as for low-cost cooking oil in China and India), implying that the market for RSPO-certified oil has yet to take off. Establishing industry-led standards also takes a long time. A period of 5 years to 10 years until an initiative becomes operational is considered respectable (de Man 2010). In a rapidly changing environment, this may be too slow to limit serious damage on the ground.

Second, the legitimacy of standards, their effectiveness in mitigating risks, and their speed and cost of operation will depend not only on them being technically sound, but also on their underlying governance structure, in particular participation by civil society. A more participative and decentralized approach has higher transaction costs but can be more robust (Synnot 2005). The FSC has broken new ground in this. It is a member-based organization with three "chambers" that represent social and indigenous organizations, environmental organizations, and economic interests, respectively, rather than a purely business-driven initiative.[4] Allowing national chapters to adapt certification rules to local conditions enhances the FSC's relevance, ensures the evolution of standards, and provides a vast pool of expertise. This has greatly increased the FSC's legitimacy, causing industry leaders to prefer it to competing schemes. In most industry initiatives, governments have a limited role despite their importance in supporting implementation. In areas that are core competencies of the public sector, including land rights and environmental protection, this has arguably reduced the effectiveness of these initiatives. For example, the RSPO is judged to have been very effective in regulating plantation management but much less so in preventing establishment of new plantations in areas of high conservation value. One response has been the addition of a government chamber in recent initiatives (such as the RSB). For land acquisition especially, industry initiatives that lack government participation will have difficulty protecting against specific risks (for example, surfacing of hidden claims), providing access to or compiling relevant data cost-effectively, and translating the experience in applying standards into broader policy reform.

Third, sustainable standards are not developed in the abstract but by learning from successful examples by industry leaders and in continual interaction with practice. In the ideal case, as indeed observed in some sectors, procedures adopted by industry leaders have provided inputs to standard development in a three-stage evolution. First, a few leading companies create internal standards and management systems to respond to new challenges in a way that provides them with a competitive edge. Then, the approaches taken by key companies are consolidated into harmonized standards and compliance systems that allow moving toward a noncompetitive industry standard. Finally these industry standards are integrated into countries' policy and regulatory framework.

Fourth, while most standards reference land issues in some form, the way this is done is often weak. Many standards' requirements for adherence to national legislation do not add anything in substance (companies would presumably have to abide by the legislation anyway) and ignores the fact that weaknesses in national law are the key reason for needing a standard in the first place. The ambition of declarations is not always matched with robust mechanisms for implementation, and independent verification of compliance is lacking. This creates an opportunity to strengthen the development of industry standards and define a workable set of principles to which other initiatives could then refer. The general nature of land-related criteria and their limited operationalization imply that their impact on the ground remains weak. To deal with this shortcoming, a focused effort to identify specific land-related criteria (rather than trying to encompass every single issue related to investment in large-scale agriculture) that could then be referenced by a wide range of industry standards could be a desirable option. The criteria should be limited to land-related issues, deal with key problem areas, and be backed by examples on the ground, guidance on disclosure, and robust mechanisms for third-party verification.

Fifth, the growing number of industry standards creates a danger of duplication and of focusing on semantics rather than discussing how principles will be applied and compliance monitored. Promoting accepted principles to govern agricultural land acquisition can have a significant impact, even if it is just voluntary initially. By providing consistent guidelines on what should be reported and allowing for third-party verification, industry leaders could provide examples of good practice. This would allow for the identification of mechanisms to set substantive standards and make land-related provisions in existing commodity standards operational. While expectations for new initiatives in this area should not be exaggerated, engagement with industry leaders, standards bodies, and governments to ensure that existing criteria can be implemented and gaps filled offer promise if they are complemented with actions by other stakeholders.

Financial Institutions (Including Commercial Banks and Funds)

Financial institutions have long had a strong interest in having their clients comply with performance standards.[5] In the end, this will minimize commercial and reputational risks caused by loopholes in legislation or enforcement capacity in countries where investments are implemented. Given the complexity of their operations and the resources at their disposal, multilateral institutions have developed such standards and provided guidance on their implementation. The World Bank's safeguards consist of 10 separate policies; six environmental, two social, and two legal. In 2006, the IFC and the Multilateral Investment Guarantee Agency (MIGA) replaced the safeguards with a policy comprised of eight performance standards distributed equally among social and environmental standards and broader community impacts and labor standards. They clarify roles and responsibilities for IFC's and MIGA's private sector clients and are accompanied by advisory services that strengthen client capacity and processes.

Principles built on these frameworks were adopted by other multilateral and bilateral institutions. In 2003, a group of private Equator Banks (currently 73) committed themselves to implementing the Equator Principles, with provisions identical to the IFC's standards (Schanzenbaecher 2010). With support from the International Monetary Fund (IMF), a 2008 Forum of Sovereign Wealth Funds adopted the "Santiago Principles" to guide its operations. The Equator Principles, which include IFC's Performance Standard 5 on "Land Acquisition and Involuntary Resettlement," provide the most specific guidance on land issues.

Experience with investment projects financed by the major financial institutions shows that effectiveness of these rules depends on the mechanisms for disclosure and enforcement that are available to assess whether actors comply with standards and to deal with cases where they do not (Kiene 2010).[6] Effective implementation also depends on the knowledge and skills of those applying the principles. This is an area where considerable expertise has been gathered. It depends on the clarity (including consultation and publicity) of the process and the capacity of affected populations to articulate and transmit concerns (or their scope for seeking assistance in doing so).

Given their coverage and the number of banks that subscribe to them, the Equator Principles offer considerable potential to address some of the challenges that have thus far limited success of industry self-regulation in the commodity supply chain within a reasonable time frame. Two areas that would need to be addressed in order to allow this potential to be fully realized relate to routine disclosure and the number of institutions subscribing to these principles.

- Limited disclosure weakens the ability to assess the extent with which performance standards are complied. While projects supported by multilateral institutions, including IFC, normally need to publish key documents and progress reports, adherence to the Equator Principles is voluntary, and no recourse mechanism is available to deal with noncompliance. Their effectiveness could be enhanced by mechanisms to improve disclosure of key facts that may include investment amounts, jobs generated, environmental impact assessments (EIAs), social impact assessments (SIAs), and payments for land to allow independent third-party verification. The current review of Performance Standards and disclosure requirements conducted by IFC is one way to address this and thus improve relevance on the ground.
- Financial sector standards will only be successful if all relevant players, including investment and sovereign wealth funds, agree to adhere to them. Getting broad buy-in remains a challenge. Nonetheless, models where countries take the lead and buy-in at the country level then requires compliance by all entities operating in a specific country offers some promise.

CIVIL SOCIETY

Civil society, producers associations, and academia can provide input in three respects, namely, (i) educating communities on their rights and helping them exercise these effectively, (ii) providing specific assistance in negotiation and subsequent monitoring, and (iii) performing a watchdog function to spot and publicize deviations from existing policy or globally agreed norms.

A key finding from case studies is that communities were rarely aware of their rights and, even in cases where they were, lacked the ability to interact with investors or to explore ways to use their land more productively. In areas with high agro-ecological potential, there will be a need to disseminate information about rights and procedures that could be used to minimize the risk of communities being unprepared when confronted with investment proposals. Local land use planning has been used with great success to document existing rights (including secondary ones) in Tanzania, for example. Benefits include specifying areas that the community may not need at the moment and can be made available for others to use and identifying potentially relevant environmental issues. In Mozambique, virtually all of the community land delimitations have been carried out by local NGOs, and efforts are currently under way to link this process to land use planning and possibly legal assistance.

If demand for investment has already materialized, more intensive assistance may be needed to screen the technical, economic, environmental, and social aspects of investor proposals. Communities will also need to identify information gaps and how investments could help provide local benefits. This requires a higher level of legal and technical skills (for example, through support by local producer organizations) and a more intensive engagement at the local level. Having local input into negotiation of agreements will make monitoring easier throughout the implementation process and help build capacity and skills. The return to investments in this area can be very high.

Civil society has traditionally performed an important role in holding governments accountable and publicizing deviations from existing legal norms. Civil society groups could have an important role in assessing investments' compliance with general principles and, more important, with specific contractual arrangements and standards. This would help to gain operational knowledge that is relevant to field realities, showcase positive examples, learn from their success, identify deviations from agreed standards, and point to reasons for deviations and ways in which such deviations could be avoided in the future.

INTERNATIONAL ORGANIZATIONS

Large-scale land acquisition affects the work of multilateral organizations because of its impact on natural resource management, agricultural growth, and poverty reduction. It also touches on global public goods in the areas of conflict, environment, and food security. Multilateral organizations have a comparative advantage in three mutually reinforcing areas. They can serve as a catalyst to bring stakeholders together in support of a common set of principles and ways to make them operational and check compliance on the ground. They can contribute to high-quality economic, financial, environmental, and social analysis at the country and the global level to help countries weigh available options and provide evidence on the impact of different actions in these dimensions now and in the future (for example, in light of possible climate change). And they can provide technical and financial support to help build institutional capacity and infrastructure (for example, land registries, roads, storage facilities) to help target as well as origin countries achieve their development objectives in a sustainable and constructive way.

Support from multilateral institutions can help stakeholders to agree on minimum principles to guide action and, more importantly, ways in which such principles can be implemented on the ground and compliance determined and monitored. This is relevant because many of the activities supported by such institutions, for example, construction of road infrastructure, will have far-reaching impacts on land values and the pressure for land acquisition in land abundant countries. Experience in other sectors suggests that the bulk of such work will need to be done at the country level, but that efforts will be most effective if they are linked to mechanisms for structured interaction among stakeholders on a regular basis. In the mining sector, the Extractive Industries Transparency Initiative (EITI) (box 5.1) provides an interesting model that can inform much-needed efforts to improve land governance.

Observers note that EITI took a long time to get off the ground and that, with weak incentives for participation, progress with country certification has been slow. To ensure that efforts to improve land governance avoid similar problems, two issues will need to be addressed.

- Any initiative in land governance will need to build on existing activities at the country and regional level and have strong political backing from the start. In Africa, these would be based on the Framework and Guidelines on

---

Box 5.1 The Extractive Industries Transparency Initiative

In the mining and extractive industries, the Extractive Industries Transparency Initiative (EITI) promotes sector-specific transparency at the global level.[7] It establishes a country-owned and country-driven process to promote accountability in an area where openness was often lacking. Participating countries fall into two categories: candidate and compliant. To become a candidate, governments must commit to implementing the EITI in partnership with civil society and the private sector and publicize a costed country work plan. To be compliant, countries need to disclose and disseminate a report that includes information on revenue streams validated by the local multi stakeholder group and endorsed by EITI's global governing body (EITI 2009).

By bringing together a multistakeholder steering group that comprises government, companies, and civil society, the process can provide a forum for dialogue and a platform for broadening reforms to promote policies contributing to good governance of resources by having different stakeholders explore specific issues and thus perform an effective watchdog function. Having civil society perform such a function should lead to more substantive involvement on the policy front or greater vigilance in the auditing of company accounts, something often described as EITI Plus (Goldwyn 2008).

Source: Authors.

Land Policy that was adopted by African Union Heads of State in 2009. In other regions, similar pronouncements are available. At a global level, Organisation for Economic Co-operation and Development Investment Guidelines and "Voluntary Guidelines for Tenure of Land and Associated Natural Resources" being put together by the Food and Agriculture Organization of the United Nations in a participatory process could also provide a starting point. Thus, gradual progress starting with existing programs will be possible.

- As countries that improve land governance will incur costs, ensuring that participation provides them with tangible benefits will be essential. Benefits could be technical, financial, or reputational. They may involve support to building capacity for project design, analysis, and dissemination, or a certification that is based on countries or investors agreeing to independent third-party verification that involves minimum levels of disclosure and the option for independent review and analysis.

In light of the fact that multilateral institutions already advise client countries on poverty reduction and broader development strategies, they have an advantage in carrying out rigorous monitoring and empirical research, both at the country and global levels. Support to evidence-based policy making in this direction, drawing on inputs from others as needed, is especially important in light of the lack of empirical evidence on large-scale land acquisition and the links to core topics of interest to development issues.

This study demonstrates the usefulness of evidence-based research in a number of respects. At the country level, it allows dispensing with prejudices on the extent of the phenomenon, the characteristics, and—to some extent—the initial impact of key deals and the actors involved (which in many cases involve local people). It also highlights the need to improve systems of data management to better inform decision makers, as well as private stakeholders and local communities, about existing deals and potential future opportunities and provides suggestions on how this may be done in a specific-country context. At the global level, it helps identify good policy in specific areas and provide the basis to compare demand for land with what may be available in different regions and countries by helping to identify potential hotspots, the need for and potential impact of complementary measures, and the possible long-term implications.

Additional evidence that multilateral organizations can help gather will be desirable in three areas, namely to (i) draw out implications at the country level in more detail and bring together information on agro-ecological potential, property rights, and infrastructure access, ideally in a process that feeds into decentralized governance at the local level; (ii) analyze the effect of country policies, many of them adopted very recently, aiming to more proactively manage the phenomenon and draw on information (for example, monitoring of project performance) that becomes available in this context; and (iii) document in more detail the productive performance of key investments, possibly feeding into a mechanism to share lessons from experience across countries.

Ultimately, governments in recipient countries are responsible for securing property rights and creating an environment that allows use of the resources available in a way that furthers social and economic development by framing and implementing policies conducive to growth and poverty reduction. There is little doubt that, in many cases, lack of capacity is a key factor that contributes to less than desirable outcomes. Although opportunities for effective capacity building may be constrained if the policy environment is not conducive, quite a number of countries are willing to adjust their policies and, in some cases, have already started doing so. This provides a starting point to assess the impact of policy reform in a way that involves all relevant stakeholders. The benefits from such activities can be large. The ability to document successful projects and policies, especially in Africa, while benefiting everybody, will help those investors confront operational and reputational challenges associated with such ventures. Finding resources to help build the needed capacity should therefore be possible.

CONCLUSION: THE NEED FOR AN EVIDENCE-BASED MULTISTAKEHOLDER APPROACH

The magnitude and often speculative nature of land transactions observed recently has caught many actors by surprise. Demand for land acquisition continues and may even be increasing. At the same time, scarcity of information on what is happening encourages speculation on a large scale. The review of empirical evidence conducted for this study leads to three main conclusions.

First, the large size of the areas that could potentially be involved (such as those not currently cultivated but with high agro-ecological potential), the concentration of such land in few countries, and the fact that there appears to be significant interest in countries with weak governance imply that the risks associated with such investments are immense. Case studies confirm that in many cases public institutions were unable to cope with the surge of demand and quickly screen out nonviable proposals and that legal provisions were unclear and not well-disseminated or known by rights holders. As a result, land acquisition often deprived local people, in particular the vulnerable, of their rights without providing appropriate compensation. In addition, consultations—if conducted at all—were superficial and did not result in written agreements, and environmental and social safeguards were widely neglected. In a number of countries, investors are treated more favorably than local smallholders, for example, in terms of tax payments and the ability to obtain land and other resources. Rudimentary project proposals, lack of technical know-how, and optimistic revenue projections together with highly opaque ways of processing and approving projects implied that many projects either did not start production at all or operated only on a small fraction of the land they had been allocated. In one country, investors had actually resorted to leasing land out to smallholder farmers. In some cases, investors who were unable to turn a profit due to unrealistic plans then started to encroach on protected areas or on land that had explicitly been set aside for use by local people, causing environmental damage and threatening local food security.

At the same time, these risks correspond to equally large opportunities. Some countries have very large areas of land that is currently not cultivated but suitable for rainfed cultivation of crops with high and growing global demand. In many cases these countries are also home to large numbers of smallholders who eke out a living on tiny plots, unable to access technology or capital, located far from infrastructure, and with yields that are only a small fraction of what is possible. Addressing the underlying constraints in terms of technology, access to capital markets, infrastructure, or institutions to allow increased productivity and effectiveness in the utilization of these assets could have far-reaching development impacts.

Second, investors could contribute to this effort in a number of ways, including through adequate contract farming arrangements. While some mechanisms for doing so have been identified in the case studies, many other options for productive partnerships are likely to be available. To realize the benefits that could be attained in this way, three things will be needed: a strategic approach that proactively engages investors, changes in land governance and policy, and greater institutional capacity. Required measures include recognition of local rights to land and associated resources, open and well-documented mechanisms to transfer these rights voluntarily instead of having them expropriated by the state, and public institutions with clear mandates and sufficient capacity to prevent negative external effects—whether socially or environmentally. Although this is a daunting list, a global review of good practices suggests that there are examples to draw from and that the benefits from doing so could be high. Although much of the suitable land is located far from infrastructure, infrastructure construction could set in motion a virtuous cycle of development. More importantly, the high global interest in this issue suggests that country governments willing to embark on this agenda should be able to draw on significant technical and financial support.

Third, while making the necessary institutional arrangements is a responsibility of governments in target countries, a pervasive lack of reliable information on opportunities, actual transfers, and the impact of large-scale investments can lead to negative impacts. Investors unaware of the location of high potential land that current owners might be willing to transfer may spend considerable time and energy searching for land or designing projects that are bound to fail. Communities who have not been educated about their rights to land and associated natural resources or the potential uses and implied value of such resources are more likely to make decisions about their divestiture that they may regret and that may not be sustainable or even lead to conflict. Limited awareness of key economic and technical parameters of relevance for implementing projects will hurt the stakeholders, as it forces them to invest in acquiring knowledge that should be easily available. Finally, weak or nonexistent information on project performance makes it impossible to identify investments that are underperforming and liquidate or transfer them to alternative uses, to ensure that environmental and other safeguards are actually adhered to, and to evaluate the effectiveness of policies with a view toward making changes to adapt them to existing needs.

To ensure that information to help make critical decisions and effectively deal with risks is more widely available, concerted multistakeholder efforts are needed to improve land governance and to define a set of parameters that would be accessible to all interested parties to provide input into planning, analysis, and policy advice. Exploring the available options and drawing on the lessons from EITI and other initiatives to move rapidly in this direction could avoid some of the considerable risks highlighted by this study. By allowing continued feedback to decision makers in public and private sectors, it could also help stakeholders more effectively use the opportunities created by increasing global interest in agricultural land.

NOTES

1. Having an inventory of clearly defined boundaries on the different types of land that may be acquired by investors (at least for land in the custody of the state) would prove very useful in this respect.

2. The RTFO includes strong requirements to demonstrate that biofuels contribute to net greenhouse gas savings and that their feedstock is produced sustainably. To minimize the cost and administrative burden of compliance, the reporting model makes use of existing voluntary agri-environment and social accountability schemes which thus have been benchmarked against an RTFO Sustainable Biofuel Meta-Standard, creating a direct link between the "voluntary" commodity standards and the obligatory U.K. standard on biofuels (The Royal Society 2008).

3. Domestic markets, however, may be less responsive to certification in international markets, as in the wood sector, for example.

4. Voting rights are apportioned to chambers equally. Within chambers, northern and southern subchambers have equal voting rights. In fact, the impetus for formation of the FSC came from civil society, with a major role played by the World Wildlife Fund.

5. The IFC supports development and implementation of commodity standards (for example, RSPO). However, although there is overlap between commodity standards and IFC's Performance Standards, the commodity standards cannot be, at any time, considered as a substitute for IFC's Performance Standards. IFC's Performance Standards are written broadly and inclusively to have global relevance across countries, sectors and project specific contexts, and their specific application varies by country, sector and project. By contrast, commodity standards are sector driven and address only environmental and social issues relevant to a given sector.

6. To improve compliance, the World Bank has an Inspection Panel to provide affected citizens and communities with access to independent recourse through the World Bank's Board of Directors, which has the responsibility to ensure compliance. Similarly, IFC has a Compliance Adviser/Ombudsman who reports directly to the President of the World Bank Group.

7. As of April 2010, the EITI was supported by 31 implementing countries, around 40 major international oil, gas, and mining companies, 80 institutional investors managing assets of more than US$14 trillion, hundreds of civil society groups and networks, and supporting countries and donors.

REFERENCES

de Man, R. 2010. "Regulating Land Investments: The Role of the Private Sector. Lessons Learned from Voluntary Standard Initiatives in the Financial Sector and in Commodity Supply Chains." Paper presented at the Annual Bank Conference on Land Policy and Administration, World Bank Washington, DC, April 26–27.

EITI (Extractive Industries Transparency Initiative). 2009. "EITI Rules including the Validation Guide." Oslo, Norway: EITI.

Goldwyn, D. L. 2008. *Drilling Down: The Civil Society Guide to Extractive Industry Revenues and EITI*. New York: Revenue Watch Institute.

Kiene, W. 2010. "Enforcing Industry Codes of Conduct: Challenges and Lessons from Other Sectors." Paper presented at the Annual Bank Conference on Land Policy and Administration, World Bank, Washington, DC, April 26–27.

Schanzenbaecher, B. 2010. "Sustainable Large-Scale Agriculture: Lessons Learned from the Forestry Sector." Paper presented at the Global Donor Platform Land Day, Rome, January 24.

Synnot, T. 2005. "Some Notes on the Early Years of FSC [Forest Stewardship Council]." Forest Stewardship Council, Saltillo, Coahila, Mexico.

The Royal Society. 2008. "Sustainable Biofuels: Prospects and Challenges." Policy document 01/08, The Royal Society, London.

World Bank. 2010. "Towards Better Land Governance: Conceptual Basis and Pilot Applications of the Land Governance Assessment Framework." Agriculture and Rural Development Department, World Bank, Washington, DC.

Methodology of and Issues Encountered in Collecting Inventory Data

C ountry level data collection was complicated by the generally limited amount of information collected from investors preapproval and especially postapproval of the investment, the lack of data coordination between different agencies and levels of government, and in some cases the complete absence or questionable provenance of important details, such as the investment's location and implementation status. The results of this exercise, along with a detailed discussion of the challenges faced in collecting information from each study country, are presented below.

CAMBODIA

The Ministry of Agriculture, Forestry and Fisheries (MAFF) created an inventory in 2006 in response to strong international pressure to increase the openness of the process of awarding concessions. This pressure ultimately resulted in the Subdecree on Economic Land Concession in 2005 and an agreement to cancel all concessions larger than 10,000 hectares (ha).[1] The government was set to release an updated inventory in June 2009 but did not do so, forcing us to rely on 2006 data.

Difficulties were encountered regarding internal consistency and the interpretation of global positioning system (GPS) coordinates included in the database. Interviews with officials in Kampong Thom province suggested that grants by local authorities continue and that capacity gaps hinder full implementation of measures that aim to promote competitive award of economic land concessions, as well as the monitoring envisaged in the subdecree. These reports are consistent with independent findings (United Nations 2007). Public information on economic land concessions remains incomplete, and many environmental and social impact assessments, if conducted at all, involve little community participation or fall short of international best practice.

DEMOCRATIC REPUBLIC OF CONGO

A national inventory includes all concessions of at least 500 ha for agricultural or forestry-based uses approved by the Minister of Land Affairs since 2005. As land records are maintained at the district level, follow-up data collection was undertaken in a selection of districts in Katanga, Kinshasa, Équateur, Orientale, and Bandundu provinces. Efforts were made to obtain information on projects involving 1,000–2,000 ha (which require ministerial approval) and projects involving more than 2,000 ha (which require parliamentary approval). Although all concessions of at least 1,000 ha must be approved by the Minister of Land Affairs, evidence from pilot data collection in Katanga and Kinshasa suggests that governors have in some cases awarded multiple concessions of up to 1,000 ha each to individual investors without the required approvals. Although the media has reported concessions of up to 3 million ha, the largest of the 40 projects listed in official data was only 163,000 ha in size. However, seven projects involved transfers of 10,000 ha or more and thus accounted for more than 97 percent of the total area transferred.

Despite speculation that projected carbon offset revenues (for example, from REDD) might set off a global land grab, particularly in the still heavily forested Democratic Republic of Congo, the sole carbon offset project identified was an 8,000 ha World Bank–funded project in the Bateke region of Kinshasa province. Initial investigations at the provincial level suggest that many of the investments approved within the past five years are either not yet operational or have only recently begun land-clearing on a limited scale. In the forest zone, only two projects (a 500-ha project for palm oil and a 4,000 ha project for rubber) approved in the past five years in Équateur province were found to be operational. A single investment was authorized during this period in Orientale province; it was not operational at the time of this study.

ETHIOPIA

As Africa's largest recipient of food aid, Ethiopia has attracted considerable media attention based on reports about private investors, especially from the Gulf States, obtaining large tracts of land for export production in a country that is chronically food insecure. The highlands, where 80 percent of the country's 85 million live, are densely populated (150 persons/km^2). But there are at least 3.5 million ha of potential cropland in the lowlands with a population density of only 30 persons/km², but with pervasive presence of pastoralists who use land virtually everywhere.[2] After unsuccessful attempts at resettlement from the densely settled highlands to the lowlands, the government now encourages investors to start mechanized production of oilseeds and other crops. Following disastrous land collectivization in the 1980s, land rights for the mainly sedentary population have recently been strengthened through certification of user rights (without the right to buy or sell land). We looked at data on 406 projects from inventories in five of Ethiopia's nine regions that together account for 1.19 million ha of leased land.

The fact that the regions can authorize land allocations below 5,000 ha required visits to five of the country's nine regions.[3] Information on existing investments from federal and regional authorities differed greatly, partly because regional investment authorities can allocate land without consulting other agencies (for example, those responsible for environmental impact and land administration) and there is no routine process for data sharing. All foreign investors, including those entering into joint ventures, must first obtain a federal investment license from the relevant ministry. Once this license is obtained, land may be requested from the Regional Investment Authority (or the Environmental Protection, Land Administration and Use Authority in Amhara), a process that domestic investors also follow. Once the request has been approved, actual land allocations are made at the district or zonal level, possibly for amounts different from those that had been requested.[4]

INDONESIA

The government views plantation crops as key to its development strategy and has supported, and is planning to support, a number of large existing and planned investments in bioenergy and plantation forestry, wood-based products, and food security (Obidzinski 2010). Given the decentralized approach to governance in Indonesia, we approached officials involved in the land concession approval processes at the national, provincial, and district levels for inventory data.[5] Given the lack of response at the national level, we organized a field visit to one of the most heavily affected provinces, East Kalimantan, to collect data from the provincial governor's office and forestry service. The limited information shared at the provincial level may be related to the delayed approval of the provincial special plan, which has prevented the allocation of land for new concessions and forced interested investors to take over existing concessions.

LIBERIA

Upon coming to office in 2006, the current government cancelled all large concessions (some of which had been awarded 60 years earlier) and established a process for renegotiating them through the Ministry of Agriculture or the Forestry Development Authority. Information on land area, rents, and tax payments is thus official and complete, although investment data relate to plans rather than actual values. GPS coordinates do not accurately reflect actual cultivated area, as concessions awarded in the past may never have been fully utilized or had fallen into disuse during the civil war.

LAO PEOPLE'S DEMOCRATIC REPUBLIC

By the end of 2009, 248,846 ha had been awarded under 1,143 concessions, including at least 398 for foreign investors. Fragmentation and lack of upstream reporting in the approval processes, together with lack of accountability with responsible state institutions, are reported to have led to significant underreporting (World Bank 2010). There is growing evidence that many concessions have failed to contribute to national economic development as expected. One study indicates, for example, that in one province only 13 percent of plantation projects approved between October 2003 and July 2007 had been developed (Thongmanivong and others 2009).

MOZAMBIQUE

Mozambique has large amounts of land that are not currently cultivated: the Food and Agriculture Organization of the United Nations estimates that of the country's 36 million ha of potentially arable land, at most 6 million ha were cropped in 2005. Following a long civil war, in 1997 Mozambique passed a progressive land law to recognize communities' land rights. It later established a mechanism to formally recognize these rights through the issuance of land use rights known as *direito de uso e aproveitamento da terra* (DUATs). The National Directorate of Land and Forests (DINATEF) can also issue provisional and nontransferable DUATs to investors based on an approved investment proposal, payment of (nominal) annual rents, and a community consultation. In theory, provisional DUATs can be converted into "definitive" rights once the investment has been implemented but lapse if the proposal is not implemented within a specified period of time. In practice, provisional DUATs are rarely cancelled, and most DUATs remain provisional.

The large areas of potentially productive land in Mozambique and their location close to ports and South African markets prompted leaders to aggressively market land resources to potential investors. Their efforts resulted in a flood of applications, with informal requests for 13 million ha received within an 18-month period, according to the investment agency. The overwhelming response, together with results from a land audit suggesting that less than half of the land awarded to investors had actually been used, led to a reversal of policy, the imposition of stricter requirements for economic analysis, and a moratorium on the allocation of land for biofuel projects until proper zoning to identify suitable land for different crops was completed. Our data include all DUATs and applications for DUATs of at least 1,000 ha for agriculture, livestock, plantation forestry, and game farms between 2004 and 2009. We have information on the status of the land rights, the investor's country of origin, and the size and location of the investment. DUATs were granted for just over 1 million ha to 259 projects; another 117 project proposals, involving more than 1.27 million ha, are being reviewed.

The application process in Mozambique requires that all projects involving more than 1,000 ha be reviewed by the minister of agriculture. Our inventory thus includes only projects above this threshold. Government records generally do not go beyond the project approval stage, with the possible exception of additional documentation required to convert short-term (2–5 year) "provisional" allocations of land use rights to "definitive" use rights valid for up to 50 years. Although formal surveying and demarcation and the implementation of proposed business plans are prerequisites for conversion to full definitive use rights, no investments included in this inventory had yet completed the demarcation process and less than 1 percent had been checked for demonstrated progress.[6] There are, therefore, no data on implementation progress, and all projects reported here have at best provisional land use rights. Our research confirms that even in cases in which investments have been cancelled or not yet implemented to their projected scale, the land acquisition process and land clearance can have negative impacts on local communities and the environment (FIAN 2010).[7]

Projects involving less than 1,000 ha do not enter the national approval process and may thus not be fully reflected in our inventory. As in the Democratic Republic of Congo, case studies identified some instances in which local approval of multiple projects was used to avoid national approval requirements. The fact that only one copy of each investor application is available created a significant bottleneck for reviewing and updating applications.

NIGERIA

All land allocations in Nigeria are decentralized to the state level. Our inventory relies mainly on data collected from 26 of Nigeria's 36 states,[8] the federal ministries for agriculture and the environment, and the Forestry Research Institute. Concession data are not maintained in any uniform manner, making it difficult to draw conclusions.

PAKISTAN

Pakistan was included because it featured highly on some investors' priority lists and because the government reportedly made efforts to attract investors.

The political sensitivities surrounding landownership did not allow compilation of an inventory. Field trips were undertaken to cross-check the projects cited in media reports catalogued on the GRAIN blog. In none of these cases could evidence of any investments be identified on the ground.

PARAGUAY

Land transactions in Paraguay are a private matter. Registration and census data were examined to explore patterns of large-scale land ownership. Census data provided information on overall land concentration. Exploring data from the registry proved difficult, because many properties are not registered and there is considerable overlap (some 10 percent to 20 percent of parcels in each department), with inaccuracies higher in areas with active land markets. Attempts to access relevant data through the public registers, where leases are registered, were unsuccessful. However, examination of the cadastre data revealed that some 2.4 million ha (4.5 percent) of the country's land resources are titled to banks. According to the latest census data, non-nationals own 28 percent of parcels larger than 100 ha.

PERU

Concessions for forestry and agriculture in Peru are processed by separate agencies with very different processes. Since the 1990s, public land for agricultural use, mainly in irrigation projects along the coast, has been divested through competitive public auctions. As investors are required to make formal bids with verifiable capital to obtain these parcels, data on the minimum bid value of the land and investment commitment were available from ProInversión, the agency responsible for running the auctions. Bids consist of a purchase price as well as an amount of investment (a significant part of which has to be deposited in an escrow account to ensure compliance), with an average concession size of 3,800 ha and investment commitments of more than US$4,000/ha (Hernandez 2010). Monitoring investors' honoring of their commitments is an integral part of this function.

Forestry concessions in Peru's interior can be allocated through bidding by small and medium-size producers, a process that resulted in granting of some 7.5 million ha of forestry concessions between 2002 and 2006.[9] Some 700,000 ha of forested areas are being used for agricultural production, including 300,000 ha for intensive production of, for example, coffee. The practice of granting agricultural concessions on former forest concessions cleared of their vegetation is a source of considerable concern and recent political unrest, discussed in detail in chapter 4.

SUDAN

Sudan illustrates the case of a fairly land-abundant country that aggressively promoted large-scale agricultural investment in response to the 1970s oil shock with mixed results. Land seems no less controversial today than it was before the decade-long civil war. Our country inventory makes up a partial list of 132 land use licenses from the Ministry of Agriculture and from investment commissions in nine states granted between 2003 and 2008. Only information on area allocated was available.

Federal and state ministries of agriculture and investment commissions can allocate large concessions. Allocation of land is the main mandate of the Government Agricultural Land Disposition Committee (GALDC), which applies the procedures for land allocation.[10] To obtain an agricultural leasehold, an applicant submits an application to the state's governor explaining the intentions behind and purpose for requesting the land, provides proof of financial capacity, and indicates the location and size of the requested area, among other information. The governor then transfers the application to the GALDC, and the Ministry of Agriculture makes a technical inspection on-site to check whether the proposed project is viable. After the GALDC approves the application, and in the absence of contestation during the publicity period, dues are paid to the Land Department and the land lease contract can be signed and sent to the Land Registration Office for recording. Although the federal Ministry of Investment is expected to maintain a comprehensive concession database, inadequate sharing of information with state-level authorities limits its comprehensiveness and currency. For this reason, we collected data in nine of the country's 25 states in the north and central regions (Blue Nile, River Nile, North Kordofan, Northern, Gedarif, Gazira, Khartoum, Kasala, and White Nile). No information on project implementation was available. Nearly half of the projects targeted irrigated crop development. Data quality suffered as a result of the transfer of responsibilities for land allocation and investment approval between ministries and investment commissions.

UKRAINE

As land transactions in Ukraine are between individual landowners and investors, there is no centralized concession database. To collect data, we interviewed by phone all 2,984 agricultural operators farming at least 2,000 ha (based on the Statistics Committee's official database of farm operators). Because the willingness to share sensitive financial information was limited, only very basic data (for example, land area, location, investor origin) could be obtained.

ZAMBIA

A list of all 100 rural properties larger than 500 ha was obtained from the Ministry of Lands to allow us to obtain the relevant information on the nature of planned investments from the Zambia Development Agency (ZDA) and investor characteristics from the Patents and Companies Registration Office (PACRO). After long delays, the ZDA provided data on 20 of these projects, most of them devoted to game viewing, hunting, or tourism; PACRO identified that only 10 of these projects were agricultural investments.[11] Although the Environmental Council of Zambia, which reviews environmental impact assessments (EIAs), was approached to obtain data on land use, the fact that few agricultural projects conduct EIAs made it difficult to obtain data of interest to this study. The small sample size and the fact that, as ZDA (which was incorporated only in 2007) is still consolidating its operations suggests there may be considerable underreporting, making it difficult to draw conclusions. However, case studies revealed that, as of late 2009, implementation had not yet started on any of the farm block projects designed by ZDA, suggesting that investor interest may be limited.

NOTES

1. Initially, provincial and municipal governors were empowered to authorize land concessions of up to 1,000 ha. The prime minister issued a declaration in September 2008 revoking this power and granting MAFF the exclusive authority to award concessions.

2. In past attempts at resettlement, pastoralist rights were often neglected. Neglect of these rights was not conducive to the success of resettlement and led to conflict (Pankhurst and Piguet 2009). Protection of pastoralist use rights in current legislation remains weak.

3. Amhara, Benishangul-Gumuz, Gambela, Oromia, and the SNNPR.

4. These findings are corroborated by a recent report on biofuels development in Ethiopia by MELCA Movement for Ecological Learning and Community Action (Mahiber 2008).

5. We contacted officials from the ministries of agriculture and forestry, national land agencies, and national investment coordination boards as well as governors and heads of districts in selected pilot areas.

6. Under Article 30(2) of the Land Law Regulations, formal surveying and demarcation must be completed within a year of concession approval.

7. The case studies reveal that many concessions have not been put to productive use and that a number of biofuel investments have gone bankrupt or halted operations.

8. The states surveyed include five in the northeast, four in the northwest, six in the north central, two in the southeast, four in the South, and six in the southwest. In each state, the lead investigator administered the inventory questionnaire to the commissioners of agriculture; natural resources, environment, and lands; and housing. A team of student enumerators cross-checked these official data with data from interviews with investors; nongovernmental organizations (farmers organizations,

chambers of commerce and industry); and parastatal agencies (the Nigerian Investment Promotion Commission, the Nigerian National Petroleum Commission, and the Corporate Affairs Commission).

9. In 2006, a moratorium on forestry concessions was put in place to allow transfer of responsibility for allocating forest concessions to regional governments in the context of the country's overall decentralization process.

10. The committee is made up of members of state-level ministries and institutions (agriculture, survey department, urban planning, forestry, irrigation, land registration).

11. Information on the remaining 70 projects was either unavailable with PACRO or projects were registered as neither agricultural nor forestry (that is, outside the purview of this study).

REFERENCES

FIAN (Food First Information and Action Network). 2010. "Land Grabbing in Kenya and Mozambique: A Report on Two Research Missions—and a Human Rights Analysis of Land Grabbing." FIAN, Heidelberg.

Hernandez, M. 2010. "Establishing a Framework for Transferring Public Land: Peru's Experience." Paper presented at the Annual Conference on Land Policy and Administration, World Bank, Washington, DC, April 26–27.

MELCA (Movement for Ecological Learning and Community Action). Mahiber. 2008. *Rapid Assesment of Biofuels: Development Status in Ethiopia.* Addis Ababa: MELCA.

Obidzinski, K. 2010. "Plantation Expansion in Papua, Indonesia: Likely Impacts on the Largest Remaining Forested Lanscape in the Asia Pacific." Paper presented at the Annual Bank Conference on Land Policy and Administration, World Bank, Washington, DC, April 26–27.

Pankhurst, A., and F. Piquet. 2009. *Moving People in Ethiopia: Development, Displacement, and the State.* Oxford: James Currey.

Thongmanivong, S., K. Phengsopha K., C. H. Houngphet, M. Dwyer, and R. Oberndorf. 2009. *Concession or Cooperation? Impacts of Recent Rubber Investment on Land Tenure and Livelihoods: A Case Study From Oudomxai Province, Lao PDR.* Vientiane, Laos: National University of Laos.

United Nations. 2007. "Economic Land Concessions in Cambodia: A Human Rights Perspective." United Nations Office of the High Commissioner for Human Rights, Phnom Penh, Cambodia.

World Bank. 2010. "Lao PDR: Investment and Access to Land and Natural Resources: Challenges in Promoting Sustainable Development." World Bank, Washington, DC.

APPENDIX 2

Tables

Table A2.1 Land Sizes and Origin of Projects in Country Inventories

Country	All projects			Domestic			Foreign		
	Projects (number)	Total area (thousand ha)	Median (ha)	Projects (number)	Total area (thousand ha)	Median (ha)	Projects (number)	Total area (thousand ha)	Median (ha)
Ethiopia	406	1,190	700	383	582	616	23	607	4,000
Liberia	17	1,602	59,374	2	117	58,323	15	1,485	98,179
Mozambique	405	2,670	2,225	274	1,402	2,000	131	1,268	3,800
Nigeria	115	793	1,500	110	769	1,500	5	24	4,000
Sudan	132	3,965	7,980	90	3,086	6,930	42	879	8,400
Cambodia	61	958	8,985	35	670	9,400	26	288	8,608

Source: Relevant ministries, national and regional investment promotion agencies.

Note: For Ethiopia, only the region of the investor was available and all investors from Africa were considered domestic. The inventory for Ethiopia covers only the five regions of Amhara, Benishangul-Gumuz, Gambela, Oromia, and the SNNPR (Southern Nations, Nationalities, and People's Region). The Sudanese inventory only covers 9 of Sudan's 25 states, predominantly in the north and central regions of the country (Blue Nile, River Nile, North Kordofan, Northern, Gedarif, Gazira, Khartoum, Kasala, and White Nile). The data was collected for application made during the five years prior to December 2009. Thresholds defining "large scale" were 500 hectares for Ethiopia, Liberia, Nigeria, and Sudan and 1,000 for Mozambique. Cambodia does not mention a threshold for its official inventory.

Table A2.2 Reasons for Country Selection and Key Insights from Case Studies

Reasons for country selection	Reasons for enterprise selection and key insights
Congo, Dem. Rep. ■ Postconflict (displacement, potential elite capture) ■ High agro-ecological potential/investor interest ■ Ecosystem vulnerable to land use change ■ New forestry law introduced social safeguards	**Maize:** (10,000 ha obtained, 2,000 ha under operation). Designed to meet provincial demand to achieve self-sufficiency (that is, may be more strategic than economic). Investor originally planned to focus on sugarcane, but chose maize because of liquidity problems. Investment displaced local cultivators, pushing them into a national park where farmers now pay guards to let them cultivate within the reserve; other farmers forced to relocate 50 km away where they rent land from local people. Mineral poor soils highly susceptible to erosion following biomass clearance. No EIA required by law; only projects supported by outside agencies (for example, World Bank) conduct EIA. **Rubber, coffee, cacao** (24,000 ha obtained, planted approximately 4,000 ha rubber; 150 ha coffee, 95 ha cacao): Colonial plantation in Équateur province recently acquired by a new investor. Currently employs all previous workers (1,282) and provides them with housing, a 230-bed hospital, clean water and electricity, primary and secondary schools, and other social infrastructure. Workers receive variable wages of some US$35 per week. No pollution was observed though there was some forest clearance for new rubber plantings, which could have negative impacts.
Liberia ■ Renegotiating concessions postconflict ■ Legislated concession process ■ Community-negotiated social contracts for forestry ■ Extractive Industries Transparency Initiative (EITI) now includes timber in Liberia	**Rice** (14,999 ha): Chosen because of role as a major food crop; picked largest rice concession on the border with Sierra Leone and Guinea to study migration effects. Economic problems caused investor to encroach on fertile wetlands, in contravention of agreements reached with the community (which cannot be enforced), displacing 30 percent of the local population. Compensation is not offered to all who lost rights. 400 full-time jobs have been created for unskilled workers (mostly ex-combatants) but there is concern about hiring foreigners who are willing to work for lower wages. As a result of deforestation, more than 50 ha of swamp have been silted from the first year of operations.

(continued)

Table A2.2 (Continued)

Reasons for country selection	Reasons for enterprise selection and key insights
	Timber (119,240 ha): After UN ban was lifted, Liberia adopted very progressive legislation requiring social agreements and could become a major player in tropical timber markets. The country's second largest timber concession was chosen because it is only concession that has implemented a social agreement so far. Social agreement clearly specifies rental payments and benefit sharing with government, but prohibition of investors' interference with good faith exercise of customary uses of timber and other forest products is not adhered to. Investment has thus restricted community access to forest products in context of increasing population and decreasing farmland.
	Rubber (32,540 ha): Rubber is Liberia's most important cash crop (20 percent of GDP) and the second largest rubber concession; the largest one (Firestone) has been extensively studied. Employees negotiated for safe water in all camps, increased number of approved dependents entitled to health care and education from four to seven. Still, despite this, productive use of the concession is made difficult by a long-standing dispute about the concessionaire's right to expand beyond the area brought under cultivation in the 2 years after award of the concession, creating great uncertainly for local communities. Situation is made worse by lack of community consultation and limited compensation.

Mexico
- *Ejido reform allocated community land rights*
- Communities negotiate with investor directly
- Government services (attorney, register of projects)

Maize: Investments in Chiapas (3,066 ha) and Jalisco (2,070 ha). Foundation (Fundación Mexicana para el desarrollo rural, FUNDAR) engages smallholders to improve their access to markets in the food processing industry and so secure industry supplies. Land belongs to *ejido* members and peasants with scant resources who receive technical assistance and financing from suppliers. Key private sector companies support project by guaranteeing harvest sales. 300 jobs created at Chiapas site. Both public and private sector actors involved in project: government programs boost productivity. Sale agreements and production support from private sector enterprises with strong corporate social responsibility mentality.

Rubber (2,970 ha): Company cultivates most land but *ejido* members act as small-scale suppliers and workers, derive clear benefits from plantation.

Mozambique

- Government solicited private investment
- Unanticipated rush of applications (especially biofuels)
- New land law (1997); community consultation mandatory
- In contrast to biofuels investments, most of which are very recent, forestry concessions have been operating for years, allowing detection of impacts

Sugarcane for ethanol (30,000 ha): Authorities awarded use rights (DUAT) to a multi-national investor based on promise of employing 2,650 workers. At time of study only 35–40 were employed full-time plus some 30 on a seasonal basis (some of them migrants from Zimbabwe). Although few benefits materialized, local people lost access to forest for fuel wood, game meat, fish. Investor uses local water supply and roads without compensation; thus negatively affecting women who gather the water. EIA noted potential negative impacts of agro-chemicals on soil, air, water and recommended mitigation measures. Also negative impact of forest clearance for sugarcane production. Project is the first that has been cancelled by government due to noncompliance with contract.

Forestry (26,000 ha): DUAT awarded to foreign investor. Unique social and ecological goals of the project benefit from private sector contributions and outside assistance. Company employed 280 people (mostly local people) at time of study, including 56 women. Work is intensive but contracts are short term; monthly salary not sufficient to compensate for lost livelihoods. Although community land delimitation was conducted, local authorities did not issue communities certificates; some of the land was then awarded to the investor. Lack of agreed boundaries led to displacement from agricultural lands.

Sugarcane for ethanol (20,000 ha): One of very few large-scale agricultural investments actually operating. Lack of information on project boundaries led to community concerns over access to grazing lands; company may have encroached on fertile lands that the communities had not wished to concede. Consultations did not include itinerant charcoal makers who were negatively impacted by the transfer of community forest lands to the investor.

Tanzania

- Recent investor interest in developing biofuels supported by government investment promotion on coast
- Agricultural encroachment on pastoral lands
- No social impact assessment required for approval
- Impacts on vulnerable groups (including those dependent on natural resources) often overlooked in planning

Teak (28,132 ha awarded, of which 7,800 planted): Sustainable teak plantation and processing facilities. Company provides direct employment to 120 people in the plantations and 110 at the wood processing facility. Since 2005, company's Social Fund has contributed US$150,000 to social infrastructure projects (for example, schools, dispensaries, teachers' houses, and village halls). Village contracted (US$25,000 annually) to prevent wildfires and poaching via patrols and boundary maintenance. Company supports teak outgrower and beekeeping programs in some neighboring communities. Land conflicts with local agriculturalists, beekeepers, other investors have damaged public relations.

Livestock and jatropha (4,455 ha at present but investor targets 18,211 ha): Joint venture between Dutch and Tanzanian companies; land belongs to four villages, who still must approve

(continued)

159

Table A2.2 (Continued)

Reasons for country selection	Reasons for enterprise selection and key insights
▪ Only nonbiofuel projects were selected for case studies given that biofuel investments are already well documented.	transfers to the investor; only one village has so far granted land rights. Investor wants to lease land directly from the local villages, in violation of the Village Land Act. Potentially negative impacts on pastoralist communities' access to grazing land, firewood, and water. Expected employment benefits not quantified. New charcoal production method consumes 1/4 the biomass of traditional methods and uses only wood obtained through pruning/thinning, which could have significantly positive impacts on local woodlands. Planned organic honey production should have limited negative environmental impacts (no chemicals used) but could increase pollination and create additional income for smallholders through honey and beeswax production. Through eradication and control of tsetse fly in this area, there will be not only a large tsetse fly-free pastureland for grazing wild and domestic animals (livestock), but also the community in this area will be free from sleeping sickness disease. Possible negative impacts include chemical pollution and exotic alien plant species introduction. Significant number of EIAs (1 per enterprise) already completed.
	Multiuse (5,000 ha): For eco-charcoal production, cattle production, beekeeping/honey processing, aloe vera and jatropha production/processing. Investor (Dutch joint venture) bought derivative right of occupancy held by two farms. Expected to employ 250 people full-time; 150 people thus far during start-up phase (over half women). Company provides water and other social services (for example, electricity, a dispensary, and primary school) for local communities. High benefits generate concern about possible in-migration.
	Rice (5,818 ha): Investor acquired derivative right of occupancy from previous investor; got into land conflict with local users who claim rights. Public-private partnership between Rufiji Basin Development Authority (Tanzania) and British company. Investor provides roughly US$38,500/year annually for community development in surrounding villages. Employs 262 workers, of which 85 percent are local.
Ukraine	**Multiple crops and pigs** (9,477 ha): EU investor leases land from local peasants; employs 5,000
▪ Unfinished land reform; no agricultural land sales	workers, almost all local people, at competitive rates (50 percent higher than average). Uses
▪ Local government supports community-investor negotiations	modern production methods; trains workers to properly operate and maintain expensive equipment.

Multiple crops (150,000 ha): Domestic investor built excellent community relations through regular communication with and training of local people (for example, regarding use of pesticides) and social infrastructure investments (for example, repairs roads, and so on). Employs modern no-till technologies; plans to increase yields to EU average (three times current levels) in three years.

Multiple crops (300,000 ha): Largest portfolio investor in Ukraine. Bad community relations due to economic difficulties that led to leaving most of the land fallow and closing down of the more labor-intensive livestock operation, apparently in breach of its agreement with the local rayon administration. This, and payment of low land rental (1.5 percent compared to national norm of 3 percent of normative land value) leads to limited community benefits.

Zambia

- Government farm bloc model: mixed large- and small-scale
- Biofuels rush; also large Zimbabwean farmers
- 2 percent of land rental proceeds to community

Export-oriented crops (155,000 ha): Government has created a farm bloc after converting customary into statutory land. However, after the investor that was initially identified lost interest, no progress has been made. Local fears about potential displacement. Potential population displacement, loss of access to forest products, including edible caterpillars. Intact miombo woodlands on site would be negatively impacted by clearing for cultivation; current environmental impacts limited to land-clearing for road and dam construction and related soil erosion.

Sugar: 17,838 ha estate + 13,860 ha outgrowers (smallholder + commercial). Investor (multinational, mostly South African and British) leases state land (formerly crown land) from Government on 99-year lease, pays rental fee of US$5/ha (soon to increase to US$20/ha) + taxes (US$1.1 million/yr cane levy, US$590,000/yr personal levy, + 35 percent corporate income tax). Roughly 300 smallholders engaged in sugar cultivation on plots of average 6.5 ha, earning roughly US$1,643/ha/year. Smallholders participate either as independent producers on their own land or as labor tenants who lease a total of 1,100 ha from the nucleus estate. Pricing mechanism works against smallholders and there allegations of the company trying to gain access to land and water rights by requiring smallholders to pledge their land as collateral in exchange for loans for input. Environmental concerns include eutrophication from agricultural chemical runoff and sedimentation in the floodplain, an important fishing area which currently produces US$23.3 million/year in fishing off-take; pollution and resulting health impacts from cane burning (roughly 1.35 g TEQ/ha and 45 g TEQ/ha of emissions to air and land, respectively); indirect impacts from loss of land to sugar plantation, including population displacement to marshlands with a heightened risk of malaria and former pastures, which leads to increased grazing pressure and human-wildlife conflicts. Nonparticipating smallholders have wider range of farm enterprises, many of higher value than sugarcane (for example, cabbage US$19,000/ha, or rainfed maize, irrigated beans and wheat US$4,464/ha).

(continued)

Table A2.2 (Continued)

Reasons for country selection	Reasons for enterprise selection and key insights
	Jatropha on 250 ha nucleus, only 65 ha planted, + outgrowers: British investor; 40 percent germination rate on nucleus; no production yet. 35 locals employed on short-term basis (US$2.56/d), lack of interest from local farmers perhaps due to poor germination rate on nucleus and the fact that their holdings are located within a Game Management area, which limits land use options and introduces oversight from environmental authority. Only 27 farmers from a nearby Resettlement Scheme (each has 25–35 ha under 14-year lease) joined outgrower scheme, with 0.25l ha each under jatropha. Investor provides inputs and buys seeds subject to a floor price and quality standards. However, insufficient technical advice given to farmers due to lack of sufficient testing of the different varieties in the area and no farmers have yet been paid for their seeds. Farmers find the crop is more labor intensive than advertized, especially because lately aphid attacks have increased production costs. Long-term contracts lock in land use, which prevents farmers from switching to higher value crops. No EIA because individual holdings are small, but collective impacts include forest clearance for outgrower jatropha production.

Source: Country case studies undertaken for this report.

Table A2.3 Projections of Global Land Use for Food, Feed, Biofuels

Source	Biofuels included?	Area cultivated	Forest cover
FAO	No	1.8	n.a.
IIASA I	No	4.5	−2.7
IIASA II	Yes	6.0	−3.3
IFPRI	Yes	10.2	−8.7
Eickhout and others (2009)	Yes	12.3	—

Source: Authors' compilation. Figures are in million ha per year.
Note: The relevant time horizon for all projections is until 2030, with the exception of IFPRI, which is until 2020. — = not available.

Table A2.4 Estimated Costs of Sorghum Production in Sudan

Technology	Size (ha)	Yield (t/ha)	Cost (US$/t)	Price (US$/t)	Net profit
Actual	400	0.4	495	215	−280
Potential	400	4.0	125	215	90
Actual	20	0.5	204	215	11
Actual	8000	0.5	277	215	−62

Source: Government of Sudan 2009.
Note: Potential yields possible using zero tillage and fertilizer.

Table A2.5 Summary of Analysis of Farm Incomes for Smallholders Relative to Wage Employment on Large-Scale Farms

	Ratio of smallholder to large scale for			Smallholder farm		Comparison		
	Yields	Labor/ha	Cost/ton	Family labor (days/year)[a]	Farm income (US$/year)[b]	Wages for equivalent large farm area (US$/year)	Farm income-to-wage ratio	Break even land rental
Sugarcane								
Zambia 1 ha irrigated	.78	4.80	0.86	598	2,118	348	6.09	1407
Oil palm								
Indonesia 2 ha outgrower	.89	.92	1.04	322	2,067	990	2.09	422
Indonesia 2 ha low input	.47	.48	1.00	192	873	990	0.88	–93
Cameroon 2 ha independent	.62	.90	.36	200	1,770	580	3.05	535
Rubber								
Malaysia 1 ha independent	.60	1.22	1.63	72	810	624	1.30	186
Grains								
Nigeria 5 ha independent maize	.50	.53	1.18	100	1,563	500	3.13	213
Zambia 5 ha independent maize	.67	5.06	.91	260	1,316	290	4.54	108
Cameroon 5 ha independent maize	.74	.84	.93	490	1,526	154	9.91	246
Sudan 20 ha sorghum	1.0	2.0	.74	200	1,994	319	6.10	81

Sources: Sugarcane and maize for Nigeria and Zambia using emerging farmer category where possible (World Bank 2009); oil palm and maize for Cameroon using high input smallholder (World Bank 2008); oil palm for Indonesia (Zen, Barlow, and Gondowarsito 2006); rubber for Malaysia (Barlow 1997); sorghum for Sudan (Government of Sudan 2009).

Note: To allow comparison, we make a number of assumptions. First, we hold constant the farm size managed by a commercially oriented smallholder for any commodity and assume that all labor employed on the farm is family labor. Second, we combine returns to capital and land. Doing so is justifiable because for most commodities, capital investments focus on land improvements, such as trees or irrigation, whereas machinery is usually hired. Third, we consider payments to land as the residual and ignore taxes.

a. Not corrected.

b. Corrected.

Table A2.6 Potential Land Availability by Country (all areas are in thousands of ha)

	Total area	Forest area	Cultivated area	Forest < 25/km²	Suitable noncropped, nonprotected Nonforest with population density of		
					< 25/km²	< 10/km²	< 5/km²
Sub-Saharan Africa	**2,408,224**	**509,386**	**210,149**	**163,377**	**201,540**	**127,927**	**68,118**
Angola	124,294	57,941	2,930	11,502	9,684	6,625	4,561
Burkina Faso	27,342	2,072	4,817	452	3,713	1,040	256
Cameroon	46,468	23,581	6,832	8,973	4,655	3,205	1,166
Central African Republic	62,021	23,496	1,879	4,358	7,940	6,890	5,573
Chad	127,057	2,280	7,707	680	14,816	10,531	7,061
Congo, Dem. Rep.	232,810	147,864	14,739	75,760	22,498	14,757	8,412
Congo, Rep.	34,068	23,132	512	12,351	3,476	3,185	2,661
Ethiopia	112,829	8,039	13,906	534	4,726	1,385	376
Gabon	26,269	21,563	438	6,469	954	927	839
Kenya	58,511	3,284	4,658	655	4,615	2,041	935
Madagascar	58,749	12,657	3,511	2,380	16,244	11,265	6,572
Mali	125,254	3,312	8,338	582	3,908	776	28
Mozambique	78,373	24,447	5,714	8,247	16,256	9,160	4,428
South Africa	121,204	8,840	15,178	918	3,555	1,754	649

(continued)

Table A2.6 (Continued)

| | Total area | Forest area | Cultivated area | Suitable noncropped, nonprotected | | | |
| | | | | Forest < 25/km² | Nonforest with population density of | | |
					< 25/km²	< 10/km²	< 5/km²
Sudan	249,872	9,909	16,311	3,881	46,025	36,400	18,547
Tanzania	93,786	29,388	9,244	4,010	8,659	4,600	1,234
Zambia	75,143	30,708	4,598	13,311	13,020	8,367	3,083
Latin America and the Caribbean	**2,032,437**	**933,990**	**162,289**	**290,631**	**123,342**	**91,576**	**64,320**
Argentina	277,400	33,626	28,154	16,228	29,500	23,835	16,856
Bolivia	108,532	54,325	2,850	21,051	8,317	7,761	6,985
Brazil	847,097	485,406	62,293	130,848	45,472	27,654	15,247
Colombia	113,112	64,543	7,339	31,313	4,971	3,776	2,838
Ecuador	25,152	11,631	3,384	3,663	638	415	313
French Guiana	8,034	7,809	6	3,554	27	27	27
Guyana	20,845	17,737	464	8,501	210	189	156
Mexico	194,218	64,447	25,845	7,206	4,360	2,857	1,719
Paraguay	39,904	19,112	5,419	10,269	7,269	6,035	5,133
Peru	128,972	68,312	3,799	39,951	496	476	438
Suriname	14,460	13,847	86	5,318	6	5	5

Uruguay	17,772	1,323	2,030	731	9,269	8,681	7,340
Venezuela, R.B.	90,531	48,345	3,912	6,167	8,966	7,725	5,891
Eastern Europe and Central Asia	**2,469,520**	**885,527**	**251,811**	**140,026**	**52,387**	**29,965**	**18,210**
Belarus	20,784	7,784	6,019	4,853	3,691	868	204
Russian Federation	1,684,767	807,895	119,985	128,966	38,434	24,923	15,358
Ukraine	59,608	9,265	32,988	2,594	3,442	394	74
East and South Asia	**1,932,941**	**493,762**	**445,048**	**46,250**	**14,341**	**9,496**	**5,933**
China	935,611	167,202	136,945	10,514	2,176	1,383	843
Indonesia	183,897	95,700	32,920	24,778	10,486	7,291	4,666
Malaysia	32,243	21,171	7,184	4,597	186	119	50
Middle East and North Africa	**1,166,118**	**18,339**	**74,189**	**209**	**3,043**	**843**	**236**
Rest of world	**3,318,962**	**863,221**	**358,876**	**134,700**	**50,971**	**45,687**	**41,102**
Australia	765,074	88,086	45,688	17,045	26,167	25,894	25,593
Canada	969,331	308,065	50,272	30,100	8,684	8,289	7,598
Papua New Guinea	44,926	29,387	636	9,746	3,771	3,193	1,917
United States	930,303	298,723	174,515	74,350	8,756	6,818	5,058
World Total	**13,333,053**	**3,706,457**	**1,503,354**	**775,211**	**445,624**	**305,711**	**198,064**

Source: Fischer and Shah 2010.

Note: "Suitable" means that at least 60 percent of possible yield can be attained for any of the five rainfed crops considered here (wheat, oil palm, sugarcane, soybean, maize). Countries are included if they have a total of at least 3 million ha of forested or nonforested suitable area for areas with population density < 25/km^2. Suitable ha per cultivated ha area based on nonprotected, nonforest suitable area where the population density of the grid cell is < 25/km^2, < 10/km^2, or < 5/km^2.

Table A2.7 Land Availability by Region for Different Crops (< 25 persons/km² and < 6 hours to major market)

	Total	Maize	Soybean	Wheat	Sugarcane	Oil palm
Sub-Saharan Africa	**94,919**	**44,868**	**38,993**	**3,840**	**6,023**	**1,194**
East Africa	57,833	29,980	22,432	2,873	2,506	42
Central Africa	20,838	6,620	9,706	253	3,270	988
South Africa	3,252	977	1,558	715	2	0
West Africa	12,996	7,291	5,296	0	244	164
Latin America and the Caribbean	**93,957**	**28,385**	**37,716**	**11,043**	**15,021**	**1,793**
Central America and the Caribbean	5,079	1,980	1,476	845	521	257
South America	88,878	26,405	36,240	10,198	14,500	1,535
Eastern Europe and Central Asia	**43,734**	**3,851**	**419**	**39,464**	**0**	**0**
Eastern Europe	40,031	3,788	321	35,922	0	0
Central Asia	3,703	63	98	3,542	0	0
East and South Asia	**3,320**	**465**	**443**	**1,045**	**500**	**867**
Southeast Asia	2,918	425	415	712	499	866
South Asia	402	39	28	333	1	1
Middle East and North Africa	**2,647**	**0**	**10**	**2,637**	**0**	**0**
North Africa	651	0	0	651	0	0
West Asia	1,996	0	10	1,986	0	0
Rest of world	**24,554**	**5,741**	**5,289**	**12,747**	**722**	**55**
North America	12,321	1,583	2,386	7,800	552	0
Oceania	8,920	3,804	2,838	2,053	170	55
Western Europe	3,313	354	65	2,894	0	0
Total	**263,131**	**83,310**	**82,870**	**70,776**	**22,266**	**3,909**

Source: Fischer and Shah 2010.
Note: All areas in thousands of ha.

Table A2.8 Wheat—Potential for Land/Yield Expansion for Key Producers and Countries with Uncultivated Land

| | 2008 production | | Land availability (thousand ha) | | | | | | |
| | Area | Yield | | Population < 25/km² | | Population < 10/km² | | Population < 5/km² | |
	1,000 ha	t/ha	Total	< 6 h	> 6 h	< 6 h	> 6 h	< 6 h	> 6 h
Countries with land available									
Russian Federation	26,070	2.45	35,722	29,510	6,218	17,219	5,991	8,610	5,593
China	23,617	4.76	1,622	533	1,120	268	925	125	667
United States	22,542	3.02	3,877	3,586	284	2,852	269	2,162	250
Australia	13,552	1.58	1,402	1,005	121	937	128	855	135
Kazakhstan	12,906	0.97	2,948	2,376	574	1,963	525	1,491	498
Canada	10,032	2.85	8,639	4,214	4,425	3,844	4,419	3,182	4,407
Turkey	7,583	2.35	1,626	1,585	41	408	9	64	4
Ukraine	7,054	3.67	2,430	2,418	12	296	1	50	0
Argentina	4,284	1.97	6,472	5,472	979	4,072	965	2,550	902
Brazil	2,374	2.48	1,345	1,329	16	905	16	431	14
Belarus	514	3.98	3,219	3,202	15	703	7	163	2
Uruguay	460	2.80	2,736	2,225	510	2,047	503	1,679	480
New Zealand	42	8.11	1,064	1,047	17	876	15	638	15

(continued)

Table A2.8 (Continued)

	2008 production		Land availability (thousand ha)							
	Area	Yield		Population < 25/km²		Population < 10/km²		Population < 5/km²	
	1,000 ha	t/ha	Total	< 6 h	> 6 h	< 6 h	> 6 h	< 6 h	> 6 h
Madagascar	5	2.44	1,069	959	63	549	50	231	39
Subtotal	131,035		74,171	59,461	14,395	36,939	13,823	22,231	13,006
Current producers									
India	28,039	2.80	0	0	0	0	0	0	0
Pakistan	8,550	2.45	1	1	0	0	0	0	0
France	5,492	7.10	850	848	2	33	0	5	0
Iran, Islamic Rep.	4,750	2.11	333	275	58	98	47	30	25
Germany	3,214	8.09	55	55	0	1	0	0	0
Morocco	2,858	1.32	515	499	16	163	4	42	0
Italy	2,289	3.87	6	5	1	0	0	0	0
Poland	2,278	4.07	266	266	0	36	0	3	0
Iraq	2,203	1.01	275	269	6	23	2	4	2

Afghanistan	2,139	1.23	85	57	28	12	5	0	2
Romania	2,098	3.42	157	154	3	40	3	17	2
United Kingdom	2,080	8.28	39	39	0	3	0	0	0
Spain	2,067	3.25	291	286	5	91	3	27	1
Algeria	1,800	1.28	93	87	6	4	7	1	4
Syrian Arab Republic	1,668	2.42	96	96	0	6	0	0	0
Ethiopia	1,425	1.73	180	30	150	0	28	0	0
Uzbekistan	1,377	4.46	277	243	34	96	15	29	9
Egypt, Arab Rep.	1,227	6.50	0	0	0	0	0	0	0
Hungary	1,126	5.02	37	37	0	3	0	1	0
Bulgaria	1,112	4.17	295	295	0	22	0	3	0
Subtotal	77,792		3,851	3,542	309	631	114	162	45
World Total	223,564		88,149	70,776	17,373	40,553	15,424	23,577	13,786

Source: Fischer and Shah 2010.

Note: Countries with land available in the table are those with 1 million ha or more of nonforested noncultivated suitable area ($<$ 25 persons/km^2) while producers are included if they produced more than 1 million ha of the commodity in 2008.

Table A2.9 Maize—Potential for Land/Yield Expansion for Key Producers and Countries with Uncultivated Land

| | 2008 production | | Land availability (thousand ha) | | | | | | |
| | Area | Yield | | Population < 25/km² | | Population < 10/km² | | Population < 5/km² | |
	1,000 ha	t/ha	Total	< 6 h	> 6 h	< 6 h	> 6 h	< 6 h	> 6 h
Countries with land available									
United States	31,826	9.66	1,647	1,538	109	1,120	85	793	61
Brazil	14,445	4.09	11,388	10,406	982	5,314	917	2,533	795
Mexico	7,354	3.31	2,029	1,732	297	1,084	269	575	226
Nigeria	3,845	1.96	1,301	876	426	40	80	0	3
Argentina	3,412	6.45	9,469	7,704	1,765	6,015	1,761	4,051	1,642
Tanzania	3,100	1.18	3,715	2,271	1,444	950	917	303	112
South Africa	2,799	4.14	1,063	911	152	452	87	174	35
Ukraine	2,440	4.69	1,011	1,008	3	96	1	24	0
Ethiopia	1,767	2.14	2,395	114	2,281	9	707	3	196
Russian Federation	1,732	3.86	2,458	2,170	288	1,338	280	856	266
Zimbabwe	1,730	0.29	1,002	851	151	145	53	28	22
Kenya	1,700	1.39	2,568	1,009	1,559	395	885	270	325
Congo, Dem. Rep.	1,484	0.78	2,657	1,185	1,472	790	1,102	447	621
Mozambique	1,400	0.92	7,592	4,206	3,386	2,004	2,322	705	1,409
Angola	1,115	0.51	4,109	1,030	3,079	522	2,489	293	1,935
Paraguay	850	2.24	3,098	749	2,348	506	2,314	337	2,214
Venezuela, R.B.	740	3.47	4,640	3,919	720	3,299	695	2,418	638
Zambia	664	2.18	5,716	2,383	3,333	1,029	2,657	329	1,039
Burkina Faso	608	1.67	2,306	1,376	930	299	332	62	80
Guinea	484	1.97	1,458	1,198	261	293	76	64	11

Bolivia	364	2.12	2,530	920	1,610	758	1,549	598	1,428
Madagascar	250	1.48	6,753	4,654	2,100	3,075	2,020	1,573	1,597
Chad	235	0.96	9,131	3,736	5,395	1,896	4,550	738	3,452
Central African Republic	130	1.09	2,405	84	2,322	38	2,194	14	1,941
Uruguay	81	4.15	2,735	2,225	510	2,047	503	1,679	480
Australia	68	5.69	18,870	2,890	15,980	3,611	15,944	3,528	15,907
Sudan	31	2.02	31,889	14,390	17,499	9,753	15,529	3,994	7,911
Mali	0		2,358	1,580	778	152	323	4	15
Subtotal	84,654		148,293	77,115	71,180	47,030	60,641	26,393	44,361
Current producers									
China	29,883	5.56	463	279	184	82	79	21	25
India	8,300	2.32	25	24	0	4	0	3	0
Indonesia	4,003	4.08	204	5	200	1	163	0	107
Philippines	2,661	2.60	1	0	1	0	0	0	0
Romania	2,432	3.23	70	69	1	19	1	7	1
France	1,702	9.29	286	286	1	2	0	0	0
Malawi	1,597	1.65	12	8	4	0	0	0	0
Hungary	1,200	7.47	12	12	0	2	0	1	0
Canada	1,169	9.06	45	44	0	25	0	8	0
Vietnam	1,126	4.02	0	0	0	0	0	0	0
Pakistan	1,118	3.61	0	0	0	0	0	0	0
Italy	1,053	9.01	0	0	0	0	0	0	0
Subtotal	56,244		1,118	727	391	135	243	40	133
World total	**161,017**		**156,828**	**83,310**	**74,419**	**48,773**	**62,690**	**26,984**	**45,516**

Source: Fischer and Shah 2010.

Note: Countries with land available in the table are those with 1 million ha or more of nonforested noncultivated suitable area (< 25 persons/km^2), while producers are included if they produced more than 1 million ha of the commodity in 2008.

Table A2.10 Soybeans—Potential for Land/Yield Expansion for Key Producers and Countries with Uncultivated Land

	2008 production		Land availability (thousand ha)						
	Area	Yield		Population < 25/km²		Population < 10/km²		Population < 5/km²	
	1,000 ha	t/ha	Total	< 6 h	> 6 h	< 6 h	> 6 h	< 6 h	> 6 h
Countries with land available									
United States	30,206	2.67	2,582	2,386	196	1,781	173	1,248	127
Brazil	21,272	2.82	22,124	20,057	2,067	11,471	1,975	5,571	1,746
Argentina	16,380	2.82	9,752	8,142	1,610	6,379	1,572	4,211	1,451
Paraguay	2,645	2.57	2,245	763	1,481	486	1,325	303	1,209
Bolivia	958	1.67	3,676	1,337	2,339	1,191	2,301	1,032	2,174
Uruguay	462	1.67	2,743	2,231	512	2,053	505	1,683	482
South Africa	174	1.85	1,669	1,449	220	691	112	257	45
Mexico	76	2.02	1,272	1,121	151	774	136	486	103
Zimbabwe	65	1.62	1,467	1,312	155	218	60	24	29
Venezuela, R.B.	37	1.62	3,693	3,076	617	2,541	597	1,765	538
Congo, Dem. Rep.	35	0.48	8,700	3,600	5,101	1,903	3,678	959	2,206
Australia	18	2.00	5,778	2,775	3,003	2,689	2,520	2,574	2,547
Cameroon	12	0.58	2,346	1,406	940	723	867	123	380
Zambia	10	1.20	6,372	2,702	3,670	1,195	2,940	361	1,139
Ethiopia	8	1.08	2,142	119	2,024	13	625	6	169
Burkina Faso	5	1.13	1,407	934	473	224	185	52	62

Tanzania	5	0.38	3,832	2,399	1,433	1,097	941	378	174
Kenya	3	0.84	1,391	612	779	252	427	159	175
Madagascar	0	1.00	6,243	4,425	1,818	2,832	1,667	1,393	1,340
Mali	0	0	1,550	1,021	529	91	210	2	7
Central African Republic	0		4,311	765	3,546	455	3,301	159	2,904
Angola	0		5,259	1,326	3,932	558	2,964	273	2,029
Chad	0		5,685	2,467	3,218	1,332	2,752	584	2,286
Sudan	0		13,698	6,694	7,004	4,839	6,038	2,478	4,057
Mozambique	0		7,340	4,040	3,300	1,935	2,273	691	1,380
Guinea	0		1,345	1,138	208	278	62	62	11
Subtotal	72,371		128,622	78,297	50,326	48,001	40,206	26,834	28,770
Current producers									
India	9,600	0.94	14	13	1	1	0	0	0
China	9,127	1.70	83	44	39	11	18	5	1
Canada	1,195	2.79	0	0	0	0	0	0	0
Subtotal	19,922		97	57	40	12	18	5	1
World total	96,870		137,711	82,870	54,841	49,379	43,575	27,401	31,125

Source: Fischer and Shah 2010.

Note: Countries with land available in the table are those with 1 million ha or more of nonforested noncultivated suitable area (< 25 persons/km^2), while producers are included if they produced more than 1 million ha of the commodity in 2008.

Table A2.11 Sugarcane—Potential for Land/Yield Expansion for Producers and Countries with Uncultivated Land

| | 2008 production | | Land availability (thousand ha) | | | | | | | |
| | Area | Yield | Total | Population < 25/km² | | Population < 10/km² | | Population < 5/km² | |
	1,000 ha	t/ha		< 6 h	> 6 h	< 6 h	> 6 h	< 6 h	> 6 h
Countries with land available									
Brazil	8,141	79.71	9,431	8,757	674	5,440	655	2,803	596
Indonesia	416	62.56	3,169	330	2,839	136	1,991	46	1,333
Argentina	355	84.37	3,808	3,018	789	2,298	773	1,368	681
Cameroon	145	10.00	1,297	665	632	337	607	63	363
Bolivia	128	50.31	1,522	588	934	567	934	528	906
Paraguay	90	50.00	1,812	818	993	537	764	347	634
Madagascar	82	31.71	2,108	1,766	342	890	164	312	82
Congo, Dem. Rep.	40	38.75	6,531	1,958	4,573	756	3,208	276	1,935
Congo, Rep.	18	36.11	1,453	117	1,336	46	1,280	12	1,092
Central African Republic	13	7.20	1,210	446	763	257	639	77	476
Papua New Guinea	9	52.94	1,035	45	990	10	835	1	443
Uruguay	6	55.33	1,055	843	213	809	213	648	209
Subtotal	9,433		34,431	19,351	15,078	12,083	12,063	6,481	8,750
Current producers									
India	5,055	68.88	1	0	1	0	0	0	0
China	1,709	73.11	8	6	2	2	0	0	0
Pakistan	1,241	51.49	0	0	0	0	0	0	0
Thailand	1,054	69.71	3	3	0	0	0	0	0
Subtotal	9,059		12	9	3	2	0	0	0
World total	24,375		41,176	22,266	18,910	13,706	15,039	7,469	10,909

Source: Fischer and Shah 2010.

Note: Countries with land available in the table are those with 1 million ha or more of nonforested noncultivated suitable area (< 25 persons/km²), while producers are included if they produced more than 1 million ha of the commodity in 2008.

Table A2.12 Oil Palm—Potential for Land/Yield Expansion for Key Producers and Countries with Uncultivated Land

| | 2008 production | | Land availability (thousand ha) | | | | | | |
| | Area | Yield | Population < 25/km² | | | Population < 10/km² | | Population < 5/km² | |
	1,000 ha	t/ha	Total	< 6 h	> 6 h	< 6 h	> 6 h	< 6 h	> 6 h
Countries with land available									
Indonesia	5,000	17.00	6,576	771	5,805	283	4,265	75	2,756
Congo, Dem. Rep.	175	6.48	4,546	849	3,697	451	2,822	223	1,731
Colombia	165	19.39	2,811	687	2,124	475	1,893	272	1,618
Ecuador	135	15.56	214	24	191	22	151	17	116
Papua New Guinea	96	14.58	2,069	53	2,016	11	1,721	0	985
Brazil	66	10.00	1,185	570	615	360	599	198	561
Venezuela, R.B.	27	12.27	286	171	115	147	113	116	113
Liberia	17	10.76	397	88	309	22	190	4	88
Peru	13	18.93	220	33	187	30	184	21	171
Congo, Rep.	7	12.50	1,222	2	1,219	1	1,186	0	1,040
Gabon	4	7.98	319	14	304	7	303	4	283
Nicaragua	3	24.00	431	105	326	71	281	42	210
Bolivia	0	0.00	287	37	250	35	249	25	235

(continued)

Table A2.12 (Continued)

	2008 production		Land availability (thousand ha)						
	Area	Yield	Population < 25/km²			Population < 10/km²		Population < 5/km²	
	1,000 ha	t/ha	Total	< 6 h	> 6 h	< 6 h	> 6 h	< 6 h	> 6 h
Subtotal	5,708		20,563	3,404	17,158	1,915	13,957	997	9,907
Current producers									
Malaysia	3,900	21.28	145	36	109	17	78	5	32
Nigeria	3,200	2.66	1	0	0	0	0	0	0
Thailand	450	17.49	20	15	5	0	1	0	0
Guinea	310	2.68	1	1	0	0	0	0	0
Ghana	300	6.33	6	5	0	0	0	0	0
Côte d'Ivoire	215	5.58	122	70	52	11	22	1	4
Subtotal	8,375		295	127	166	28	101	6	36
World total	14,586		21,760	3,909	17,851	2,100	14,474	1,059	10,235

Source: Fischer and Shah 2010.

Note: Countries with land available in the table are those with 1 million ha or more of nonforested noncultivated suitable area (< 25 persons/km²), while producers are included if they produced more than 1 million ha of the commodity in 2008.

REFERENCES

Barlow, C. 1997. "Growth, Structural Change, and Plantation Tree Crops: The Case of Rubber." *World Development* 25 (10): 1589–1607.

Eickhout, B., H. van Meijl, A. Tabeau, and E. Stehfest. 2009. "The Impact of Environmental and Climate Constraints on Global Food Supply." In *Economic Analysis of Land Use in Global Climate Change Policy*, ed. T. W. Hertel, S. Rose, and R. S. J. Tol. London: Routledge.

Fischer, G., and M. Shah. 2010. "Farmland Investments and Food Security: Statistical Annex." Report prepared under a World Bank and International Institute for Applied Systems Analysis contract, Luxembourg.

Government of Sudan. 2009. "Study of the Sustainable Development of Semi-Mechanized Rainfed Farming." Ministry of Agriculture and Forestry, Khartoum.

World Bank. 2008. "Cameroon Agricultural Value Chain Competitiveness Study." World Bank, Washington, DC.

World Bank. 2009. *Awakening Africa's Sleeping Giant: Prospects for Competitive Commercial Agriculture in the Guinea Savannah Zone and Beyond*. Washington, DC: World Bank.

Zen, Z., C. Barlow, and R. Gondowarsito. 2006. "Oil Palm in Indonesian Socio-Economic Improvement: A Review of Options." *Oil Palm Industry Economic Journal* 6 (1): 18–29.

APPENDIX 3

Figures

Figure A3.1 Yield Gap vs. Relative Land Availability, Africa

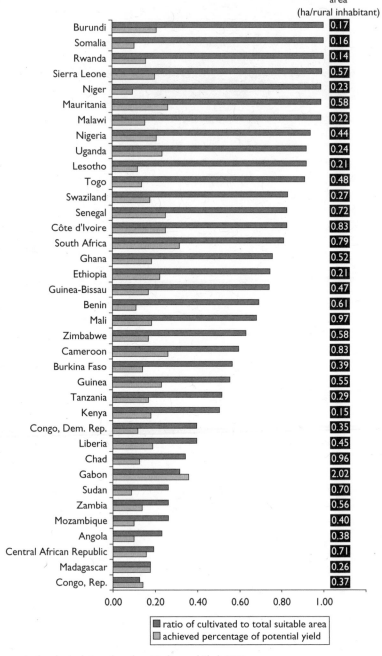

area
(ha/rural inhabitant)

Country	area (ha/rural inhabitant)
Burundi	0.17
Somalia	0.16
Rwanda	0.14
Sierra Leone	0.57
Niger	0.23
Mauritania	0.58
Malawi	0.22
Nigeria	0.44
Uganda	0.24
Lesotho	0.21
Togo	0.48
Swaziland	0.27
Senegal	0.72
Côte d'Ivoire	0.83
South Africa	0.79
Ghana	0.52
Ethiopia	0.21
Guinea-Bissau	0.47
Benin	0.61
Mali	0.97
Zimbabwe	0.58
Cameroon	0.83
Burkina Faso	0.39
Guinea	0.55
Tanzania	0.29
Kenya	0.15
Congo, Dem. Rep.	0.35
Liberia	0.45
Chad	0.96
Gabon	2.02
Sudan	0.70
Zambia	0.56
Mozambique	0.40
Angola	0.38
Central African Republic	0.71
Madagascar	0.26
Congo, Rep.	0.37

0.00 0.20 0.40 0.60 0.80 1.00

■ ratio of cultivated to total suitable area
▢ achieved percentage of potential yield

Source: Authors' calculations based on Fischer and Shah 2010.

Figure A3.2 Yield Gap vs. Relative Land Availability, Europe and Central Asia

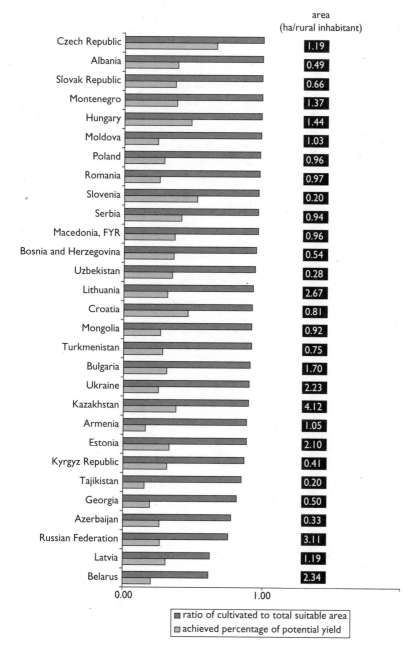

area
(ha/rural inhabitant)

Country	area
Czech Republic	1.19
Albania	0.49
Slovak Republic	0.66
Montenegro	1.37
Hungary	1.44
Moldova	1.03
Poland	0.96
Romania	0.97
Slovenia	0.20
Serbia	0.94
Macedonia, FYR	0.96
Bosnia and Herzegovina	0.54
Uzbekistan	0.28
Lithuania	2.67
Croatia	0.81
Mongolia	0.92
Turkmenistan	0.75
Bulgaria	1.70
Ukraine	2.23
Kazakhstan	4.12
Armenia	1.05
Estonia	2.10
Kyrgyz Republic	0.41
Tajikistan	0.20
Georgia	0.50
Azerbaijan	0.33
Russian Federation	3.11
Latvia	1.19
Belarus	2.34

0.00   1.00

■ ratio of cultivated to total suitable area
□ achieved percentage of potential yield

Source: Authors' calculations based on Fischer and Shah 2010.

Figure A3.3 Yield Gap vs. Relative Land Availability, Latin America and the Caribbean

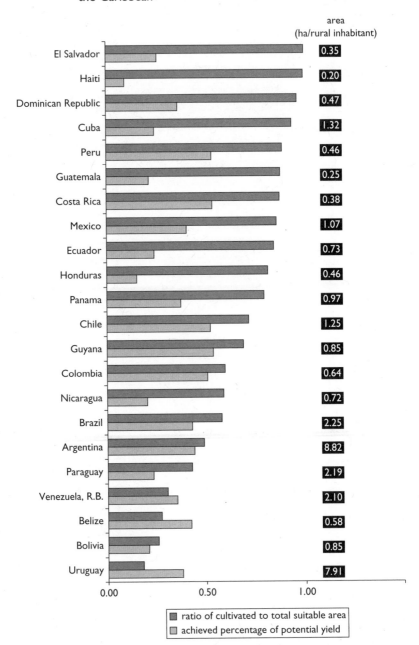

Source: Authors' calculations based on Fischer and Shah 2010

Figure A3.4 Yield Gap vs. Relative Land Availability, North America, Northern Europe, and Oceania

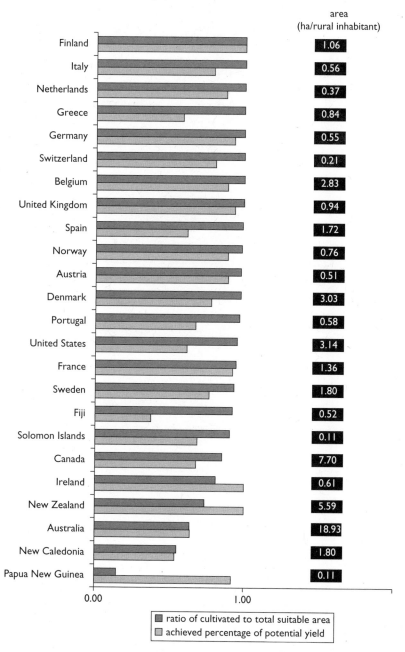

area (ha/rural inhabitant)

Country	area (ha/rural inhabitant)
Finland	1.06
Italy	0.56
Netherlands	0.37
Greece	0.84
Germany	0.55
Switzerland	0.21
Belgium	2.83
United Kingdom	0.94
Spain	1.72
Norway	0.76
Austria	0.51
Denmark	3.03
Portugal	0.58
United States	3.14
France	1.36
Sweden	1.80
Fiji	0.52
Solomon Islands	0.11
Canada	7.70
Ireland	0.61
New Zealand	5.59
Australia	18.93
New Caledonia	1.80
Papua New Guinea	0.11

0.00   1.00

■ ratio of cultivated to total suitable area
□ achieved percentage of potential yield

Source: Authors' calculations based on Fischer and Shah 2010.

Figure A3.5   Yield Gap vs. Relative Land Availability, Selected Countries

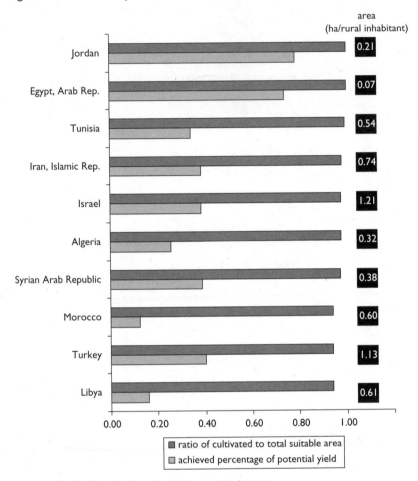

Source: Authors' calculations based on Fischer and Shah 2010.

REFERENCE

Fischer, G., and M. Shah. 2010 "Farmland Investments and Food Security: Statistical Annex." Report prepared under World Bank and International Institute for Applied Systems Analysis contract, Luxembourg.

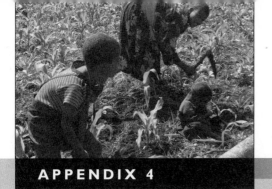

APPENDIX 4

Maps

Map A4.2.1   Mozambique Concession Overlap with Community Claims

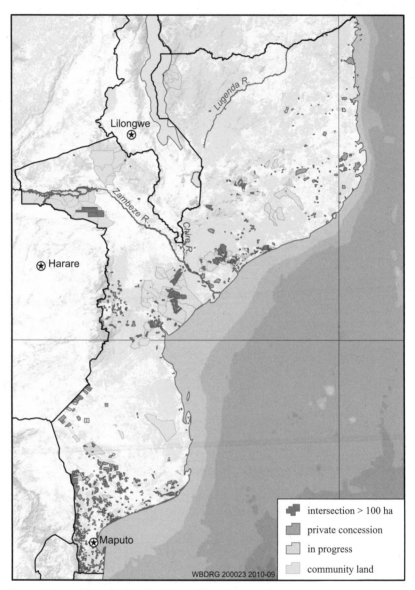

Source: Authors, elaboration based on Mozambique inventory data.

RISING GLOBAL INTEREST IN FARMLAND

Map A4.3.1　Maximum Potential Value of Output for Africa (US$ per hectare)

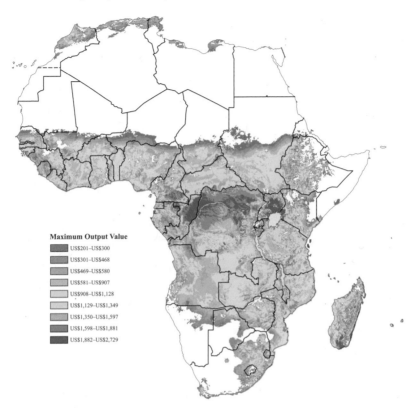

Maximum Output Value

- US$201–US$300
- US$301–US$468
- US$469–US$580
- US$581–US$907
- US$908–US$1,128
- US$1,129–US$1,349
- US$1,350–US$1,597
- US$1,598–US$1,881
- US$1,882–US$2,729

Source: Fischer and Shah 2010.

Map A4.3.2   Maximum Potential Value of Output for Latin America and
             the Caribbean
             (US$ per hectare)

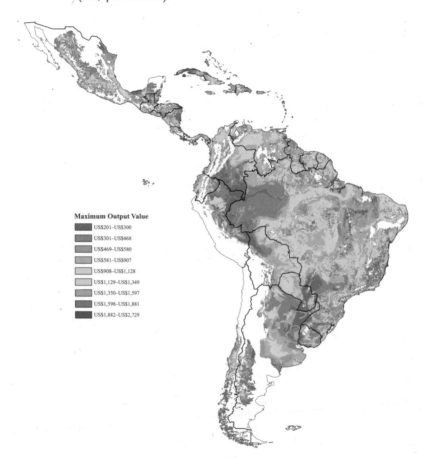

Maximum Output Value

- US$201–US$300
- US$301–US$468
- US$469–US$580
- US$581–US$907
- US$908–US$1,128
- US$1,129–US$1,349
- US$1,350–US$1,597
- US$1,598–US$1,881
- US$1,882–US$2,729

Source: Fischer and Shah 2010.

Map A4.3.3 Maximum Potential Value of Output for Europe
(US$ per hectare)

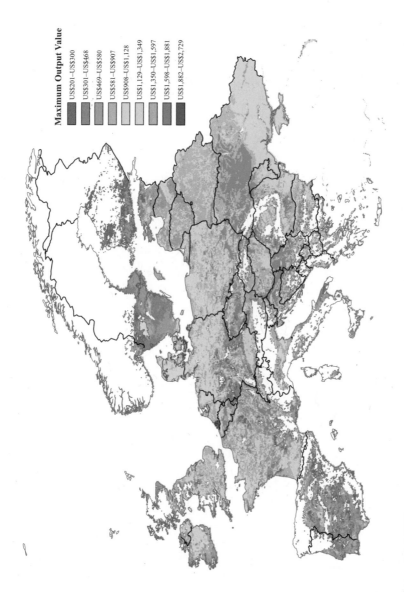

Maximum Output Value

- US$201–US$300
- US$301–US$468
- US$469–US$580
- US$581–US$907
- US$908–US$1,128
- US$1,129–US$1,349
- US$1,350–US$1,597
- US$1,598–US$1,881
- US$1,882–US$2,729

Source: Fischer and Shah 2010.

Map A4.3.4 Maximum Potential Value of Output for the Middle East and Asia
(US$ per hectare)

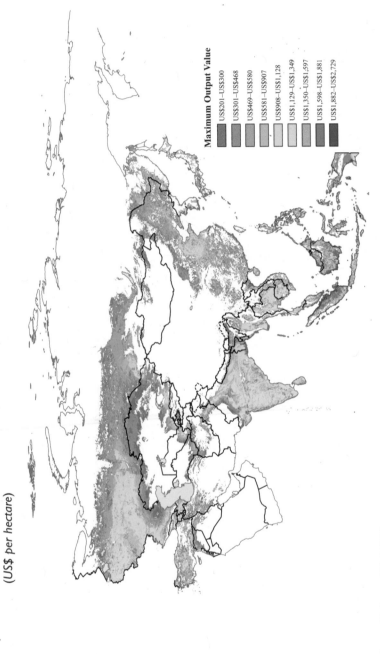

Maximum Output Value

US$201–US$300
US$301–US$468
US$469–US$580
US$581–US$907
US$908–US$1,128
US$1,129–US$1,349
US$1,350–US$1,597
US$1,598–US$1,881
US$1,882–US$2,729

Source: Fischer and Shah 2010.

Map A4.3.5 Maximum Potential Value of Output for Oceania (US$ per hectare)

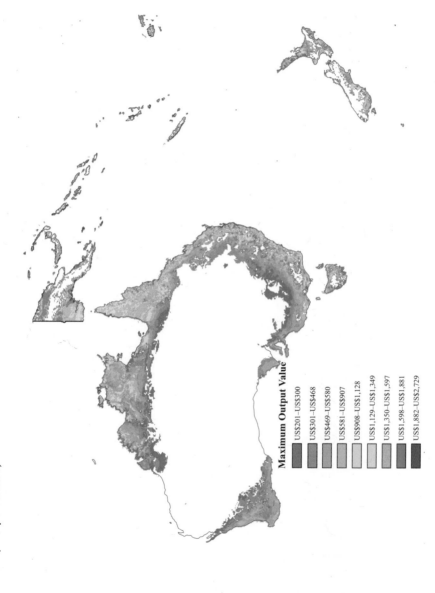

Maximum Output Value

- US$201–US$300
- US$301–US$468
- US$469–US$580
- US$581–US$907
- US$908–US$1,128
- US$1,129–US$1,349
- US$1,350–US$1,597
- US$1,598–US$1,881
- US$1,882–US$2,729

Source: Fischer and Shah 2010.

Contributors

Valuable inputs throughout the process were received from Vera Songwe (MDO), Werner Kiene and Reinier de Man (independent consultants), Lorenzo Cotula and Sonia Vermeulen of the International Institute for Environment and Development (IIED). Rabah Arezki (IMF) worked closely with the team on regression analysis, and Charlotte Coutand and Caroline Silverman assisted with coding blog postings. The team is also grateful to Thierry Mayer (CEPII), Jacques Ould-Aoudia (French Ministry of Finance, Economics and Industry) and Jean-François Eudeline for providing access to useful data sets. Communication support was provided by Fionna Douglas, Gunnar Larson, and Elizabeth Petheo (ARD), Roger Morier (SDNCM), Merrell Tuck-Primdahl (DECOS), and Jane Zhang and Swati Mishra (DECRG). Pauline Kokila and Raja Manikandan (DECRG), Felicitas Doroteo-Gomez, Jane Jin Li, and Cicely Spooner (ARD) contributed excellent administrative support. Superb publication and editing support was provided by Patricia Katayama, Santiago Pombo (EXTOP), Bruce Ross-Larson, and Mary Fisk.

The team would like to thank Justin Lin (DECVP); Kathy Sierra and Hart Schafer (SDNVP); peer reviewers Gavin Adlington (ECSS3), Keith Bell (EASER), Hans Binswanger, John Lamb (ARD), Paul Mathieu (FAO), Robin Mearns (SDV), Stephen Mink (AFTSN), Paul Munro-Faure (FAO), John Nash (LCSSD), and Steven Schonberger (AFTAR); and members of the World Bank–wide working group on large-scale agricultural investment.

The team would also like to thank the following World Bank staff members who provided insightful comments on the draft report: Theodore Ahlers

(ECAVP); Gokhan Akinci, Kusi Hornberger and Xiaofang Shen (CICIG); Menberu Allebachew, Amadou Oumar Ba, Oliver Braedt, Karen Brooks, Frank Byamugisha, Indira Ekanayake, Achim Fock, Li Guo, Chris Jackson, Alex Mwanakasale, Mohamed Osman Hussein, Shobha Shetty, and Martien van Nieuwkoop (AFTAR); William Battaile (AFTP2); Garo Batmanian (LCSEN); Mohammed Bekhechi, Charles di Leva, and Una Meades (LEGEN); Rajesh Behal, Oscar Chemerinski, Andrew Hamilton, Richard Henry, Alzbeta Klein, and Vipul Prakash (CAGDR); Eustacius Betubiza (AFCCD); Benoit Blarel (ECSSD); Carlos Alberto Braga (SECVP); Milan Brahmbhatt (PRMVP); Marjory-Anne Bromhead, Peter Dewees, Azeb Fissha, Edgardo Maravi, Mark Sadler, and John Spears (ARD); Timothy Brown (EASIS); Catherine Cassagne, Chris Richards, and Bruce Wise (CSIAS); Malcolm Childress, Laurent Debroux, Erick Fernandes, Jorge Munoz, and Ethel Sennhauser (LCSAR); Luis Constantino and Julian Lampietti (MNSAR); Edward Cook and Grahame Dixie (SASDA); Pamela Cox (LCRVP); Jose Antonio Cuesta Leiva (PRMPR); Steven Dimitriyev (AFTFW); Mark Dutz and Lili Liu (PRMED); Paavo Eliste, Patrick Labaste, Magda Lovei, Juan Martinez, Guzman Garcia-Rivero, Iain Shuker, and Giuseppe Topa (EASER); Dereje Feyissa (consultant); Emmanuel Doe Fiadzo (AFTP4); Cyprian Fisiy (SDV); Melissa Fossberg and Sumir Lal (EXTOC); Hans Jurgen Gruss (LEGVP); Isabel Guerrero (SARVP); Jeffrey Gutman (OPCVP); Maks Kobonbaev (PRMPS); Mark Lundell (LCSSD); Euan Marshall (CSISI); Paul Martin, Carole Megevand; Nyaneba Nkrumah, Idah Pswarayi-Riddhough, and Simon Rietbergen (AFTEN); Galina Mikhlin-Oliver (INTSC); Richard Mills (EXTVP); Stephen Mink (AFTSN); Edgardo Mosqueira and David Varela (LCSPS); Fred Nickesen (EAPCO); Juri Oka (SECPO); Vincent Palmade and Marilou Uy (AFTFP); Djordjija Petkoski (WBIGV); Anwar Ravat (COCPO); Daniel Runde (CPAPD); Uli Schmitt (EASCS); M. Srinivas Shivakumar (consultant); Alassane Sow (AFMSD); Amy Stilwell (EXTCC); Dina Umali-Deininger (ECSS1); J. W. van Holst Pellekaan (IEGCR); and Michel Wormser (AFRVP).

Valuable inputs were received at various stages of preparing the report from the following people outside the World Bank: Mohamed Abdelgadir, Jean-Philippe Audinet, Kevin Cleaver, Henock Kifle, Mylene Kherallah, Harold Liversage, Cheryl Morden, Rasha Omar and Philippe Rémy (IFAD); Kwesi Ahwoi (Minister of Food and Agriculture, Ghana); Roberto Albino (Director, Center for the Promotion of Agricultural Investment, Mozambique); Liz Alden Wily (Independent Consultant); Mario Alegri; Clarissa Augustinus (UN Habitat); Tilman Altenburg (German Development Institute, DIE); Brian Baldwin and Monika Midel (Global Donor Platform for Rural Development); Kevin Barthel, Richard Gaynor, Jolyne Sanjak, and Jennifer Witriol (Millennium Challenge Corporation, MCC); Margarita Benavides (Instituto de Bien Comun, Peru); Jozias Blok and Philip Mikos (European Commission and EU Working Group on Land Issues); Tony Burns and Kate Dalrymple (Land Equity International); Bruce Cabarle (World Wildlife Fund); Joe Carvin (Altima); Cazenave and Asociados SA (Argentina); Wade Channel, Timothy

Fella, and Gregory Myers (USAID); Paul Collier (Oxford University); Ladd Connell (Conservation International); Kaitlin Cordes (Columbia Law School); Luiz Felipe Jansen de Melo (Cosan); Ertharin Cousin (United States Ambassador to United Nations Food Agencies); Fred Cubbage (North Carolina State University); Issoufou Dare (West African Economic & Monetary Union); Abdoul Karim Mamalo (former permanent secretary of the Rural Code, Niger); Alain de Janvry (University of California–Berkeley); Philippe de Laperouse (HighQuest Partners LLC/Soyatech LLC); Madiodio Niasse, Laureano del Castillo, and Michael Taylor (International Land Coalition); Reinier de Man (Sustainable Business Development) Olivier de Schutter (United Nations); Mika Torhonen, Nasredin Elamin, Ibrahim El Dukheri, and Daniel Gustafson (FAO); Dominic Elsen (independent consultant); Laurène Anne Feintrenie, Krystof Obidzinski, Pablo Pacheco, and George Schoneveld (Centre for International Forestry Research, CIFOR); Beth Gingold and Craig Hanson (World Resources Institute, WRI); Martin Grass and Tim Loos (University of Hohenheim); Gustavo Grobocopatel (Grupo Los Grobo); Mario Hernandez (ProInversión); Thomas Hertel (Purdue University); Thea Hillhorst (KIT, Netherlands); Leonidas Hitimana (Club du Sahel, Organisation for Economic Co-operation and Development [OECD]); Julie Howard and Emmy Simmons (Partnership to Cut Hunger & Poverty in Africa); Shunichi Inoue (Japanese Ministry of Foreign Affairs); Laxman Joshi (World Agroforestry Center); Akin Adesina and Joan Kagwanja (Alliance for a Green Revolution in Africa, AGRA); Alain Karsenty (CIRAD); Arvind Khare and Augusta Molnar (Rights and Resources Group); Werner Kiene (Former Chair, World Bank Inspection Panel); Michael Kirk (Marburg University); Lasse Krantz (SIDA); Thorben Kruse, Tanja Pickardt, Dorith von Behaim, and Oliver Schoenweger (GTZ); Tim K. Loos (University of Hohenheim); Alejandro Lopez (Adecoagro); Carin Smaller, Nathalie Bernasconi-Osterwalder, Eduardo Manciana, and Howard Mann (International Institute of Sustainable Development, IISD); Nathaniel Don Marquez (Asian NGO Coalition for Agrarian Reform and Rural Development); Ruth Meinzen-Dick, Don Mitchell, Regina Birner, and Tidiane Ngaido (International Food Policy Research Institute, IFPRI); Anne Miroux, Hafiz Mirza, and David Hallam (United Nations Conference on Trade and Development); Virginia Morales Olmos (Weyerhaeuser); Hubert Ouedraogo (African Union); Sushil Pandey and David Raitzer (International Rice Research Institute, IRRI); Susan Payne (Emergent Asset Management); Kim Pfeifer and Robin Palmer (Oxfam); Lionel Vignacq, Caroline Plançon, Sujiro Seam, and Benoit Faivre-Dupaigre (French Ministry of Foreign and European Affairs); Vatché Papazian (French Development Agency); Alejandro Preusche (NFD Agro); Andrea Ries (Swiss Agency for Cooperation and Development, SDC); Angus Selby (formerly Morgan Stanley); Frits van der Wal (Dutch Ministry for Foreign Affairs); Willi Zimmerman (Technical University, Munich); Isolina Boto (Technical Center for Agricultural and Rural Cooperation ACP-EU); Michel Merlet and Mathieu Perdriault (aGter); Jun "Saturnino" Borras (Saint

Mary University); André Tioro (Réseau des Organisations Paysannes et de Producteurs de l'Afrique de l'Ouest ROPPA); Rivo Ratsialonana (Land Observatory, Madagascar); Ruff Hall (Institute for Poverty, Land and Agrarian Studies, PLAAS); and Annelies Zoomers (Utrecht University).

Insightful comments on earlier drafts of the study's findings were received from key policy makers at the national and state levels, multilateral and bilateral development partners, academia, civil society, and international organizations during a series of workshops and conferences: the World Bank Annual Bank Conference on Land Policy and Administration (April 2010, Washington, DC), the Trust Fund for Environmentally and Socially Sustainable Development Workshop (May 2010, Helsinki), the West and Central Africa as well as Eastern Africa Regional Consultation for the FAO's Voluntary Guidelines on Responsible Governance of Tenure of Land and other Natural Resources (June 2010, Ouagadougou; September 2010, Addis-Ababa) and private sector consultation (January 2010, London), the Central Africa Rural Development Briefing of the ACP-EU Technical Centre for Agricultural and Rural Cooperation (Yaoundé, September 2010), the Centre d'Analyse Stratégique (March 2010, Paris), the "Land Tenure and Development" joint technical committee of the French Ministry of Foreign and European Affairs and the French Development Agency (May and November 2009, Paris), the World Forestry Congress (October 2009, Buenos Aires), and the CIRAD "land day" (September 2009, Montpellier). In the evolution of the study, valuable inputs were received at a side session to the United Nations General Assembly (September 2009, New York), the Land Day in conjunction with the Annual Meeting of the Global Donor Platform (January 2010, Rome), the European Development Days (October 2009, Stockholm), and a Chatham House Conference (November 2009, United Kingdom), and in various nongovernmental organization and private sector conferences and workshops, including the "Commercial Pressures on Land: Rethinking Policies for Development" conference co-organized by the Centre for Development Studies, University of Groningen, Utrecht University, Oxfam Novib, International Land Coalition, and the Dutch Ministry of Foreign Affairs (July 2009, Utrecht) and the Global AgInvesting Conference (June 2009, New York).

This work would not have been possible without generous support from a number of partners. Funding of the inventory and legal analysis components of this research was provided by the Program on Forests (PROFOR) with a view toward identifying possible implications of future land expansions on forested areas. Significant support was received from the Swiss Agency for Cooperation and Development (SDC), the Trust Fund for Environmentally and Socially Sustainable Development (TFESSD), the Hewlett Foundation, and the Bank Netherlands Partnership Program (BNPP) to support in-depth social, environmental, and economic case studies. We are also very grateful to the French Ministry of Foreign and European Affairs and the French National Institute for Agricultural Research for their support in the form of a seconded staff to the World Bank.

INDEX

Boxes, figures, maps, notes, and tables are indicated by *b*, *f*, *m*, *n*, and *t* following page numbers.

capacity building, recommendations
for, xli–xlii, 130, 132, 140, 141
carbon emissions. *See* climate
change; REDD
case studies, 64–70, 65–66*t*
implementation status and viability,
xxxi–xxxii, 67–68
methodology, 64–67, 157–62*t*
socioeconomic impacts, 68–70
cattle ranching. *See* beef
cereals. *See* grain production
CGE (computable general equilibrium)
models, 16
Chad
availability of uncultivated
land, xxxiii
maize yields, 84
soybean yields, 85
China
Congolese rainforest for oil palm,
interest in, 67
cropland expansion, xxvi
distribution of projects and
investors, 53
past processes of land expansion, 13
transfer of property rights, 104
water availability, 15
civil society's role, xlii, 55, 130, 137–38
climate change
crop yields and, 15
deforestation and, 21, 21*f*
land conversions and, 43*n*1
Colombia
farm management companies, 33*b*
unprotected forested land, 81
commodities, 83–86. *See also*
specific types
past processes of land expansion
and, 11, 12*t*
standards, 134–36
commodity prices boom (2007–08),
xxiii, xxix–xxx, 1
linked to interest in foreign land
acquisition, 50, 51*f*, 55
community involvement. *See*
consultation with local right
holders; local decision making
on property rights

compensation
Corporate Social Responsibility
principles and, 126*n*2
from transfers, 107–9
competitive processes. *See* auctions of
public lands
compulsory acquisition approach, 104
computable general equilibrium (CGE)
models, 16
concessionary agreements, 113,
115, 126*n*4
cancellation of, 133
conflict management, 132
conflicts with local communities,
67–68, 70, 100, 103
Congo, Democratic Republic of
availability of uncultivated land,
xxxiii, 79–80
case study, 65*t*, 67, 157*t*
conflict over concessionary
agreements, 113
cropland expansion, xxviii
Forest Code (2002), 126*n*4, 126*n*6
information collection and
disclosure, 117
job creation from land
investments, 64
maize yields, 84
methodology and data
collection, 146
monitoring of implementation of
investments, 118, 119
project review and approval,
114, 126*n*7
soybean yields, 85
sugarcane yields, 85
taxes from forestry sector, 113
unprotected forested land, 81, 126*n*4
urgency of approval concession
applications, 115
consultation with local right
holders, 70, 71, 106–7,
123–24, 125, 141
contract farming, 33*b*, 34, 124
corn. *See* maize
Corporate Social Responsibility
principles, 126*n*2
Cosan (Brazilian company), 31

country inventories of land, xxx–xxxi, xxxi*t*, 3, 56–64, 72–73*n*11. *See also* recording of existing property rights
administrative processes, 4, 56–61, 58–59*t*
land sizes and origin of projects, 156*t*
large-scale land acquisitions, 61–64, 62*t*
country typology, xxiv, xxxii–xxxvii, 7, 86–91, 86*f*
little land available, high yield gap (Type 3), xxxiv–xxxv, 89, 90*f*
little land for expansion, low yield gap (Type 1), xxxiii, 87–88, 87*f*
suitable land available, high yield gap (Type 4), xxxv, 89–91, 91*f*
suitable land available, low yield gap (Type 2), xxxiii–xxxiv, 88–89, 88*f*
crimes against the environment, 122
crop insurance, 32
crop yields, 14–15, 14*b*
country typology and. *See* country typology
maximum potential yield, 81, 82*t*, 190*m*
yield gap, defined, 93*n*1
yield gap vs. relative land availability, 181–86*f*
customary land rights, 99–100, 103

D
deforestation
Amazon region, xxvi, 17–19, 18*f*, 120–21
cropland expansion and, 76, 81
social impacts of, 19–22, 21*f*
demand for land. *See* land rush
Democratic Republic of Congo. *See* Congo, Democratic Republic of
developing countries
employment potential, 38–39
past processes of land expansion and, 13
disclosures, open and publicly available, 96, 116–17
displaced persons, 70

dispute resolution, 132
Doing Business 2009 classification of investment protection, 54, 72*n*5

E
East Asia
availability of uncultivated land, 79
past processes of land expansion, 10
Eastern Europe and Central Asia. *See also specific countries*
availability of uncultivated land, xxxii, 79
cropland expansion, xxix
frequency distribution of projects and total land area, 52
little land available, high yield gap (Type 3), xxxv
methodological approaches, xxiv
superfarms, 26–28
yield gap vs. relative land availability, 183*f*
Ecological Economic Zoning framework (Brazil), 123
econometric analysis of agricultural investment projects, 54–55, 55*t*
economic viability. *See* technical and economic viability
Egypt
availability of uncultivated land, xxxiii
distribution of projects and investors, 53
EITI. *See* Extractive Industries Transparency Initiative
elites, land grabbing by, 68, 102
El Tejar (Brazil and Argentina), 32
employment
expectations related to land deals, 63–64, 68, 124
females and other vulnerable populations, 70
labor laws, 123, 124
large-scale investment and, 38–39, 39*t*
smallholders' incomes in relation to wage employment on large-scale farms, 164*t*

enforcement of agreements and
    contracts, 116
environmental and social sustainability,
    xxxix, 96, 119–24
  enforcement of policies and
    standards, 121–22, 127n13
  social standards, adherence
    to, 122–24
  unsuitable areas, protection of, 120–21
environmental challenges, 16–19.
    See also climate change;
    deforestation
environmental impact assessments
    (EIAs), 57, 121–22
"Equator Banks," 130, 136
Equator Principles, 136–37
ethanol. *See* biofuels
Ethiopia
  biofuels development, 152n4
  boundaries unclear for
    government lands, 120
  compensation from voluntary
    transfers, 108, 109
  domestic investors, 63
  environmental permits, 122
  expropriations, 105
  frequency distribution of projects
    and total land area, 52
  incentives for investors, 116
  job creation from land
    investments, 64
  large farms, 24
  large-scale land acquisitions, 62
  maize yields, 84
  methodology and data
    collection, 146–47
  monitoring of implementation
    of investments, 118
  protected lands, 120
  reporting on land use, 60
  transfer of property rights, xxx,
    xxxviii, 104
eucalyptus, 19
European Union. *See also*
    specific countries
  biofuels and, 12
  past processes of land
    expansion and, 13

publicly listed companies, 29
  trade preferences, 26
evictions, 105
evidence-based multistakeholder
    approach, xxiv, 140, 141–43
expropriation of land prior to
    voluntary transfers, 104–6,
    126n3
Extractive Industries Transparency
    Initiative (EITI), 139, 139b,
    143, 144n7

F
fairness and targeting of
    proceeds from voluntary
    transfers, 107–9
family-owned and operated
    farms, 28–30, 28t
farm management companies, 33b
financial institutions, 136–37
Food and Agricultural Organization
    (FAO), xxiv, 15, 16
  "Voluntary Guidelines for Tenure of
    Land and Associated Natural
    Resources," 140
forest dwellers, 101
forestland
  concessions, regulation of,
    126n4, 153n9
  cultivation of. *See* deforestation
  failure to map and identify
    boundaries of, 120
  maintaining, xxvii
  plantations. *See* plantation forests
  unprotected, 81
Forest Stewardship Council (FSC),
    134, 143n4
Forum of Sovereign Wealth Funds
    (2008), 136
future demand for agricultural
    commodities and land,
    xxiv, xl–xlii, 6–7, 13–16,
    129–44, 163t
  civil society, xlii, 137–38
  evidence-based multistakeholder
    approach, need for, xxiv, 141–43
  international organizations,
    xlii, 138–41

future demand for agricultural
commodities and land
(*continued*)
investors, 133–37
commodity standards, 134–36
financial institutions, 136–37
key areas for government
action, 130–33

G

Ghana
disclosure of public information, 117
environmental permits, 122
frequency distribution of
projects and total land
area, 52
inaccurate or unavailable
records, 117
incomplete projects, effect
of, 126*n*9
large farms, 25
local decision making, 103
oil palm yields, 86
tax rebates and incentives, 113–14
government action
approval of projects by
government agencies,
114–16, 125
environmental challenges and, 19
key areas for, xl–xlii, 130–33
partnerships between small farmers
and large investors, 38
targeting countries with weak land
governance, 55, 141
GRAIN blog on large-scale land
acquisition, 50
grain production
employment generation, 38–39
large farms, xxix, 23, 32
pricing, 15
superfarms, 27
"green deserts," 13
greenhouse gas emissions.
See climate change; REDD

H

Hertel, T. W., 43*n*2
horticulture, xxix, 34

I

incentives
enforcement of agreements and
contracts with incentive
recipients, 116
tax, 113–14
India
availability of uncultivated
land, xxxiii
cropland expansion, xxvi
distribution of projects and
investors, 53
expropriations, 126*n*3
large farms, 31
maize yields, 84
indigenous people's rights, 123.
See also long-established
property rights
Indonesia
boundaries unclear for
government lands, 120
conflict
over concessionary
agreements, 113
over land claims, 70
consultation of affected
populations, 107
cropland expansion, xxvii, 42
customary land rights, 100
deforestation, social impacts
of, 19–21, 21*f*
forest estate and state ownership, 99
frequency distribution
of projects and total land
area, 52
inaccurate or unavailable
records, 117
incentives for investment, 126*n*8
land regulation, 61
methodology and data
collection, 147
migrant labor, 69
recording of property rights, 100
infrastructure
large farms, provision by, 32
proximity to, 37*b*, 40
initial public offerings (IPOs) of
superfarms, 27